gabriel's fire

gabriel's fire

luis gabriel aguilera

The University of Chicago Press / Chicago and London

The University of Chicago Press, Chicago 60637
The University of Chicago Press, Ltd., London
© 2000 by The University of Chicago
All rights reserved. Published 2000
Printed in the United States of America

9 8 7 6 5 4 3 2 1 00   1 2 3 4 5

ISBN: 0-226-01067-8 (cloth)

Library of Congress Cataloging-in-Publication
Data
Aguilera, Luis Gabriel.
    Gabriel's fire / Luis Gabriel Aguilera.
        p.   cm.
    ISBN 0-226-01067-8 (alk. paper)
    1. Aguilera, Luis Gabriel—Childhood and
youth.   2. Mexican American youth—
Illinois—Chicago Biography.   3. Mexican
Americans—Illinois—Chicago Biography.
4. Mexican Americans—Illinois—Chicago—
Social conditions.   5. Chicago   (Ill.)
Biography.   6. Chicago (Ill.)—Ethnic
relations.   7. Inner cities—Illinois—
Chicago.   I. Title.
F548.9.M5A38   2000
977.3′110046872073′0092—dc21
    [B]   99-16610
                                                    CIP

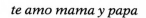

te amo mama y papa

preface

*F*ollowing my graduation from the University of Chicago in June of 1995, I commenced work on a writing project stemming from the baccalaureate essay I had recently completed. The topic of the academic paper was an in-depth cultural study of one of Chicago's largest "street gangs," the Latin Kings. The present autobiographical work, entitled *Gabriel's Fire*, concerns itself with issues that go beyond the essay's subject.

Gabriel's Fire is set during the years when I was between the ages of thirteen and eighteen. It is a glimpse of the life my family and I underwent as a people of Mexican descent in a predominantly Polish, blue-collar community on Chicago's South Side. This is not to say that the memoir focuses on any single area of interest, be it either issues pertaining to race relations, the immigrant's plight, the dilemma of social and class identity for a "minority" family living in an American city, or those stereotypes that oversimplify, degrade, and dehumanize inner-city life. One of my aims is to show that there is so much more happening in the "hood."

Dialogue rather than descriptive narrative is a device used extensively throughout the work for a variety of reasons. One of them is to display the world as it was presented to me then—in words. It was not until I was eleven or twelve that I truly started to become both familiar and comfortable with the English language.

Prior to those years I relied more on intuitive thought and feelings to decipher the world around me. This was not necessarily a bad thing. The frustration and problems came when I could not communicate fully my own views to others. This, coupled with a sometimes hostile environment, meant that I was very much confused and frightened as a child. Once I grew into the language, however, it was as if a new toy had been handed to me. From then on, everything seemed to move quite rapidly for me. With a newborn's enthusiasm for life, I was able to wander and situate myself with a variety of groups and individuals in the following five years, making a good many mistakes along the way.

With dialogue I have also sought to be as realistic and accurate about the time period mentioned, relying primarily on memory, with the addition of journals as secondary sources of what took place (I have kept them since the age of twelve). Conversations presented here are obviously not full-body transcripts of what proceeded, but they are as close as possible to what I would recall then and now. Indeed, one of the most tremendous rewards I have ever received in life came to me by way of memory during one of my writing sessions. I remember closing my eyes and sensing the sights, sounds, and smells of a record shop I used to frequent in my early youth. How gloriously real it seemed.

Ultimately, the events of this work are what I deem to be some of the most important in the shaping of my life at that age. Other happenings have been left out so as to maintain the structural and thematic integrity of the work as it is. Omitted too are incidents that would, at best, have served only to reaffirm the more sensitive themes but would, at worst, have steered the work toward unwanted sensationalism. The names of certain characters have been altered for reasons of legality (but note that Rivas is in fact Rivas). I feel neither ill will nor pity for any of the "malicious" characters depicted. They were who they were; they contributed to my formation. Despite the hurdles of the period, I understand how fortunate I am to have experienced those times and how much I have learned from them. In retrospect, things may have gone far worse for me but I don't think they could have been better.

The work has helped me to deliberate upon a tumultuous past. There are, of course, many other ideas of which the book speaks both softly and loudly, but I will let you decide that for yourself. I hope you find this journey rewarding and insightful. I am grateful for those who have been supportive in this endeavor, particularly Professor Tom Cummins of the art history department at the University of Chicago for initiating the spark, Aida Herrera for her love and patience while I wrote this, the Visual Resource Collection of the art history department at U of C where I spent my days editing (thank you, John), David Brent, executive editor at U of C Press, for his faith in me, and the liberty I received from the Press in making this genuinely my own.

January 13, 1999

twilight collects

1985

I

"What are you thinking?"

I was staring at a shadowy ceiling when Israel's quiet voice startled me. It was unlike him to still be awake, I thought. From my corner space I leaned over to take a look at him.

The ten-year-old's bed lay parallel to mine, to my right. His body, motionless, was wrapped tightly inside the same sort of thin white sheet now half-covering me. I pictured a photo of Israel in a grasshopper outfit our mother had made for him a few years ago. That frozen image of him happily parading in the Halloween costume felt tranquil. Sincere.

"Come ahhhhhn, what are you thinking?"

"Oh . . . umm . . . nothing," wanting to explain but for various reasons unable to do so with words. "I'm not thinking nothing," becoming frustrated.

"So how come you don't close your eyes?"

"Because," gathering myself together, "I'm listening to what they're saying."

"Who? Who are you listening to?"

I sat up in bed, placed the pillow behind me, against the headrest, and fell back.

"The people outside," I answered. "Can't you hear them? Fernando and his girlfriend Deborah? They've been arguing since like Ma told us to go to sleep."

"Oh."

I turned left, focusing on the room's wallpaper, lit by the muddy combination of blue and orange hues coming from outside. Save for the present situation, the rest of our Polish neighborhood was fast asleep now.

I squinted and tried to make out the details of every Peanuts character I saw lined up horizontally on the wall. I centered in on Snoopy, pretending to be a tennis player. I drew back my gaze and pinpointed him again in another spot. There was the ace with scarf and goggles. Now he was an airplane pilot. A war hero. He was whatever he wanted to be. Never just a dog.

And there was Charlie Brown with a baseball glove and a red cap covering his big bald head. He looked unusually old, it seemed to me, like a person who had gone through too much. I wondered why his friends thought there was something wrong with him. Why did they tease him so?

Linus was there too, dragging his favorite blue blanket on the ground! And Lucy. Her agitated look. Why did she always appear so cross?

"I don't hear anything," Israel announced. "I just hear wind."

"Yeah," coming back to him, "well," now hearing the whistling breeze myself. "I think Fernando went back into his house or something 'cause a heard a door close before."

"Hey."

I stared over.

"Remember we have to go to serve Mass tomorrow. So you better go to sleep because Ma's going to wake us up real early."

"How early?"

"You know. Like always. Five."

"Five again?" I groaned, "Oh maaan!"

"Shhh, stop yelling. You're going to wake everybody else up. Just go to sleep already. Then you won't be mad like you always get in the morning."

"But I can't go to sleep."

"Yes you can," Israel tugged on his sheet, "you do it all the time. I hear you do it in class too."

"Yeah, well . . . I can't go to sleep now."

I slid back into bed and turned to my left, away from him. I lifted one of my bare legs and placed it against the wall. I felt a thin layer of cool moisture cover the wallpaper's grainy surface. The landscape felt pleasant. I caressed it until the spot became annoyingly warm for me. Then I simply shifted to another area.

"Hey, you want to know something?"

"What?" his interruption irritated me. I felt he was asking and saying too many things.

"Why don't you count sheep like they say you should do in school so that you can go to sleep? Miss Kim tells me that that always works for her."

"Who?"

"You know," he said, "Miss Kim, the fifth-grade teacher."

"Isn't that your new teacher this year?"

"Uh-huh . . . she's real nice. She's helping us so we can sing the Super Bowl Shuffle in front of everyone at school this year. We're even going to dress up like the real Bears. She's cool."

"Oh yeah, right. Cool enough to still count sheep?"

"Hey, don't make fun of her. It works!"

"Are you kidding?" I began to play with my bedsheet, shaping it into a miniature mountain range. "That doesn't really work," scaling the terrain with my eyes. "That's stuff for little kids."

"Well then how are you going to get to sleep?"

"Man, it don't matter," pulling back on various parts of the cloth, making my imaginary snow peaks higher and sharper. "I don't need to sleep."

"Everyone needs to sleep."

"Not me," spreading out the sheet again to start over, "the only thing I n . . ."

The faint sound of a metal door slamming shut cut me off. Fernando's, I thought.

"Why don't you close the win . . ."

"Shhh," gesturing for him to remain quiet, "let me hear."

I heard a set of footsteps walking slowly over wooden stairs. I heard a girl's voice. Yeah, I told myself, Fernando's. They were the only ones who had long wooden stairs on our block.

I slouched back into bed and waited for something to happen. No one said a word.

Minutes passed. The crashing music of the leaves getting caught in the wind rose. Soon, I thought.

"Oh, just go back to sleep," I said moments later, completely unaware of how rude I had been to my younger brother.

He didn't say a word.

"Isi?" The Spanish nickname his mother and father had given him. "Isi? Are you asleep?"

The only thing that came from him was a light snore. Man, he's probably mad at me because I told him to be quiet. Man, I didn't want that to happen. How come I always make him mad?

But I didn't understand. Only the steady and familiar guilt remained of having done something wrong to someone I enjoyed spending time with.

An hour or so after our last words to each other, an argument broke out between Fernando and his girlfriend Deborah. Periods of tense whispers erupted into shouting matches. Their fighting jolted my spirit, making me feel nervous. Yet, as disturbing as it was, their arguing was too interesting for me to ignore.

"You better watch it, Deborah!" Fernando yelled. "If that baby you're carrying turns out to be a fuckin' addict, I'm gonna fuckin' blame it all on that little fuckin' habit of yours! You fuckin' hear me?"

"Will you shut the fuck up, Fern! Stop acting like a goddamn little fairy!"

"Man, I mean it, Deborah! Don't you know that snorting all that shit up your nose is gonna fuck up the baby?"

"Well, motherfucker, I don't see you giving anything up."

"That's different, I'm not having it. Besides, I'm thinking about our baby."

"Oh yeah, that's right, *our* baby! Now you want to call it *our* baby! Let me ask you something, Fern. Did you even once think about telling that bitch that was by your crib the other day that you already had a lady? Huh?"

No answer.

"You fucking lowlife! See, you can't even be straight with me. What a pussy motherfucker! Now who's being jive? Shit, Fern! Is it just me or are all you fucking spics the same?"

"Hold on, bitch! Watch who the fuck you call a spic! Don't even say that shit in front of my crib! Shit, whatever I do with Cindy has nothing to do with your dumb ass!"

6

"Oh yeah, well what about those fucking gangbanging friends of yours? Huh, Fern? How 'bout getting yourself a real job! Did you ever think about that? Shit, you think I like seeing you hanging out on that street corner making chump change with those fucking braziers?"

"You better fuckin' watch what you say about my friends, you stupid white bitch, because what I do with them is none of your fuc . . . none of your business."

"Whoa," she sneered, "what's the matter, Fernie? You can't say 'fuck' because your ma's at the door? Fuck, if she's really that tough, I wish she would do something about those friends of yours. Her sorry ass don't do nothing but complain about you going out with me. What about them losers?"

"Shut your blonde dumb ass up. You don't know what you're talkin' about." He hesitated. "See, Ma, this is what I was telling you about. You see how she gets when she's drunk? She gets stupid!"

"Fuck you, Fern! I bet your mom doesn't even know you're going to have a kid."

Silence.

"I didn't think so. So what do you expect me to tell *our* baby when it's born and asks me what daddy does for a living? Am I going to tell it that he's some little thug . . . peddling dope on some street corner 'cause he ain't *man* enough to get himself a real job? And how about . . ."

Ever since we had moved here, there was something I didn't like about Fernando. Something I felt inside. I didn't like her either. I wasn't sure why, though. Was it the way she looked at me with her bulging blue eyes? Or was it that fake cracked smile she always gave?

As she kept bringing up Fernando's faults, all my suspicions about him became confirmed. He *did* sell drugs, I thought. She said so herself. But I wasn't too sure what drugs were or what they were for. I had heard about them.

I recollected seeing a film at school showing some boy jumping up and down on a bed, hollering that he was Superman. I remembered the narrator's voice calmly explain that the boy had ingested something called *ah-sid*. Ah-sid, my teacher Miss Barbara added, along with Mary Iguana were what the devil himself had put on the planet to take us away from Jesus. As the film rolled, I

7

wondered how she could possibly know so much about what the devil put here for us.

A car door closed. On the third try, an engine cranked out a rattling noise. Wheels peeled, putting an end to Fernando's presence. His mother came out of the house and bluntly screamed for Deborah to leave. She was no good for him, she said in Spanish. She had ruined her son. Had taken him away from them, the family, and her. I was convinced otherwise. They were all wrong, I told myself. And as I lay there, I regretted not having gone to sleep instead.

Their screen door banged shut once more. I felt viscous ripples of hate encroach me, throwing me off inside once more.

I heard Deborah say something about how fed up she was with "Fernie."

"Fuck this motherfucker," she ripped, "this is the last time. Fuck all you motherfuckers! You can all go fuck yourselves!"

I backed away from the windowsill, quivering. They made me so angry. Why did people have to fight so much? I began to think of my own problems. I couldn't understand why they hated me at school. What did I do to them?

I searched for a solution to the pain. Eventually, I found what I wanted. I had been pondering the whole thing for some time. And I was convinced no one would care if I died. Why would they? They didn't care that I was alive.

Things had passed by the time a familiar rumbling came through the screen windows. Our mother yelled for us to close them. I didn't. I loved the rain and the rest of the sounds that came with it. I prayed for more thunder.

Drops of water splattered over my face.

More pleeeasse . . .

A response.

I jumped out of bed and went directly to the living room, tiptoeing lightly, hoping my mother wouldn't find me up. It felt like a good storm to me. Not to be missed.

In the living room I poised myself on the brown-carpeted floor in front of the largest window. It could easily cover six or seven of me. I pulled the gold-laced curtains apart and placed my palms on the glass. The pane trembled. I pressed my right cheek against it and waited for the worst of it. Out there the trees swayed violently, leaning toward ground. I was half-afraid, half-hoping they would fall. They always seemed like they were about to drop, even though I never witnessed it. I sighed.

Suddenly, the sharp cramp in my stomach returned. My eyes watered. I crouched forward, holding myself in, expecting to throw up the filth. If Mom even found out that I was up past my bedtime she would be so upset with me, I told myself.

I cried. I felt I couldn't do anything right. As the storm made its final attempt at something grand, I heard her voice.

"Luis! Ya vete a dormir!"

"Ya voy, Ma!" I yelled, covering my pain. She had known all along that I was awake. "Un poquito mas por favor!" I wondered what else she really knew. All the awful things I had done?

"Luis!"

"Okay, okay! I'm going."

I left the living-room floor and sped past the clock in the kitchen, which read a little past three.

"Five," I muttered. "Five."

Because our mother didn't believe in having us close our bedroom doors and because our room was directly in front of the kitchen, Israel and I were always subjected to the brunt of the noise my mother made every morning.

First, she fiddled from station to station until the Spanish voice came over the radio. Then she would attack the kitchen, producing a clinking and clanking, making it clear to everyone that this time for rest had met its end.

"Muchachos!" her high-pitched voice sounded, "ya es hora que se levanten!"

Israel shuffled out of his covers and landed on the open floor between us. I heard the refrigerator and pantry doors open. She was preparing our father's lunch. Good, I thought, maybe she'd somehow forget about me. If she did, I'd have another ten minutes to rest.

"Isi!" my mother yelled, in the gentlest manner one could yell, "fíjate si ya se levantó tu hermano!"

Ugghh, she was calling on her loyal soldier to investigate the situation.

"No, Mom," Israel responded, "todavía está dormido!"

"Entonces dile que se levante!"

"Si, Mom!"

Israel tapped me on my shoulder. "Mom says to wake up."

"Maaan," holding the sheet over my face, "I heard her already! Why did you tell her I was asleep?"

"Because you are."

"You know I'm not!"

"Then how come you're still in bed?"

"Because I don't want to get up," annoyed at his peculiar zeal in carrying out her orders. "Maaan, you should've just told her I was already awake. I need more tiiiime."

"Time for what? So that . . ."

A nearby voice stopped him.

"Luis, por que no le haces caso a tu hermano? Por el amor de Dios, levantate!"

She was in the doorway now. I pulled the sheet away from my face. My puffy eyes prevented me from seeing her. Yet she was there. Despite the barriers. And she was frowning. Of course she was. She was waiting to see what I would do. Hoping to distract her, I asked her what time it was.

"Ya pasan de la cinco," she replied.

A little after five? "Pero la misa no empieza hasta las seis."

"Si, por eso *apúrate*, porque se te va hacer tarde."

"*Late*, I'm never late." I clutched my pillow and bitterly threw it off to the side. "Maaan, when am I late?"

She left her station, obviously satisfied with the results of her visit.

"I hope you're not going to take forever in the bathroom," scratching the side of my head.

"What?" Israel answered mildly, reaching down to pick up the school uniform he had neatly folded the night before, "you're the one who's not even out of bed." He gave me a disapproving glance. "How come you're already kicking me out of the bathroom?" He gingerly placed his clothes on top of his bed.

"Man, just hurry it up."

"*You* hurry it up," putting on his slippers, "I don't want to be late for Mass again because of you."

10

"Man," I grumbled, "they should be happy that we even get up this early to go to church for them. We serve like every other week."

"Well no one's forcing you to go." He left the room.

The grogginess threw me right back in bed. I drew the white sheet over my face. "Come ahhhnn, God, give me five more minutes. Just five more. Pleease."

"Mom sent me to get you out of bed!"

"Oh noooo . . . another soldier!"

"What are you talking about now, goofy ass?"

I uncovered myself, turned on my right, and saw Jose's face. My older brother was fully dressed in his school uniform. He was wearing the navy-blue cardigan sweater our mother had recently bought for him.

"Oh, so you think you're cool with your brand new sweater?"

"Shut up, nerd. Stop changing the topic. You're just jealous because you didn't get one and you don't have your own room like me."

"Man, no-no. I don't even like those kinds of sweaters."

I actually did like those types of sweaters, I thought. They just didn't seem to go well with my skinny body.

"Anyway," I continued, "Ma says you only got it because you're in eighth grade. She says I'm going to get one next year when I'm in eighth grade."

"Yeah, you'll probably get this one."

"No way! I'm not tall like you, Big Bird."

"Oooh, that really hurt, you little dork."

"You're the dork . . . Hey, is Israel out of the bathroom yet?"

"He just got out," stepping closer to my bed and grabbing my wrist. "Are you coming or do I have to pick up your little ass and throw it in the shower?"

"Stop it! I'm going! Wait!"

Jose's frame was tall and muscular. I didn't even dare to say no to him. Not that I was scared, but I felt too sick to challenge him.

"You better hurry it up then before you get Mom mad at you and make her come over here for you."

"She already came."

"Oh," he tightened his hold, "so you want her to come back again?"

11

With that, I bolted out of bed and left the room barefooted, passing my mother on the way.

"*Ya,*" I said, bitterly responding to her soundless stares through words, "ahorita mismo me voy a ir a bañar, Ma."

I walked a few more steps down the hall and turned into the bathroom. I closed the door behind me and bent over the bathtub. I turned the knob to let the water out and then yanked on another lever, immediately sending the clear liquid through the shower-head. I stooped forward to take a long drink.

Once I felt the water warm, I stepped into the tub and closed the sliding glass door behind me. Remembering my underwear, I removed them and tossed them out. I took a quick shower, scrubbed sporadically, went back to my room, dressed, and eventually sat down at the kitchen table with my two brothers. They had begun to eat without me.

My mother came over and spread her fingers through my wet hair.

"Hay, Luis! Ni siquiera te secastes el pelo!"

"Man, Ma," pushing her hands away, "ya no soy un niño. Why do you keep talking to me like I'm a little kid? I don't need to dry my hair. It's fine."

"*It's fine, it's fine,*" she said sarcastically in broken English. "Y eso es lo que me vas a decir cuando te enfermes, eh?"

"No. Yo nunca me enfermo, Ma."

She turned around and walked back to the stove. Yeah, I repeated inside, I never get sick.

"Sí, como no," she turned a corn tortilla over the open blue gas flame. "Si el otro día ya te estabas muriendo. Recuerdas?"

"What? Oh, yeah," watching the tortilla bubble up. "That was a long time ago, Ma . . . I guess sometimes I get sick."

"Cómo?" coming over to hand me a concoction of semi-raw eggs and lime juice.

I drank it down. "Nothing, Ma," looking at the rest of my food. Maybe it would be best to keep quiet and eat.

"Wow," snickered Jose a few seconds later, "he's really going to shut up. Amazing. I'm amazed. Aren't you amazed, Mom? How about you, Isi?"

"Shut up," I said.

"Ooops," he snapped his fingers, "spoke too soon. Damn!"
Israel laughed sheepishly.

By five-thirty we were outside, waiting in that familiar place between night and day.

"Están seguros que nada se les olvida?" our mother asked us. She was standing at the top of the concrete stairs of our South Side Chicago home. What the real estate agency called a "ranch" model.

I could sense in our mother's voice how difficult it was for her to let us go alone even though we had already talked about it at the beginning of the school year. The three of us had convinced her we were old enough to go by ourselves. And ever since grandfather had left for Mexico, there was no one else to take us.

"Pues," she presented us with an umbrella, "aquí tienen la sombrilla, por si acaso llueve."

None of us seemed too enthusiastic about taking the small pink umbrella.

"Ma," looking up at the sky, trying to dissuade her, "ya no creo que va a llover. It's not cloudy anymore."

"Pero dijeron en el radio que iba a llover en la tarde," she explained.

"Ma," deciding to tell her the real reason why none of us would take it, "la umbrella se ve *dorky*."

"Cómo?" a baffled look appeared on her face. "Ah, mira. A mi no me importa si la sombrilla se ve '*dorky*' o como tu la quieras llamar. Con que no se enfermen es lo que a mi me importa. Está bién?"

"Yeah," waving the umbrella away, "I know you don't want us to get sick, Ma, pero yo no la voy a cargar. Let Isi or Jose carry it."

"No way," Israel said. "Not me."

"Dámela a mí," Jose took hold of it, "porque este," he pointed to me, "es *chicken*."

I felt my face redden.

"Shut up! I'm not chicken!"

"Ya dejen de pelear," our mother said to us both. "Son hermanos."

Somehow her calling us brothers in Spanish seemed to have

13

much more meaning for me just then than its English counterpart.

"Yeah, Jose," I said, "stop fighting with me. We're brothers."

"Dork, you're the one who's fighting."

I gave my mother a good-bye kiss on the cheek. She returned the peck. Israel did the same.

We then began to descend the short concrete steps, leaving Jose behind to talk to her. We were almost at the bottom when our mother called out to the two of us.

"Muchachos!" We both turned around. "No se les olviden que su papá también los tiene que persignar."

We had forgotten about our father. Her reminder prompted Israel and me to run back up. We headed straight for our parents' room. Underneath the bedcovers was a huddled mass in fetal position. I gave a forceful shake, asking him to bless us. Half awake, he rose and chanted a quick prayer in Spanish. He ended the blessing, making the sign of the cross on my forehead, lips, and chin. I stepped back. He went on to Israel, who graciously thanked him as soon as he was done.

"Ya están?" my mother asked us as we reappeared outside.

"Yeah. He did it."

My mother looked at Israel. He nodded in agreement.

"Bueno," she smiled, "vayan con Dios."

Israel and I plunged back to our front walk. Jose continued speaking with her and looked back at us from time to time, nodding his head to my mother. I wondered if they were still discussing the umbrella.

As we waited I crossed our lawn and headed to a nearby streetpost. Stationed in front of our home, the long green metal fixture overlooked 33rd Street. The orange glow of the streetlight began to fade. A dull opaque white shell replaced it. I wondered who it was that turned it off and on.

I smelled traces of gas. Across the street was the gasoline station, the only building on that peculiar triangular-shaped block. It wouldn't be open until later in the day, yet even now the fumes were present.

I watched Jose coming over to us. As he neared, I begged him to tell me what she had said.

"Stop being so nosy," he waved a last good-bye to her.

Her face appeared anxious. It was as if she wanted to say good-bye to us once more. Her lips smiled, but her eyes gave her true emotions away. I turned away from them. I didn't know how to respond. What could I do? Why was she so sad? I looked down on the ground and turned elsewhere.

"No, come on," I pleaded, "tell me what she said to you, Jose. Tell me what's wrong!"

"Okay, just wait."

Jose began to walk down the street. Israel and I followed him. When we were out of earshot range, he pulled me close.

"Well," in a quiet tone, "she just told me to make sure that you guys didn't go off on your own and . . . ," smiling wryly, looking back as if to see if anyone was listening. His eyes opened wide, "and that you don't get yourselves into trouble. *There*, are you satisfied?"

"You mean that's it? You mean she didn't say anything else?"

"What else did you want her to say, goofy?"

"Man, I thought it was going to be something important."

"No, that's it. So are you finished asking me a million questions?"

"Yeah. I guess."

"Don't guess, dork," Jose shook his head. "Are you or aren't you?"

"Yeah. I am."

"All right then, let's go. Israel looks like he's getting tired of waiting for us."

I was beginning to realize our morning walks reminded me of the times when our father would take us to the forest preserves past the city limits. I remembered how he would methodically point up to the trees, aim at the inhabitants of the thick green, and tell us stories of his hunting days in Mexico. The difference between hunting for pleasure and hunting for necessity.

He would explain to us the vast reality he saw, show us life I would normally have missed. I was in awe of him. Not only for his skills in detecting what was around, but for his ability to transform himself into a friend and to relate to us his insight.

"Cool," skipping and scrambling from side to side.

"What's up, Louie?"

15

"Nothing, Jose. I'm just thinking something."

I thought about the baby squirrel that had once bit my finger. My father had said I had deserved it for bullying something so small. I argued I hadn't bullied it. Then what was it doing in your baseball glove? he asked. How did it get there? What gives you the right to imprison it? To hurt something that hasn't done a damn thing to you?

I looked down at the ground. All I wanted to do was protect it, I answered.

From what? From its life?

I kept silent and learned from him what not to do.

I lifted my head to see where we were. We were less than a block from 37th Street. Ever since we had left home, the three of us had kept to ourselves. This was beginning to occur more often, I thought. It worried me. What would happen when Jose started high school next year? Would this make for more loneliness?

"Aw shit!" sniffing the air around me.

"What?" Jose asked.

A greenish-brown mush lay pasted over the edge of one of my black shoes.

"What a dork!" Jose hailed Israel, who was getting far ahead of us, to wait. "You stepped on dog shit again?"

"Yeah, and my s-s-s-school shoes . . ."

"Spit it out."

"They're brand new," I clenched my teeth.

"Well," grinning, "I guess they're not new anymore."

"Man, Jose, what am I going to do?"

He set his schoolbag down and began seemingly to check a vast expanse. "Man, Louie, that's what you get for running around like a monkey all over people's grass. Now you know why Mom said not to let you go on your own? To listen to me?"

The stench climbed up from below, becoming more intense. My eyes began to fill with tears.

"Stop being such a little baby. You're always crying about something."

I lowered my head in disgust.

"Listen, dork," softening his tone, "why don't you go across the street and clean it off where that puddle is?"

I was reluctant to see what he was talking about.

"Look," he persisted, "that'll help."

"Okay."

I strolled over to the other side of the street.

"Hey, dork!" he said halfway through my light jog. "Will you stop and make sure you look both ways before crossing the street? I don't want to tell Ma you got killed by a stupid car! Then she's going to get pissed off with me!"

"Okay, okay!"

I reached the water and dipped my right foot into the dark lagoon. I imagined the Loch Ness monster pouncing up. I had seen a television show about it the night before. The horror never materialized.

When I found bottom, I made a circling motion and then front to back. When I was through, I went over to someone's lawn and rubbed my shoe into the moist green. The dew on the surface of the grass helped wipe away whatever was left. I sat on the front steps of a stranger's porch and initiated a more intense inspection. I was afraid someone at school would pick up on my clumsiness.

"Cool." It had all come off. Only bits and pieces of grass were now stuck within the grooves of the black rubber sole.

I drew the tip of my nose along the bottom of my shoe. I relaxed. Not a tinge. I rose up and returned to my brothers.

Israel hadn't said a thing throughout my ordeal. Instead, he was swinging his open schoolbag in the air, making full circles with it. He seemed more impressed that nothing dropped out of the bag.

"What?" he stopped playing.

"Nothing!" speaking now with an air of regained confidence.

Israel shook his head. "I don't know what your problem is, Louie. You've been in a bad mood ever since you woke up today."

"Yeah . . . So?"

"You don't like it when people talk to you in a mean way. You think I like it? Huh?"

"I know," whispering, "I know. I'm just . . ."

"You're just what?"

"Nothing! I don't know."

We resumed our walk. Israel led. Jose and I lagged behind.

"Hold your horses, Israel, we still got time."

"No we don't," checking his watch. "It's already six and Mass is suppose to start at six. What are we supposed to tell Sister when she sees we're late?"

"Sister Consuela isn't going to say nothing."

"Cut it out, you two," Jose intervened. "You sound like the assholes from last night."

"Awww," Israel commented, "you said a bad word."

We turned onto Paulina Street. St. Peter's was less than a block away. The red brick elementary school, rectangular shaped, stood well above the trees. Past it was the rectory's front lawn, meticulously manicured. And right next to it was the church. A white concrete cross was delicately suspended on top of its steeple, seeming anxious to break off at any moment.

The gutters on the roof of the church provided a haven for a gang of pigeons bobbing back and forth. They were prepared to make their drops on some unsuspecting victim below.

"Look, dork," Jose pointed to the residents, "more shit for you."

"So? Dad told me if you step on shit, it means that you're going to be rich one day."

"Oh yeah," he laughed, "so then you're probably going to be a billionaire!"

"Asshole." I returned my gaze on the school building. The window shades had all been left perfectly half-raised. A pitch-black void came from the bottom half of the windows, provoking more questions than answers. The black holes they talked about in school, I imagined. I feared not knowing their truth.

"Hey, Jose," I called out, nearing the building, "you think ghosts live in the school?"

"Yeah, and if you don't shut up they're going to come out and get your stupid ass."

I kept quiet, believing someone or something was staring back at me from the windows. A feeling of guilt emerged.

"Look, I don't know if there's ghosts in there or what," Jose added. "But hurry it up. Speedy Gonzalez over here is going to get mad again and start complaining again about how late we are."

"Dogs get mad, people get angry." I said. *Remember?*

"Huh? What the fuck are you talking about now? Oh man," he said, "you're such a geek. Don't tell me you're starting to sound like them. Man, do you always believe everything they say? People get mad too, just in a different way."

"No, no," I implored.

"Why do you say that? Because they say so?"

"Yeah, they're the teachers."

Jose threw his arms out. "So? That doesn't mean they know everything. Does it?"

"I didn't say that. You're getting it all wrong."

"Hey, goofy ass! Did you ever think that maybe *they* sometimes get it wrong?"

"No. Why are they going to lie to me?"

"Man, Louie, I didn't say they lied all the time but I bet they make mistakes like everybody else. I bet they don't have all their facts straight. You see what I mean?"

"I guess."

"Damn, bro'," sounding disappointed, "you still have a lot to learn."

"Well, why don't you teach me instead of make fun of me?"

"I don't know if you can learn, goofball."

"I can learning anything. I just want you to teach me."

"Maybe. But not yet."

"Why not?"

"Because. You're still too little. When you get older, we'll talk."

We passed the front of the school. I tried opening the steel doors.

"Leave it alone already," Jose said. "*Relax*, you're going to be in there in about two hours. Wait like everybody else."

"Maaan, I just want to see if they're open."

I tapped on the thick glass of one of the doors and looked inside. I couldn't see much, except for a dim set of emergency lights in the middle of the hallway. An army of goosebumps began to crawl up my arms and neck. I thought about the stories my father would tell us at night about the scary and strange things he saw when he was living in Mexico. I heard a click. Jumping back, I frantically moved ahead of the others.

"Oh my God, dork, don't tell me you got scared?"

I kept going.

"A-ha!" Jose sang. "Louie got scared! That's what you get, dork!"

19

"Shut up!" yelling back. "You know how I get when I see dark places," covering my ears with my hands, hoping it would protect me from whatever it was I felt coming after me.

He said something. I lost a few of his first words but eventually gave in to the temptation of taking my hands off my ears.

". . . why do you talk about shit like ghosts for, then? You know you're going to get like this."

"I don't know," completely dropping my hands down. "I just like to think about stuff like that."

"Man, Lou-Lou, quit being such a scaredy cat."

He turned to Israel. "Isn't he being wimpy?"

"I don't care," he answered. "All I know is we're going to be late."

"Oh my god! Another dork!" Jose pointed to me. "This one talks too much." He looked at Israel. "And this one doesn't think of anything else but getting to Mass on time." He looked up at the sky. "Why did you give me a couple of dorks for brothers? *Why?*"

Israel and I kept quiet. The teasing hurt.

"Come on," Jose grabbed hold of Israel's arm and turned to look at the time. "Oh shit, Mickey's hands say we're late."

"I told you," Israel quipped. "Let's gooo . . ."

After opening a pair of tall golden doors, we found two old Polish women in the dark lobby, whispering excitedly to one another. Each of them was wearing a babushka. One was a violent pink-colored one, the other a swirling pattern of earth tones. A few inches from the women was a bulletin stand at which they took simultaneous glances.

"See," I jeered, "they haven't even gone inside to sit down."

"That doesn't mean we're not late," Israel confided. "Maybe they're waiting for us."

Jose shook his head.

Both women peered over our way. One of them—I think her name was Stephanya—was always saying hello. She smiled, adding the Polish greeting "dzien dobry."

Her friend remained still, treating us as a nuisance. I went ahead and waved hello. Stephanya bowed her head. The other one remained grim.

"Come on, dork," Jose undid his sweater, "you always want to talk to everybody. Don't you see they don't like us?"

"Wait." I took a better look at the bulletin's announcement. George Pincze. The date of his funeral was for today at 11:30. Hopefully, Sister Therese would pick us to serve the Mass. That would make the day go by quickly.

"Oh, by the way," Jose said, "I heard you told Miss Rhonda you were God."

"What? Who told you that?" surprised he knew about the incident.

"Ah," opening the glass door leading to the left aisle, "I got spies everywhere."

"No, come on, Jose, tell me who told you."

"Don't worry about it," walking slowly ahead, "just tell me what happened."

"Well, it started like this. See, I told Miss Rhonda that I was God, sort of. But it wasn't my fault. Sister Albian had asked me to take care of Miss Rhonda's class during choir rehearsal. They were making a lot of noise and I told them to stop. Then when Miss Rhonda finally showed up to take over, she asked me what gave me the right to give her class orders. You know, she didn't even give me time to answer." Jose gave a sympathetic nod. "Anyway," breathing in, "she asked if I thought I was special and she even asked me if I thought I was God. I was so pissed off that when she did let me talk, I told her what Miss Barbara had told me; that God is everywhere. And I told her that since God is everywhere, God must be inside of me everywhere, and if that's true, then I must be God all over. So I must be God."

"What? What a dork!"

"Wait a minute. I'm not finished."

"All right, what else did you say?"

"Anyway, I told her that it was Sister Albian who had given me permission to take care of her class and that I wasn't doing anything wrong."

"You told her all of that?" Jose appeared unconvinced.

"Yeah," I answered proudly.

"And then what did she do? Did she tell on you with Miss Barbara?"

"No, she didn't. Miss Rhonda didn't do anything except send me to Sister Albian's. She said I should tell Sister what I told her and that that would get me off my high horse."

"And when you went down to the office, did you tell Sister Albian everything you had said to Miss Rhonda?"

"Yeah. Why not? I didn't do anything wrong."

"And what did she say?"

"Man, she just laughed at the whole thing."

"You're sure you didn't get in trouble?"

"No way, she just said to be more *ca-ahn-shi-en-chus*. Is that the word?"

"That's it."

"Yeah well, she told me to be more like that when I say things to people."

"Man," Jose shook his head, "you're lucky. I would have gotten in trouble."

"That's because you're a smart ass, Jose. I'm just smart."

"Yeah, right."

The interior of the church was even darker than the lobby. There were really only three areas from where light shone. Two strips of fluorescent lighting were at the front of the room, hanging alongside the main altar's crucifix. Soft bouncing light came from the north and south wings, where two side altars were in place.

At the wings, statues lay elevated atop wooden vigil-light stands, facing each other directly. There was fifty feet between the life-sized man and woman. I felt an apprehensive fear every time I crossed the path of these two pale and morbid saints. What if they were to come alive? What would they do?

They stood four feet above, policing the air in front of them, never looking down. On top of the stands sat three rows of perfectly lined candles, honoring these creatures who always appeared miserable at their posts. The highest row, closest to the statues, seemed never to be without a lit candle. The lowest row would normally only have a few. Why were they unequal? What did it matter which candles were lit?

I tilted my head at a higher angle. During the day, the sun illuminated sets of colorfully stained glass windows, which ran along the uppermost part of the church's side walls. But at the moment, every biblical image appeared bleak and lifeless. We walked on.

The sacristy, our next stop, was buried next to the main altar. Before we entered this room, we came to a spot where we were required to genuflect before a gigantic blue and white statue of the Virgin Mother Mary. She stood behind a banister, about fifteen feet away from us and nearly six feet above the tiled floor of the side altar. Like falling dominoes, we knelt to the routine. Israel went first. Jose and I rushed forward.

Inside the sacristy we found Sister Consuela cleaning a set of chalices. The plump woman was shining them to a bright gold. Her cheeks slightly flushed. We tried darting past her.

"Why are you boys coming so late?" she heaved, snorting a tremendous grunt, "I hope this doesn't become a daily habit." We smiled at each other. "Yes sir, after the meeting Sister Therese put together at the beginning of the year, I was hoping we were all going to work together this year and make things go by smoothly."

"Excuse me, Sister," Israel interrupted kindly, "this is the first time we're late."

"That's why I'm asking why you're late."

Jose took me before her. "Well, Sister, Luis stepped on some dog shit outside and we had to wait for him until he cleaned it off."

"Shhh!" putting a finger to her lips. "Jose, you should know better than to cuss in the house where baby Jesus lives!"

"But I thought you said Jesus was in heaven, Sister?"

"Now, Jose," throwing the cleaning rag over her shoulder, "do you want trouble?"

"No, Sister."

"Then don't come knocking on the door asking for it. I may be getting old for you little rascals but I'll show you a thing or two if you keep it up." She climbed a stool and placed a half-empty bottle of red wine in the cupboard above. "I've put bigger boys than you over my lap," she continued. "Yes sir, it wasn't too long ago I gave you a spanking."

I could see she was still upset over what had happened the last time she tried belting Jose. It was during one of her traditional reprimands. In evading her, Jose had quickly stepped aside, and Sister Consuela's hand had landed on a concrete post in front of him. They were still laughing about it at school. Jose had grown quite popular because of that incident and others like it.

"Is that true, Louie? Did you really step on dog sh . . . poop outside?"

"Yes, Sister," calmly resisting the temptation to laugh.

"You sure you took it all off?" She looked down at my feet.

"Yes, Sister. Do you want to see?"

She picked at my trousers, looking me over carefully.

"Looks swell to . . ."

"But," Jose objected, "he still smells like dog shit, Sister."

"Jose, that's enough from you," scrunching her face like a bulldog. "If we needed clowns we'd go straight to the circus . . . yes sir, to the circus."

"But I'm telling the truth, Sister."

"Of course, you always do, Jose, but you should know better than to say such devilish things in front of your younger brothers. Think of the things they'll pick up from that mouth of yours." Sister Consuela began to roll up one of her sleeves, holding a naked fist in the air. "I should take that mouth right now and wash it out with a bar of soap. Yes sir . . . now go on, all three of you, get dressed before Father Peter walks in and finds us all standing around, twiddling our thumbs." She began to chase after us. "Then we'll all be liable to be in hot water with Sister Therese."

We hurried out of the sacristy, running through a curved corridor leading to the dressing room. There was something pleasant about the journey through this plain parabola-shaped hallway painted cream. I felt unequivocal freedom here. I would move forward, and for what felt to be a boundless time, I would not see the other side. At times I would touch the concrete walls and be astonished to find things so flat and harsh instead of soft. In this jubilant race, mine was the only movement there was. Sometimes I would even step back to repeat the trip. Not today, I thought. Our responsibilities came first.

When we reached the dressing room, I opened wide the closets.

"They're over here," Jose pointed out a rack of recently cleaned cassocks. "Man," Jose said to me, "I can't believe you. After all this time you still don't know where the things are?"

"How come they're not in the same place?"

"Doesn't matter, goofball. You should always look around before you ask for help."

I took a look at the clock on the wall. It read 5:58.

"Hey, Israel, I thought you said it was six? I think your watch is fast."

"No, I always fix my watch like that," he said. "That way, we're never late."

"Oh."

I left the room dressed in black and white. I took a short cut across the main altar. Halfway along the path, I knelt before the main crucifix hanging six feet above the altar. I slowly made the sign of the cross.

"Jose, since you're bigger, you're responsible for carrying the cross. Do you hear me, Jose?"

"Yes, Sister."

"Now," turning to look at Israel and me, "you two boys grab the candles. Make sure you don't tilt them. I keep having to clean wax off the floors and your uniforms. Pretty soon I'll be sending them to your mother to get them washed."

"Oh man," I moaned, "you know it's not us who's doing it, Sister. Some of the other altar boys don't even take showers every day. They're the ones who keep messing up."

"Well, I may not have evidence to say who is being a slob," putting her fist against an imaginary wall in the air, "but when I find out, someone's going to be in *big* trouble."

"Yeah, well it ain't us, Sister."

"Louie, what did I tell you about the word *ain't* the other day?"

"I forgot."

"Well, I hope you start reminding yourself. Now go wait quietly with your brothers by the door."

Father Peter arrived at 6:05. At 6:10, he lined up behind us at the entrance of the sacristy's side vestibule and motioned me to begin. I gave a quick tug on a string. A sharp ring echoed. The people rose. Jose began the procession at a slow pace, hoisting the cross as high as he could. Show-off, I thought.

From their missals, the churchgoers, mostly women, sang a short Polish hymn. As usual, Sister Therese, Sister Consuela, Sister Evencia, and Sister Albian were seated in the front left row.

25

After parading up the steps of the main altar, we each went to our designated areas. The towering priest went toward his armchair, before which was a stand. He tilted the head of its microphone toward him.

He spread his arms out and looked to the left and right at the congregation of six or seven parishioners scattered among empty pews. I thought it strange how even Stephanya and her friend prayed apart.

"Pan z Wami," his thick raspy voice boomed from a set of lips that could barely be seen because of a full-grown beard.

Jose responded by bringing a thick red book to him. Father went on with the rest of the introduction, every word Polish. I had begun to repeat and give meaning to some of the words in my head.

As soon as he was finished, Jose returned to his chair, and the gray-haired priest, in monk's robes, withdrew to the center of the altar, where he knelt slowly, one hand on his leg, before the cross.

He stepped over to the side where Israel and I were sitting and wrapped his large body around the lectern. He clicked on a small brown lamp that lay perched on the lectern. The soft yellow glow of the bulb revealed ancient caverns and valleys on his face. His eyebrows, contemplative, came close to one another. It was taking him some time to begin. Why?

His fingers trembled, more so than ever. He drew Jose's attention and pointed to his eyes. He had forgotten his spectacles.

Jose went over to where the priest had been sitting, bent down, and peered into the priest's armchair. In a matter of seconds, he produced a set of glasses. He brought them over and handed them to Father Peter who gave a stern nod of approval and initiated the Readings.

At the end of Mass, when we informed Father Peter that we were staying on for the 7:00 Mass and then the school Mass at 7:30, he called us his last angels.

His words of appreciation meant a great deal to me. I smiled. For now, his eyes seemed to say, that was enough.

ב

*M*aaan, I can't stand serving all the time anymore."

"Dude, I don't know why you're still an altar boy. Just quit."

"For what?" I hung my father's handmade schoolbag on the closet hook. "So that Sister Therese or Miss Barbara will get on my case? Man, the last time I told Sister I was going to stop being an altar boy she put her crucifix in front of my face and asked me if I loved Jesus."

"She does that to everyone, dude. She did it to me. You see me still being an altar boy?"

"Yeah, just watch," I said, "as soon as she starts needing more people she'll come to you, and I'll bet you won't say no to her again."

"That's what you think." Alfred left.

"Everyone . . . take your seats."

Miss Barbara's command brought the rest of us into the classroom. With the exception of a few boys, the rest of my seventh-grade class sat in silence. At my desk I hunched over, dully observing the cream-colored intercom speaker box hanging on the front wall. Our principal's voice came through. Sister Albian's muffled greeting crackled good morning. Her words were repeated throughout the entire school. The shrill yells primarily came from the lower grades.

"Didn't anyone hear Sister?"

We continued sitting still.

". . . and please remember that this year's first raffle takes place at the end of this month. So don't forget to sell whatever is left of your raffle books. I know it may at times feel discouraging to go from door to door and have people shoo you away or tell you . . ."

"'Shoo you away?'" someone complained. "They don't even do that anymore. They just slam the door on you."

". . . remember, we're proud of each and every one of you. Especially when you sell all of your tickets. If neighbors don't want to buy any tickets from you, ask your mom and dad to take the tickets to work. Maybe their friends there will buy them. So far the second-graders have the lead in the number of tickets sold . . ."

"Did everyone hear Sister?" Miss Barbara paced up and down the aisles. "My goodness, I can't believe the little petunias are beating us. Aren't we embarrassed?"

"No!" everyone unanimously cried.

Sister's voice came back on.

". . . I was just reminded to tell you boys and girls that the monthly skating party at Disco Wheels, sponsored by the Mothers Club, will be next Friday. Tickets are still available here in the office. Remind your parents they'll save time and money if they buy them here. And while I'm on, I might as well remind you again of the family Mass that Miss Barbara was mentioning at the end of today's morning Mass. An open house follows for everyone to attend, where the Mothers Club will be selling their delicious cupcakes. Thank you and have a nice day . . ."

"Well, I know every one of my seventh-graders and their parents are going to be present at the family Mass," our teacher stated. "Mr. Schwartz? You will be at Mass this time? Won't you?"

"Yes, Miss Barbara." Mark pushed back his shaggy brown hair. "I'll make sure my mom doesn't forget this time."

"I hope *you* won't forget, Mark, because I don't believe Mr. and Mrs. Schwartz would be happy if I gave them another call at ten in the evening. Would they?"

"No."

Miss Barbara began to walk up and down the room, her arms folded in front of her chest. She came up to my desk.

"Both of your parents are going to be there, aren't they, Mr. Aguilera?"

"My mom can go but I don't think my dad will come."

"And why not?"

"He can't. I already talked to Sister Albian about it."

"Oh, that's right. Sister spoke to me about your father's problem before, about his being too tired to come to Mass on Sunday." She shook her head. "I don't know what this funny business is about, Mr. Aguilera."

"My father works six days out of the week," I snarled back. "Sunday's the only day he can rest, Miss Barbara, and that's why he can't make it for Mass. I already said that to you when the year started."

"Mr. Aguilera, I'm sure everyone's fathers here work as hard as yours. He's a carpenter? Correct?"

"No," agitated. "He's an upholsterer. It's not the same thing."

"It doesn't matter. Everyone else's father comes to the family Mass so I see no real reason why yours can't attend."

"What about Charlie's? You don't say anything to him."

"He has special circumstances. And we're not talking about Charlie . . . But I suppose if Sister Albian says it's okay for your mother to accompany the three *Aguileras* all by herself, then I don't see why I should go against her better judgment. But I really wish . . ."

A new voice came over the intercom. It was Sister Therese, reminding the altar boys of their future obligations. At the end she asked to see Israel and myself in her eighth-grade classroom. I stood up immediately, ready to leave.

"Mr. Aguilera, wait until I've given you permission."

"But I have to . . ."

"I'm not deaf, Mr. Aguilera. I know what you have to do. Besides, Sister Therese can wait a couple of minutes. It's going to take her a few extra minutes to get back to her classroom. In any case, what do you say before you leave?"

"Can I please go downstairs?" edging toward the door.

"*May* I."

"Miss Barbara, *may* I please go downstairs so that I *may* see Sister Therese? *May* I?"

"Marvelous," she said dryly, "You do *comprende.*"

Why was she so mean?

After we completed our tasks, the funeral director came over to the sacristy and handed us a sealed envelope. Once undressed, we divided the three two-dollar bills and made our way to the church's basement, where the school's cafeteria was. On our descent, I watched a flock of students being herded back to class. They filed past us without a single hello, their vacant eyes pointing straight ahead.

The cooks, irritated by our coming, seemed as if they couldn't care less what we ate. We were so hungry that we would eat anything they had to offer.

At one, I found myself standing beneath the doorway of the fifth grade, searching through my front shirt pocket for the folded piece of paper Miss Barbara had told me to deliver. The stiffness of my sky-blue shirt reminded me that the short sleeve was new. The same was true of the dark navy-blue pants I wore.

I surveyed the mint-green classroom. All the students pretended to be concentrating on their work. Their light whispers gave them away, though.

A considerable number of the desks that stood in the middle of the room were empty. Where were those students? They couldn't all have been sick or out running errands. As I stood there, some sensed my presence and turned.

"Hey, Iz," my cousin Gus pointed, "check out your brother Lou."

"Yeah?" Israel shrugged his shoulders. "I saw him a little while ago."

Feeling the relaxed mood, the afternoon class began to joke around a bit more. Until . . .

"What is going on here?" The voice came from a corner tucked away at the top of the room. "I hear some of us are staying after school!"

The room fell to its former silence. Their teacher stood up and came forward, with book in hand, from an area resembling a compact living room. Two hunter-green bookshelves, perpendicular to each other, were its walls. From the corner opening you could see a chair, rug, and short broad-leafed fern that served as furnishings. So this, I thought, was what Gus had meant when he mentioned the "romper room" to me the other day. He said it was a time when Miss Kim provided special lessons for those doing poorly.

"So what kind of gifts do you come bearing?" the teacher came closer, smiling wholeheartedly.

Her casual behavior seemed genuine. Miss Kim didn't present herself in the authoritative manner that other teachers did. I took a better look at her.

Her droopy, innocent-looking face, a pale white color, was spotted with light freckles. Makeup outlined her eyes and lips, crisply separating her features. She appeared younger in age than any of the other teachers in the school. Certainly much younger than Miss Barbara.

"What's wrong? Cat got your tongue?"

"No, Miss McGregory."

She wore a red plaid skirt, running slightly below her knees, and a baby-blue shirt. It was unlike the long dresses Miss Barbara wore or the brown uniforms of the Sisters.

Her shirt's top two buttons were unbuttoned. A scarf made of some translucent material was wrapped around her neck, loudly draping down to her chest. The way she wore it made her very attractive to me. I had never thought of anyone older or younger in that way. I noticed a strong sweet perfume coming from her.

Different.

I handed her the pink slip of paper.

"Why, thank you."

She read the note and asked whether I was Israel's older brother. I told her I was.

"Say, Iz," turning to him, "why didn't you warn me that all the *Aguileras* were such handsome young *caballeros?*"

An unsettling warmth came over me. I heard Israel being teased. I was hoping it wouldn't pass on to me.

She went back to the note. With one finger raised, she signaled for everyone to quiet down. Few paid attention. It angered me to see someone as nice as her being ignored.

"Please, let Miss Barbara know it's fine with me."

"Uh-huh," heading out the door. She stopped to ask for my name.

"Luis."

"No second name? I thought that was a big Spanish thing."

"My middle name is going to be Gabriel. That's the name I'm picking for my confirmation."

"*Luis Gabriel.* Sounds nice to the ear."

I stood amazed. She pronounced Luis the way it was meant to be. The way my mother, who spoke only Spanish, said it. Even I had begun to stop saying it that way.

"Seriously, the name *Luis Gabriel* has a wonderful feel to it. Did you know that a great many French kings were named Louis?"

"Yeah. Didn't one of them have his head cut off?"

"Impressive. How did you know about that?"

"It's in books. I like reading."

"You know there's also an angel named Gabriel."

"I know; that's why I picked it."

"Why?"

"Ummm, I don't know. It's like something told me to pick it."

"Interesting . . . you could have picked Michael. You know, I'll have to remember that name combination when I'm in the process of naming my children. Of course, that won't be for another few years. And I guess I'll need a husband for that to happen. Which I currently don't have," she laughed at herself. "Come to think of it, I'll probably need a boyfriend first. But I'll really have to consider the name Luis Gabriel as a candidate. What if I just call you Luis? Is that good with you?"

"That's cool."

"So, Luis, what does your father do for a living?"

"Oh, ummm . . . my dad's an apostle."

Her eyebrows tightened together. "Excuse me? Your dad does *what?*"

"You know. An apostle. Someone who puts new material on top of old furniture."

She began laughing hysterically. What was so funny, I wondered.

"You mean he's an upholsterer!"

"That's what I said!"

"No, Luis, you said *apostle,* the same thing your brother Israel told me when school started." She continued to laugh. "Boy, you two are a riot! I can't believe both of you answered in the same way." She looked over to Israel, who seemed leery of his teacher's

32

attention. It was obvious his classmates were seasoned to use anything to their advantage.

"It's as if you both think on the same wavelength," she remarked. "Now *that* is strange."

The class commenced ridiculing the two of us.

"I wasn't aware we wanted extra homework for the weekend!" Miss McGregory moved away from me. "You don't think that they need extra homework?" turning to face the class. "Do you, Luis?"

I smiled at her giving worth to me.

"Luis," picking up a brown bucket sitting against the wall near the chalkboard, "will you do me a big favor? Will you please fill this up with lukewarm water?"

"Yeah, it's cool."

"*Cool?* God, I'm beginning to see that's your favorite word?"

"Sort of," stepping forward to take the empty container and immediately rushing to the boys' washroom. When I returned, the classroom was in an uproar.

"Hey, Iz," someone broke out, "I guess your brother is going to take away your spot as teacher's pet."

"Shut up," Israel retorted.

Teacher's pet? I had never been a teacher's pet.

A student came over to collect the bucket. I looked for Miss Kim. From within "romper room" she let out a thank-you. I left, thinking about what had just taken place. I thought about her saying thank you to me. About her compliments. Her words. Did she really mean them? And if she did, what did she mean? Silly, I thought, I was just being silly; nothing was going to come out of this! All the other girls thought I was ugly and had a big nose. Even Imelda, who I loved, thought I was ugly. And she was two grades lower than me! I probably acted like a dork anyway. Yeah, she probably saw I was a fuckin' dork! Apostle! Oh my God, I said apostle! But she did ask *me* for a favor. She could have asked anyone else in the room, but she asked *me*. Why?

I walked back to the seventh grade. By now, Miss Barbara was busy explaining our math homework. I took my seat.

"Hey, Lou, how come you're smiling like crazy, dude?"

I kept quiet.

"Why'd you take so long? Miss Barbara almost sent one of us to look for you."

"It's Miss McGregory. The fifth-grade teacher. She's *bad*. I'll talk to you about it later."

"Mr. Aguilera." Miss Barbara glared at us from across the room. "Is there any reason why you and Mr. Fernandez are having a conversation in the middle of my lesson?"

"No."

"And by the way, where exactly have you been for the last ten minutes?"

The class looked back. I sat up to explain.

"Fine, but next time be advised that your main priority is here in this classroom, not running around doing favors for anyone else. You've practically missed an entire day of school. I'm sure Miss Kim has enough people to help her out."

"Yes, Miss Barbara."

"Now, let's see how much you've missed," turning her attention to the green chalkboard. "Can you come up here and show me how to solve this problem?"

"I already know how to do that."

"Really?"

"Yeah. I was looking at that problem after I finished doing my homework last night."

"Well then, why don't you come up here and explain to the class how it's done."

I sighed. The thought of standing in front of everyone unnerved me.

Miss Barbara looked up at the clock. "Forget it, Mr. Aguilera. It's time to go. Everyone, get your things and be ready in line for when the bell rings."

"Where do you think you two boys are going?"

Miss Barbara held an oversized poster board. Alfred and I had been working on it for the last two weeks.

"I thought you said we could all go home." I was waiting in front of the closet.

"Well, I was under the impression that you boys were going to stay and finish drawing St. Francis today. We need it ready for the open house on Sunday."

Alfred and I looked at each other. We knew what the other was thinking. The picture of St. Francis was going to take at least a week or so more if she wanted it done right.

"The pens and markers are over there," she pointed across the room to an open cigar box on her desk. "The sooner you get started, the sooner you'll be home doing whatever it is you feel is so important . . . If you need anything else, go ahead and ask. What I don't want though is for things to be flying all over the room and disappearing."

Alfred was solemn. It didn't seem as if he were going to say anything. What we had talked about yesterday apparently didn't mean much to him, I told myself. Why didn't he care? What stopped him from making an effort to say what he felt?

"Miss Barbara," becoming frustrated, "does this mean me and Alfred have to keep practicing with the choir too?"

She frowned. "Of course. Is there any particular reason why the two of you shouldn't have to sing with the rest of us?"

I swung my eyes over to Alfred. Nothing.

"Man," I fired back, "I don't think it's fair. No one else here has to draw anything for you."

"I've noticed since you've gotten here that there's a lot of things you don't think are fair, Mr. Aguilera. Really, I'm growing tired of your little complaints."

"I mean," trying to ignore the lump in my throat, "I really like to draw but everyone else gets to do their homework whenever we have to work on a project. How come we can't have time to do our homework too?"

"But you do have time to do your homework. After school. Like everyone else. Isn't that right, Mr. Fernandez?"

Alfred kept quiet. I stared at him. Shit! He wasn't going to say anything at all?

"Man, Miss Barbara, you know what I mean."

"Watch your tone with me, Mr. Aguilera. I don't think what I'm asking will impair you in any way. So let's get to work. Come on," snapping her fingers, "the more time you waste, the later you'll both get to go home."

I shook my head in disgust.

"Is there a problem, Mr. Aguilera?"

"I'll do it. But I'm not going to sing anymore."

A dead calm shot through the room.

"Jennifer, please take the class downstairs."

"Yes, Miss Barbara."

"Mr. Aguilera," raising her long thin finger as the last student left. "You *are* going to sing. Whether or not you want to. And if I hear one single word from you I'll make sure that your mother receives a phone call from me."

"Call her."

"Pardon?"

"Yeah. Tell her whatever you want to tell her. I'll tell her the truth. I'll tell her how you make us stay to work on something we don't have to do. And like how you don't give us time to do our work while everyone else gets to do theirs."

"I'm warning you, Mr. Aguilera. That's enough."

"No, it's the truth," feeling a consuming hate. "I don't care. I'm not your slave. Call her."

"Do you feel the same way, Alfred?"

Alfred let out a hollow "no."

I felt betrayed. But I had expected it. It wasn't the first time something like this had happened between us.

"It seems, Mr. Fernandez, that Mr. Aguilera is acting very childish. I suggest you work on it alone. Can you manage?"

"Yes," Alfred promptly answered. "I think so."

"As for you, Mr. Aguilera," turning coldly, "get all of your things and go home. Some of us would like to get some work done around here."

I grabbed my things from my desk and marched out of the room. Miss Barbara pursued. Outside of school, she overtook me and went straight to Jose, who had been waiting for Israel and me to be let out of class.

"Mr. Aguilera, you make sure to tell your mother that your younger brother misbehaved today."

"What did you do now, goofy?"

I came over beside him.

"Well, apparently young Mr. Aguilera has the ridiculous belief that he can excuse himself from doing the work he's supposed to do. As if he doesn't need to dedicate any of his time to the Lord. Do you, Mr. Aguilera?"

I gritted my teeth. Take the name of the Lord in vain, I thought. Thou shall not . . .

"Don't worry, Miss Barbara," Jose blurted out, "I'll make sure my mom knows what happened."

"Thank you, Jose. Now you boys go on home before your mother begins to miss you."

On the way back home, Jose didn't appear overly concerned. I asked him whether he was going to tell Ma about the incident.

"Man! Who cares? Don't let her get to you. She tried doing the same shit to me last year. Fuck, I can't stand that b-i-t-c-h! She's all nice to you when she wants something from you but when you don't want to do something for her, she'll fucking treat you like you're the one that's doing something wrong. Forget about it. Besides, Ma knows how she is."

"You don't think she'll call Mom and tell her a lie?"

"No, goofy ass! You didn't do shit. Except you probably didn't know how to tell her off. Look, all she can say is that you didn't want to draw her stupid drawing."

"But I wanted to finish the drawing. It was starting to look good."

"You can't have it both ways, dork."

"Why not?"

"Because you can't. You see the way they treat us. Like fucking dogs. They're never going to change. It's always going to be them against us. They're always going to think they're right. How can you argue with people who think that way? They don't even really think."

"I don't know. But you think she'll mess with my grades?"

"Hey, goofy ass, you always get A's in art, don't you?"

I nodded.

"Then don't worry. The worst thing she'll do is probably give you a B. If she gives you something lower, tell Ma about it and have her talk to Sister Albian. You know Ma sticks up for us when we're right . . . But you better be right. Don't fuck it up by saying something stupid like you always do."

"Man, Jose, I don't say nothing stupid! I just say what I think."

"Don't you get it, goofy? They . . . don't . . . care. How many times do I have to tell you? They're just looking for any reason to fuck with you. Don't get into it like they do. You'll see later on I'm right."

When we crossed 35th, the shouting began.

"Hey, taco breaths, chinga tu madre!"

Running feet.

"Go back to Mexico! You fuckin' spics!"

The familiar yells drew closer.

"POPES nation!"

I remembered Alfred's friend, Tony, had once mentioned that name. I asked him what POPES meant. He said every letter in the name stood for something. He said *P* stood for Protect, *O* for Our, *P* for People, *E* for Eliminating, and *S* for Spics. I asked him what it all meant.

"Dumbass, like I said, it means protect our people by eliminating spics. Asshole, if you ever hear someone say that shit to you, you better fucking run or your ass is dead."

"Really?"

"Yeah, really. They don't like people like you."

"What do you mean people like me?"

"You know."

"No. What?"

"Tell him, Alfred. This faggot doesn't know jack shit."

"Mexicans, P.R.'s, fags, niggers, anybody who isn't white," Alfred said, "c'mon, Lou, wake up."

"You mean this group . . ."

"Gang, asshole, it's a gang!" Tony shouted. "Haven't you ever seen *The Outsiders* or *The Warriors*? Don't you know what a gang is?"

"No. What's that?"

"Oh, that's right," Tony began to laugh, "Alfred told me your *mommy* makes you guys go to sleep at nine and she only lets you guys watch little-kid shows. I bet you've never ever seen a girl's tits."

Alfred laughed.

"Shut up," I told him. "So these gangs go around and beat up people just because they're not white?"

"Well, that's what this gang does," Tony said. "Other gangs do it for other reasons. You know, to protect their turf. The place where they hang out."

"That's stupid!"

"Oh yeah," he pushed me, "I wanna see you tell 'em that. Let's see if you've got big enough balls to say that to their face."

"Maaan, how come you have to be so mean?"

"Don't be such a sissy. You little fag."

"When my dad was in Mexico, he was in something like a gang."

"No shit," Tony exclaimed. "What? The Cheech and Chong Gang?"

No, I thought. The Scorpions. But he never spoke about them getting into fights. The only stories he'd tell were of the adventures they had and the things they did to make money because their families were poor. He said they were a good gang.

He would tell us of the times he hunted for rattlesnakes in the dry lands of the state of Guanajuato. After catching them, he would sometimes eat the meat, he said, and let their skins dry out in the sun. Once they were good and dry, he would either sell them in the markets of his hometown, Irapauto, or grind them down to a fine powder. It was for medicinal purposes, he'd say. For the skin. To purify the blood.

"And no one cared that you killed them?" I asked in Spanish.

Sitting cross-legged, one hand picking at the lobe of his ear, the other on his lap, the thinker would tighten his jaw and shake his head.

"The ranchers were glad we killed them," he'd say. "They'd prefer to lose a few snakes rather than lose one of their horses or workers . . . You might think something so small as compared to a horse would be harmless, but people strong as bulls fall from the bite of a rattlesnake. And with no doctor around," he whistled, "then where are you? Nature's a funny thing. It gives even the smallest something to fight with."

"Even something small like me?"

He smiled and threw his head back. "You haven't finished growing. Let's just wait and see how you come out in this life."

"And what if I don't grow?"

"Then God will give you something else to fight with."

"But . . ."

"Slow down. If you're in a hurry, you're going to end up like the rattlesnake that bites way ahead of its time," shaking his finger at me. "Dead."

I sat thinking about what he said.

"But don't worry," he laughed and nodded. "At least your death will make a good medicine for someone else."

Jose and I turned around. Always from the back. Cowards.

The majority wore mustard-colored shirts and brown pants. School uniforms. They weren't POPES! They were from Our Lady, the other Catholic school a few blocks from St. Peter's. Why were they screaming POPES for?

An older, broad-shouldered boy with dark sunglasses stepped in front of the rest. Sprinting forward, he smacked me right in the stomach. I buckled and fell. I felt shoes knock against the side of my ribs. I heard a tear.

"Hey, motherfuckers, why don't you pick on someone who's your own fucking size?"

The kicking stopped. I looked up. Jose grabbed one of the smaller ones by his shirt collar and threw him to the ground.

"So," yelled the one with the sunglasses, "you think you're *bad*, you fucking dirty ass spic?"

"Yeah, motherfucker! You and me!"

"Shit, I'm going to fuck you up and then I'm going to fuck your little pussy friend up even more."

"Okay," Jose boldly stated, "stop talking about it and do it."

I felt a rush. The pain withdrew. I used a tree next to me to stand up and limped over to a nearby gate and leaned against it.

"Kick his ass, Jose!" I cried out, encouraged by my brother's defense.

The ringleader lunged. Jose jerked to the side. He missed my brother altogether and hit the gate alongside of me.

"Come on, I thought you were going to kick my ass?"

He went at him again. Jose cocked his arm back and let it go. I heard glass shatter. A streak of blood began to flow on the ringleader's cheek. And then a shriek.

"Holy shit," I mumbled.

Stunned by the early demise of their prize fighter, the rest seemed confused as to what to do.

"Come on, goofy ass," Jose picked up my jacket. "Let's go. This was stupid."

A block away from the scene and the body aches returned, this time more insistent than before. I became aware of a salty taste in my mouth.

"Dork," Jose surveyed, "you ripped your shirt."

I looked down and saw one of my sleeves torn. Shit, Mom was going to get angry. I started to whimper.

"What am I going to tell Ma?"

"Tell her the truth, goofy ass. It wasn't your fault that a bunch of assholes wanted to fight us."

"Yeah, but I didn't even wanna fight."

"That's why you should let me do the fighting. Why do you think they call me machine gun at school?"

"I don't know. I feel dumb."

"Don't. That's the way it is. Not everyone can do the same thing. Some people have to do other stuff."

I stumbled to the front of our home, swallowing the warm mixture of tears, blood, and saliva. The gooey substance somehow had a comforting effect.

Instead of going in, I sat up at the top of our steps where the small glass plates on the aluminum screen door of our home lay open. I heard the tortillas being dipped into the frying pan. Soon they would be converted into cheese-filled enchiladas. A dense steamy fragrance of my mother's orange-colored rice came through as well.

More comfort.

"Y donde está mi *Flaco*?" my mother asked.

Israel answered, letting her know I was sitting right outside. Jose added that I didn't want to come in.

"Por qué, qué pasó?"

Jose explained the fight to her. She asked whether we had done anything to provoke them.

"No, Ma," Jose protested, "ellos fueron los que empezaron a decirnos nombres."

"Que clase de nombres?"

"Como siempre, Ma. They called us spics and stupid shit like that."

That's right, Mom, I thought angrily, after seven years the same fucking shit!

"Y después qué pasó?"

Jose explained to her about my shirt.

"That's how come no se quiere meter. He's afraid that you're going to be mad."

"Nada mas por eso?" she said in disbelief. "Hay, dile que se meta y deje de hacerse el ridículo. Que no me voy a enojar con el."

I tied my arms around my shins and buried myself between my knees. I hid myself in the dark cave. It reminded me of night where I would sometimes feel safe.

"Hey, goofy ass," Jose pressed his nose against the screen door. I remembered how enjoyable that was to do, feeling the metal web gently scrape against skin. "Ma says for you to come in already and to stop being such a baby."

"Is she mad?" looking up at him.

"Are you kidding?" he smiled. "*Only dogs get mad.* Remember?"

I felt calm once more.

"Don't worry, Louie, she's more angry at those assholes who started the fight."

"You promise?"

"Man, get in already."

I got up and walked in. I went no further than the living room and sat on our old-fashioned couch, the one my father had recently worked on. My mother came to my side.

"A ver, dejame ver," holding up my chin. She insisted on taking a look. She began to count out loud the number of cuts I hadn't even noticed.

"Así que alguien te pegó y caístes al suelo?"

"Man, Jose told you I fell to the ground?"

"Cálmate, cálmate," she said. "No tiene nada de malo que te caigas al suelo. Que te crees? Superman?"

"No," looking away. "I'm not Superman."

"Mira," smoothing out my hair, "te dás un baño para que puedas comer agusto. Está bién?"

"Yeah . . . I'll take a bath."

After cleaning up I went over to eat. Once I was done, I asked my mother if I could go back to school.

"Y que vas a hacer en la escuela?"

"Voy a ir a hablar con la maestra de Israel," I answered. "Miss Kim is cool, Ma."

I was met with an odd stare from her and Israel.

"Por que no te metes a la alberca en vez?" she asked, "después va hacer frío y no vas a tener la oportunidad de hacerlo."

I let her know I didn't feel like getting into the pool. That I'd go in with my father later on at night.

"Y si está cansado?"

"Dad isn't going to be tired to go swimming tonight. No way, man."

"Deja de usar esa palabra," lifting her face. "Yo no soy un *man.*"

"I'm not saying you're a *man,* Ma. Anyway, man isn't a bad word. Entonces si puedo ir, Ma?"

"Está bién, pero ten cuidado, no quiero que vengas con otra camisa rota. Que hora vas a regresar?"

"Six," I replied, "I'll be back a las seis."

"Conste."

"Yeah, Ma!" I ran out of the house. "Don't worry! Nada me va a pasar."

Outside, I took a quick glance at my plain pony sneakers. I had yet to put on the thick fluorescent-green and black shoelaces my dad had bought for me at the flea market. One of these days I would. And I would design them in checkerboard fashion to make them look the way the older boys at Maxwell Street had. I'd even learn how to break-dance like them. Yes I would, I thought.

One day.

"You're still here?"

"What was I going to do?" Alfred sat up and looked out of the window. "She wants the poster by Sunday."

The late afternoon sun was shining fiercely. I thought about the pool and how autumn was just around the corner. Maybe I should have stayed home.

"How come she wants it by Sunday?"

"You know how she is. She wants it for the open house so

everyone can see how *good* her seventh-grade class is. So all the teachers can see how she has us by the nuts."

"Oh, yeah, that's right. The open house is right after Mass."

He went back to the floor and crouched forward on his knees. I looked about. I saw a box of pastels next to him.

"She wants you to use *those?*"

"Dude. What do you think? She says she wants most of St. Francis done in pastel and I should do the highlighting in markers."

"Man, that's cheap. I'd rather use markers for the whole thing. People can see it better then.

"Yeah well, *you* aren't doing it."

"Look, man, don't get pissed off with me. I thought we were supposed to tell her we weren't going to work on her art projects anymore if she made us sing. Since you didn't say anything . . . oh well. That's not my fault."

He went back to the drawing.

"Didn't I tell you to go home over two hours ago?"

Miss Barbara stood before the doorway.

"I did."

"So what are you doing here? I hope you're not interrupting Mr. Fernandez from doing his job. Or are you here to help finish?"

"No, Miss Barbara, I just came to see Alfred. His mother asked me to find out when he was going to be home."

"You can tell Mrs. Fernandez that Alfred is going to be here for a long time. Especially since you're not helping him."

"Okay," glad she hadn't noticed Alfred shaking his head in disagreement.

"Better yet, why don't you go downstairs, Alfred, and give her a call instead."

"Yes, Miss Barbara."

"Now, Mr. Aguilera. If there isn't any other reason why *you* should still be here, I suggest you go on home."

"But I also came over to help Miss McGregory with some of her work."

"Is that so?"

"Yeah," I continued. "I told her I was coming in later on today after I went home and had something to eat."

Her head went back in astonishment.

"Well then, Mr. Aguilera, you should go on and help Miss McGregory. What I can't understand is why you would leave poor Alfred stuck with all this work. Do you, Alfred?"

He didn't answer. Man, Alfred, I thought, why did you have to be such a wussy? Why can't you be mean to *her*?

"Why are you *Aguileras* so hardheaded? This holier-than-thou attitude is beyond me. I'm just praying Israel won't give me the same kind of trouble."

I shrugged.

"So it was okay that I told her I was helping you?"

"I can't really say. I'm still somewhat astonished by your behavior," Miss McGregory smiled. "Maybe it wasn't the best way to handle that situation."

"Is that a yes or a no?"

"Boy, you're really not into the wishy-washy answers."

I stared quietly.

"All right. I think you did the right thing. Not so much the lying, but the standing up for yourself."

"Yeah, I knew you knew."

"How so?"

"Because, you're not like the other teachers here."

"What do you mean?"

"Well, when I came over to deliver the message today, I knew you were different because you were real friendly. You said thank you in a nice way."

"Is that so?"

"Yeah. I could tell right away you weren't mean."

"Luis, you're always going to meet different sorts of people in your life. Good and bad. But how does saying 'thank you' make me such a different person?"

"No. You don't understand. It's not that. I mean, you looked at me like I was a real person. You didn't look at me like I was some weird thing or like I was nobody."

Miss McGregory sat up. "Who looks at you that way?"

"Some of the other teachers and people. They do."

"How can you tell?"

"I don't know how to say it. I can. Something inside tells me."

"Listen, Luis, I don't think they see you in that way. I think you're picking up on something that isn't there."

I shook my head. "No. I know what I feel. I remember when my grandfather used to take us to the park . . ."

"Which one?"

"The one here. McKinley Park. Anyway, he used to take us there when we were kids, before he died, and one time a bunch of guys starting calling us names and . . ."

"Like what?"

"You know," embarrassed to say them. "Anyway, my grandfather told them to leave us alone."

"Did your grandfather speak English?"

"Oh yeah, he knew better English than us because he used to work in a steel factory in the United States and used to talk to all the people all the time. Anyway, they kept calling us these names and then started throwing rocks and sticks."

"Oh you poor dear."

"Ah, my grandpa Ventura took care of them. But what I really didn't like was the way they looked at us. I don't know, it was different. Like the times when the old ladies grab their bags close to them when we pass by them. Or like the time we went by some big buildings downtown in our station wagon and a bunch of little kids threw bricks at us. One of them even spit on my face. It sucks. You know?"

"Yes," Miss McGregory said, "I know exactly what you mean. Believe me, the Irish have had their fair share of problems in that respect."

"I know. One time I saw an old black and white picture in a U.S. history book where it said 'no dogs allowed,' and below it it said 'no Irish allowed.' That's jive."

"That's what?"

"You know. Jive. It means something that's messed up."

"Oh, I thought it's the way some people speak."

"No that's something else."

"Oh geez, I'm not as up-to-date on this new street lingo. I used to do counseling at the county jail over by 26th Street—dealing with urban street gangs—so don't think I'm totally in the dark."

"Man, that's cool. Anyway, before we came here, we used to go to another school—Ruben Salazar."

"Was that a public school?"

"I think so. I know it was a real cool place. They taught us how to read and write English. They also taught us the same things in Spanish. Everyone was real nice too. None of the teachers acted the way they act here. Like they really cared. I mean, they kind of care about us here, but not in the same way. You can tell when it's fake. Ruben Salazar, now that place was cool."

"Sounds like paradise. So why did your parents decide to take you out of there?"

"They moved it far away to another neighborhood by 18th Street."

"That's a Spanish neighborhood?"

"I guess. I think they call it Pilsen. All the stores over there have their stuff in Spanish. All the people I see look Mexican. We go to church with my mom over there a lot. It's not that she doesn't like English Mass. She just likes helping out a lot over there. But whenever we have to serve Mass at St. Peter's on Sunday, we still go to the Mass over there."

"And here you feel out of place?"

"Sometimes. It's not too bad anymore but some of the teachers and people still kind of look at us funny. They treat us weird."

"But in what way?"

"They get mad at us whenever we talk in Spanish. I remember when I was in second grade and one of the teachers told us not to talk in Spanish. She got real mad."

"Was it during class time?"

"No. It was after school—outside—when it happened."

"And you weren't saying anything to get you in trouble?"

"No!"

"Are you sure?"

"I was just talking to my cousin Carlos. Except after she told me that, I asked her if this was a communist country or what."

Miss Kim laughed. "Well, Luis, you're going to have to understand, some people are slightly paranoid. They've had things stay the same for so long that any type of change is seen as a threat to their way of life. They probably felt just as scared as you did when they first arrived."

"I don't know. I didn't feel scared when I got here. I was sad I didn't see my mom and dad when I came to school. I remember crying about that. But I wasn't scared about the people here. I don't think so. All I know is that I didn't do anything to them. I was just talking in Spanish. Why can't they leave us alone?"

"It just doesn't seem to work that way."

"Yeah," growing angry, "but they can talk in Polish whenever they want? That's not fair. Why do I have to take shit like that?"

"No. You don't have to take anything from anyone. You do the best you can in whatever task you set for yourself. Trust me. I'm telling you as your new friend. Things will work themselves out for you. I promise. Who knows? You might not even end up living in this country twenty years from now." Miss Mc-Gregory stood up and placed her hand on my shoulder. "Now what's wrong?"

"Oh," feeling light-headed. "I was just thinking about Miss Barbara. I can't stand when she tries to make me feel like I'm doing something wrong."

"Well, why don't you go talk to Sister Albian about it? She may be able to help."

"Sister Albian! The principal? No way! They're like this," I lifted my hand and crossed one finger over the other.

"That close, huh?"

"Yep."

She frowned. "It's not *that* bad here? Is it?"

"Nah, at least Sister Consuela and Sister Therese like us. They're kind of cool."

"There you go. And I thought you said I was the only one who treated you with decency?"

"I guess they're there too. But the rest of them are assholes."

"Luis!"

"I'm sorry, Miss McGregory. I'm just pissed off at everything right now. I mean, I don't understand. They tell us at Mass to forgive our brothers seven times seventy-seven, but how can you forgive people if they keep doing shitty stuff to you? I wouldn't mind if it was just words, but it's more than that. Even the words hurt a lot too. You know?"

"Well, don't use that as an excuse to vent your frustration in vulgar fashion. It's not becoming to a young gentleman like yourself. You have a lot going for you. I've talked to you for one day and already I see you as charming, well spoken, and far more mature than your peers. All these great things. My God, if you were twenty-five I'd probably ask you out on a date."

"Are you serious?"

It was then that Miss Barbara appeared at the door.

"Miss McGregory, may I have a moment with you?"

"Certainly."

"Luis," she winked, "give me a second."

Miss McGregory rose from her seat and stepped out to the hallway. She returned, closing the door behind her. Miss Barbara was gone.

"Don't worry. I covered for you."

"What did you tell her?"

"I told her that when you brought the note earlier in the day, I had asked you to come after school to help me arrange some things in class."

"Man, I knew you were cool. But I didn't think you were that cool. You even lied for me."

"Well, just don't go around and announce it to the world. I wouldn't want anyone to think I'm a pushover. And I wouldn't want to lose my job either. *That* wouldn't be cool."

"That's okay. I can keep secrets pretty well."

"I bet you're filled with little secrets."

"I am."

"I can tell. So why the little secrets?"

"Because people are always saying I'm weird or something."

"Why? Because you think and question everything around you?"

"I guess. I know people in my class got mad at me once because I started making like these files of them for myself. Like I was studying them . . . I knew I shouldn't of told Alfred. People just don't understand."

"Files, huh?" shuffling the papers on her desk. "What a great imagination. Well, don't worry. Anytime you need to talk to someone, I'm here."

"Thanks."

"I'm just doing what I'm supposed to be doing."

"So do you like music, Miss Kim?"

"That's an odd question. I love music. Doesn't everyone? Why do you ask?"

"Well, I've been listening to this music late at night for a while now and it sounds real different."

"How so?"

"It doesn't have too many voices in it like other stuff they put on in the day. It's like it sounds the same but not really. They call it house music."

"Now see, there you go again. Starting to make me feel old. But yes, I think I know what you're talking about. It's a bit repetitive. A steady stream of beats. Soothing actually. From the small bits and pieces I've heard, it makes me feel calm inside. You know, another type of music that may place you in that dreamy state of mind is probably Floyd."

"Floyd?"

"Pink Floyd."

"I want to hear that," saying this enthusiastically.

"Maybe I'll bring you some of their music one of these days. How's that?"

"That would be cool."

"Cool, huh?"

"Yeah, real cool."

"But here's the real question now. You think you're ready for something that emotionally stirring? It's not as simple as house music."

"I don't think house music is *simple* if you really listen to it, Miss Kim. But I can try Floyd. Right?"

"Right," she smiled. "You sure can. So what other type of music do you like to hear?"

"I like to hear Genesis . . . Pat Benatar . . . Joan Jett . . . Duran Duran . . . the Beatles . . . Kiss . . ."

"Woah, quite a mix of pop culture you have going there."

"I just like to hear a lot of different things. Sometimes I even flip to the classical station when I'm bored. That stuff's good really late at night."

"You know, Luis, I play the flute. I'm playing this Sunday for the family Mass. Are you going to be there?"

"Only if you play something for me."

"I'll play my heart out for you."

"Then I'll go."

Half-asleep, I heard the squealing of my father's crickety old station wagon as he turned the wheels left and right. When he walked into the house, I popped my head out of the bedroom and asked whether he still wanted to go for a swim, even though it was past ten o'clock. He had promised the day before we would.

"Que no estás cansado?"

"Come on, Dad. Pleeease. I'm not tired."

"Seguro?"

"Yeah," hanging from the doorway. "Let's go!"

"Esta bien."

I had been waiting in my swimsuit, so it was only a matter of seconds before I hurried out the back door and was outside. While waiting in the backyard for my father, I stared at the dark space in front of me, trying to guess where the next green bursts of the lightning bugs would be. And when it would happen. The latter was simple. The former always seemed much more difficult.

Growing restless, I climbed the pool ladder to the top and then slowly made my way into the dark waters, which had been warmed by the afternoon sun. Inside the liquid, I eventually felt the sensation of being brought up against my will. I pressed earnestly against the pool walls, making sure I would not rise. I lifted one of my hands, threw it out into space, and indulged in the marvelous contrast produced by the cool night breeze meeting my warm wet hand.

I was sad to come up. Only the sight of my father, who had taught me how to swim, restored my joy. He was gliding peacefully across the black space, uninterested in the challenge below.

Then came a mild distraction.

From my parents' bedroom window, our mother smiled, waved hello and good-bye. Even after the lights in her room had been turned off, I was certain she wouldn't go to sleep. Not until we were both inside. That was very much her character. And she would keep at it, with the same sort of stamina she had the day she taught me how to ride a bike.

I was just beginning to understand this thing about her. To love her in reason.

sunrise

1986—1987

3

I knelt on the living-room carpet in front of the stereo system. With frantic twists, I turned the radio's aluminum knob, toying with the static. I teased the gaps of fuzzy air with quick bursts of noise. And then I slowed down.

Green, orange, yellow . . . red lights bounced in sync with the sounds of the mids, highs, and lows. The beams of colors danced up and down on a clear black panel that lay between the controlling knob and the tape deck. I crossed my eyes.

A flickering glow lay reflected on my nose. The cool fire silenced me, making me unaware of everything, including myself.

Eventually I stepped off. Someone brought me back. Armando's voice. I had found what I was looking for. The Friday night mix show on 102.7 FM . . .

"W-B-M-X," echoing the last part of the station's announcement with a deep voice.

I popped in a cassette. This was the fourth time I had recorded over it, even though each recording was as good as the last.

I heard it announced that Kenny "Jammin'" Jason was doing the mix tonight. I spread myself, face down, over the floor. The rest of my family had already gone to sleep. Lifting and shaking my right foot nervously, I longed for the chatter of commercials to go away and for Kenny to go on.

I smiled. Last year I thought Kenny "Jammin'" Jason consisted of three dj's. Ken, Jan, and Jason. I was embarrassed when my friend Rudy pointed out the error, in front of his brothers even.

I was ashamed my senses had said differently. But that day was so far away. Last summer. Hmmmm.

Ohhh, that's right . . .

I breathed in and yawned.

That's when I kissed you, Carrie!

I felt a shiver. With the edge of my fingertips, I calmly stroked my bottom lip and rode over to the top.

You were so soft . . . your lips so real to me.

That night, last year, when Israel and I were playing catch, I had gone over to help you water the tree in front of your home. In fun we lifted the hose upright and allowed the water to fall on us. We pretended to be in a storm. Our own storm, we said. And we kissed.

I spread my fingers straight through your thin, long golden hair and rubbed your head. The way I enjoyed it done to me. I hugged you, handing to you everything I had.

The next day, I went knocking at the house you lived in. The one that looked identical to ours in every way. I was greeted by that bratty brother of yours, Kenny, telling me how your mother felt about you kissing a "wetback." Idiot. He smiled when he delivered the message. Especially when he said "wetback."

We were forbidden to see each other. Why? Your mother wasn't like this before?

That's right, I thought. Before. Before was different.

I slid over to one of the wooden cabinets, placing my left ear against the speaker. The first song was a somber piece. It included the soft repeating line, "I'm waiting for my angel." The apocalyptic track reminded me of today's funeral. Of the small white casket I had seen rolled down the center aisle.

The front two pallbearers had been a middle-aged man and woman. The second pair behind them were much younger, near my own age, but the look in their eyes informed me that they too were no longer boys. At some point, things had failed them as well. The only exception was that I commanded my youthful existence to disappear. They hadn't. I told it *no more*. What for? You're useless. Your promises turn to lies with the change of time. So I told myself that I wouldn't care. That I would do whatever I wanted to do. Regardless of anyone or anything. Because there was too much suffering already. And I was tired of it.

I rolled on my back.

What surprised me most was to see the way the adults acted at the funeral, their proper composure completely stripped. Maybe the death of their daughter Danielle was enough to bring them out of their stupor. Shit! Why did it have to take this for people to understand the time they wasted arguing and being fake?

Stupid people. You only care about yourselves, I fumed.

Strange, placing my hands behind my neck to use as a cushion, this time Father Peter had asked me to say the Readings. As far as I knew, this had never been done. I was nervous. God, every word came out choppy. I knew I skipped a few. No one seemed to mind, though. Or maybe they just weren't paying attention to words at all.

Yes, this group was different than the rest. Most actually smiled and said thank you at the end of Mass. I wondered if they would have been just as polite on any other day? Hmmm.

I rolled on my side and rubbed my nose.

Man, I wasn't even sure if I should have accepted the money offered to me. There was something eerie about it. But I knew if I hadn't, the director would have kept it anyway. He wouldn't have returned it. I was accustomed to seeing him put money intended for the altar boys in his pockets. And the excuse of him forgetting to give it to us? I'm sure he wouldn't forget about collecting his. He didn't seem like that sort of person.

Besides, I needed the money. I wanted to start buying records. Jose and Israel had already initiated a collection, just not the music I wanted to spend money on.

I steered back to the house music, slipping away from the day's events. As I listened, I thought about the beats. There seemed to be carefully selected patterns here and there. The generic pieces in the mix were uninspiring thuds of sound. But the rest would express heavy emotions at times and then move on to playful sessions. I found that the only way I could enjoy, appreciate, and understand the music was to let myself go. Real house music didn't seem to have an attitude, I felt. If it did, it was more of a humble sentiment of peace. A hello.

4

She grabbed a stack of papers and set them down in front of us. I asked whether she had any other work for me to do.

"Why, Louie?" Miss McGregory sat back at her desk. "You don't want to help correct the homework anymore?"

"No, I'm getting tired of doing that, Kim. I do it every time I come here."

"Don't worry, Miss Kim," Alfred's voice came from the other side of the room, "Louie's always getting bored doing things."

The fifth grade teacher rose and motioned me to the classroom's closet.

"Well all right then," slightly upset, "how about cleaning up the room for me instead?"

"Cool. I can do that."

"You sure?" I walked over to her. "See," pointing to a pile of open boxes, brooms, dustpans, and other things strewn on the floor, "this is what I'm talking about. Since you're good at organizing, it shouldn't take you too long. After you're done, I'll take you boys out for some burgers. Sounds good?"

I agreed.

As I cleaned, Alfred stayed in the other room helping her with the paperwork.

"It's great you two have been helping me out lately."

"Hey, it's better than helping Miss Barbara out. Did Louie ever tell you how she treated us last year?"

"Yes, I'm sure she took you boys for granted. You know, it's kind of funny. Ever since I arrived, I've heard nothing nice said about that woman, except from maybe one or two of the girls. Honestly, is she really that horrible?"

"No," Alfred strongly objected, "she's worse. And then Louie doesn't know when to be quiet."

"See, now I don't understand. Why do people like that get into teaching? Actually, what am I talking about? I do understand. They probably get off from it. Especially since they know full well the awesome power of teaching and the effects it has on young impressionable minds. Well one thing's for sure, she doesn't seem to be very happy with you and Louie coming over. She almost seems jealous. I bet a lot of her bitterness comes from the fact she's from the old guard."

"What do you mean 'old guard,' Miss Kim?"

"Well," breathing in, "you know, she's kind of ancient in a lot of her ideas. To be honest, I think she believes life here will revert to the way it was in the fifties if she works hard enough at it. Whatever that means . . . I have a hunch the majority of the teachers here still hold dear to that mentality."

"But I thought the fifties were suppose to be good?"

"Sure," she replied, "so long as people like you and Luis weren't around to disturb the *pristine* environment."

"So you think Miss Barbara is racist?"

"I wouldn't necessarily call her a racist, Alfred, but I wouldn't put it past her to be a bigot. To tell you the truth—and this will not leave the room—the way some of them talk about things in the teachers' lounge in the cafeteria makes me think twice about sticking around here myself."

"Why?"

"Well, some of the teachers have pretty disturbing issues concerning the way the neighborhood is changing."

"Really? I don't think it's that different. There's more Hispanics moving in but that's about it."

"Well, they may not see it as peachy as you do, Alfred."

"I hope you don't leave. Then there'll be no one left to hang out with after school."

"Thanks, but I'm sure you won't be hanging out with me too long after you graduate. Especially with all those young attractive Hispanic girls who'll be knocking at your door."

"You're not old, Miss Kim. Miss Barbara is old."

"See," she laughed, "you already have the lines down . . ."

Starting from the pit of my stomach, a peculiar anger began to surge inside. I felt as if they had forgotten all about me.

I began to work quickly. Each time I heard strong laughter come from either of them, the unsettling feeling seemed to become more concrete. I leaned forward to listen in on their every word. The words I didn't understand increased my madness. My thought was to get back in the classroom and put an end to whatever it was I felt was taking place between them.

I was so overwhelmed by emotional turmoil that I was unaware that partial blame for the situation lay on me. After all, I was the one who had decided to separate from them.

I wound up dropping the metal dustpan. The heavy clank sounded like the loudest and only noise in the world.

She asked how everything was going.

"Everything's okay! I just dropped the pan by mistake!"

But nothing was okay.

I walked to the doorway. "Miss Kim, I think I'm gonna go now. I think my mom is going to get worried if I don't get home soon."

"Do you need me to give you a ride?"

"Naw," turning around, "it's okay. I can make it on my own."

"Are you sure?"

"Yeah."

I took a deep breath and headed straight for the closet door, not giving them any opportunity to say good-bye.

"What's wrong with him?" I could hear Alfred ask.

Man, I fumed, reaching the stairs, can't you see? I was the one who brought you here in the first place. I was the one who told you all about her. And now you want to just take her away from me! Do you always just want to take, Alfred? Don't you ever want to give? Don't you mean people ever want to give?

As I ran away, I heard her pleading for me to wait. I went even faster than before. I needed escape. Outside, I picked up even more speed. I was nearly a block away when I heard the sound of a car engine being turned on. Kim's car.

"Fuck 'em, fuck 'em all," I said to myself. Why was he talking to her like that? Couldn't she at least see what I was feeling? We had talked about it before. Didn't she understand?

I entered an unpaved alley. The crisp crunch of wheels touching stone was right behind. Not too far away now, I thought.

I stopped to look back and saw her white Monte Carlo nearby. Shit, I thought, putting one hand behind my neck, this was so stupid. I was acting like a little boy!

I turned around. Alfred yelled for me to stop. I crouched over. Fuck! My heartbeat raced as they pulled up beside me. I began to cough.

"Where do you think you're going, young man?"

I didn't answer. Instead I rose and started to walk away, feeling her words and tone to be condescending.

"Hold on, Luis! I'm sorry! Don't go! Let me talk to you."

I stopped. They were both now staring at me from behind the car's windshield. Alfred with a blank face. She with a scared look in her eyes.

"Hey, Alfred, let me talk to Kim alone."

He swung open the door, leaving by the passenger's side.

"I'll see you later, dude," he said with an air of coolness. "I don't know about you."

"Yeah? No one does." I walked over to the car.

"Now what?" she smiled. I stood fast. "Are you getting in," her eyebrows went up, "or are you going to run another marathon?"

"Only if you let me."

"Get in."

She asked where I wanted to go.

"Wherever . . . Uh, you know what. Let's go to McKinley."

"You want to go to the park? Don't you think that's sort of weird?"

"I like going there . . . Unless you want to go somewhere else?"

"All right," an annoyed look on her face. She gripped the gear shift and put the car in reverse. "McKinley it is."

At the park I ended up telling her once again how I felt. Months ago she had said it would only be temporary. Her doubt only persuaded me to think of her even more.

"Te amo, Kim," remembering she liked it when I spoke in Spanish.

"I hope you're not saying what I think you're saying."

"De verdád," leaning forward, repeating it in her ear. "Te amo and I want to make love to you."

"Come on, Louie," pushing me away, "you can't do this."

"Why not? I'm not lying."

"Geez! You can't possibly comprehend what you're saying. You're too young! You're barely an eighth-grader!"

"Shhh. I know you feel it too. I know you can see it . . ."

"God, why did I let you kiss me last time," she murmured.

". . . If you didn't want it to happen, then why'd you let me work with you all this time?"

"Honestly, you're experiencing puppy love."

"No. That's the second time you say that. I know what I feel! You feel it too. If there's anything in life I have it's my feelings. They're like the only things I have that let me see the truth."

"So then you should be able to see the truth about this. I'm twice your age. What can we possibly do together?"

"I don't know. We get along. You're even going to teach me how to play backgammon. Remember? I mean, you're the one that's always saying how I act a lot older than the rest of the kids in school and even people older than you. You're the one who tells me the inside is what counts," pointing to my chest. "You say all this shit. Not me. So why are you taking it back? Huh? Man, you're just like everybody else. Fuckin' liars."

"Luis," placing her hands on top of my shoulders, "an adult relationship is a bit more complicated than . . ."

"No!" I snapped, throwing her warm gesture away. "People make things complicated. It's easy. Just don't lie. Look, you're not going to change my mind, Kim. No one can do that anymore. I don't believe stuff just 'cause you say it. I believe it because this is how I feel about things too. Don't you understand? You just help me put it in words. Look, if you don't love me, say it to my face."

She let out a half-hearted moan.

"See, you know it," playing with her ear. "You do love me. Seriously, I can see it. Since the first time I met you I felt something weird. And I'm not going to stop until you believe in me. I'm different now. I'm never going to let people tell me what to do anymore. Fuck that. I know who I am. I don't need people that aren't going to be there for me. Fuck that. I'm here for me now. Louie."

5

Man, Carlos," plopping next to my cousin on the apartment steps. We had recently come from soaking ourselves at a nearby water hydrant. "You're not going to believe this. They're all giving me shit at school about Miss Kim."

"Still?"

"Yep. And now they want me to go see Father Tom about it."

"Are you serious? Is Miss Barbara still on your ass?"

"Yep."

"Maybe she's just jealous 'cause she's not getting any. I remember how you told me that she would sometimes get up behind some of you guys in class and massage you guys. Weird."

"Man, she would rub her middle part against the back of my head sometimes too, Carlos. I'm not going to say I didn't like it, but it was strange . . . I guess the new principal, Sister Odelle, saw me and Miss Kim coming out of school the other day. I don't know, I'm pretty sure that's why she told me to go see Father Tom. Man, and this is after all the shit Miss Barbara told me. I bet she got Sister Odelle on my back. Shit, I wish Sister Albian was the principal again."

"Right, right . . . And, Lou, I remember all those crazy arguments you and your mother had about you going over to see her so much. Now you got to deal with this crap. Hey! Your mother still doesn't know what's going on, does she?"

"Are you crazy? You think she'd let me go out with Miss Kim if she knew what I was doing with her?"

"Don't know." He whipped off his wet T-shirt and tightly wrung it in front of him. "I don't think your mother knows what to expect from you anymore."

"Man, what are you talking about?"

"Look at you, Lou," slapping the shirt on his back, "you're a wild man. Everyone knows it. Even I still can't believe you're going out with Miss Kim. She's what? How many years older?"

"Thirteen."

"Fucking Lou . . ."

I could hear the admiration in Carlos's voice. He was always the one leading me, I thought. My guru navigator.

". . . you're pretty bold with this whole thing. If I were you, I'd be more careful with hanging around the neighborhood in her car."

"Why? I'm not going to get in trouble."

"Oh brother," brushing the water from his forehead. "Fucking Lou, I'm not talking about you. I'm talking about her. Don't you know that it's against the law for you guys to be having sex?"

"So? No one sees us," pulling off my wet tank top.

"How do you know?"

"What do you think? We do it in school when everyone's around? Duh! We wait until everyone's gone or sometimes we go out in her car and drive to some place where no one can see us. Did you know that there's a shitload of places to hide over by the factories around 37th Street?" I straightened my arm out and pointed to the street.

"Don't tell me you do it over there, Lou! By Panther's Lair? No fucking way!" He scratched his head viciously. "Where we all use to go when we were kids to play? That's nuts!"

"Hell, yeah! Around six o'clock no one's really around. Except for the people who drive the big trucks. Those guys don't care. And security doesn't stop or anything when they see her car parked. I think it's because it's brand new."

I scrunched the tank top into a ball, raised it to the sun, and squeezed it hard over my head. I then unwrapped it and draped it over my head. With fist poised up, I pretended to be some sort of prehistoric warrior advancing to battle, the kind I had seen on television.

"You mean you two will be doing it in the car and they don't even stop to check?"

"Nope," leaping up, "even when the windows get fogged."

"Like I said, Lou. You're a wild man."

"Hey man, I just really love Miss Kim."

He began to laugh.

"What are you cracking up about? You've seen me naked like this before," continuing to play.

"That's not it. Didn't you notice just now how you still call her Miss Kim and not Kim?"

"So?"

"Nothing. I just think it's funny. You don't think it's weird, Lou?"

"Aw, man, I call her Kim to her face all the time. I don't know why I just called her Miss Kim . . . Seriously, Carlos . . . I love her. Why do you think I spent so much time trying to get her? It took me like six fucking months for her to even listen to me!"

"So how does it feel for her to be your first?"

"What do you mean?"

"Sex. Did it feel strange to be that close to someone?"

"To tell you the truth, I don't even remember how it felt the first time."

"That sucks. Is it at least different every time?"

"I guess. Actually, it kind of always feels the same. *Real good.* But check it out, I wasn't too sure what I was doing at first."

"So how did you know if she liked it or not?"

"Oh, I always ask her if she likes it. She says she does. So I guess it's cool."

"Crazy." He stood up and began walking down the stairs. With every pace, his gym shoes made a squishing sound. We would be soaked for a while, I thought. "So, Lou," Carlos turned and gazed up, "what do you think about your new place?"

"It's all right," looking behind at the two-story building. "At first it hurt when Mom told us we were selling our house. But, hey, things change, and you got to make the best out of what you get. I didn't even think about where we were going. I thought it'd be bigger. Guess not. No biggie."

"I'm sorry. If I had what you guys lost I would've been crying my eyes out right now. Your house was like a little palace. You had a nice pool in the backyard. A tool shed. Your father had his work-place in the basement where he kept all his upholstery tools and stuff. Even your mom had a little garden where she grew peppers, tomatoes, and other things for you guys. I remember the time when we stayed with you guys for a couple of months. That was kick ass."

"Yeah," I sighed, "that was when you guys first got here from California."

"Uh-huh. I thought I had gone to heaven when I saw your house."

"Shut up."

"Seriously, Lou, you guys had it pretty good. Back in Mexico when we use to live in the ranch—La Noria—you would never see a pool. I think the closest thing there was to a pool were these huge ditches that got filled up during the rainy season. Gus and me would go into these muddy things, jump in with the rest of our friends and cousins, buck-naked."

"And you didn't mind that it was all muddy inside?"

"Lou, we were little. You don't care about anything like that when you're little. You should know that. I mean look at you. You still pick your nose in front of everybody. I tell you, as long as we got to do anything we were totally happy. You can't even imagine how boring La Noria is. The only thing that was even anyway near being exciting was when my uncles would let us take the trucks out on the roads."

"Naw!"

"Seriously, Lou, driving a truck over there is no big deal. It's more like something you need to know how to do so you can help on the ranch. It's not like here where you go to school forever. No, over there the ranch and family comes first and, if you're lucky, you then might go past grade school."

"Man, Carlos, that sounds real fucking cool."

"Sure, Lou, real cool. That's why people want to move over here so bad."

"Is that how it is in my mother's town?"

"Irapuato?" Carlos scoffed, "Lou, that's not like the Noria. It's not as big as Chicago, or have skyscrapers like Chicago; it's a small, teeny-weenie city. At least there the roads are paved."

"So it's just like here?"

"No, the streets are paved but they get dusty as hell in the summertime. When it finally feels like raining, the street sometimes get flooded. I wish you could see it. Those storms are wicked in La Noria. When those clouds come in, they look big and puffy like giant marshmallows! They look like they're going to fall right down on you. And the lightning bolts. Holy fucking shit! They light up the sky like you can't believe. At night, it gets so dark on the ranch that you can even see the stars. No, Lou, it's a different world. There's even mountains close by."

"For real? Everywhere in Mexico it's like that?" awestruck by the images I began to produce from his descriptions.

"Don't know. Haven't been everywhere."

"Do you like it better over there or over here?"

"I like it better here." He let out a laugh. "After having lived with you guys, I know I like it better here. I don't think my aunt is ever going to forget that place."

"Fuck!" jumping the top stair and landing next to him. "I still can't understand why they had to sell our house! Mom says we only needed a few more years to pay it off."

"I thought you said it had to do with your relatives coming over from Mexico?"

"I don't know, Carlos. I think so. I hate talking shit, but when my uncle first got here, everything was cool. Then the rest of his family came and things started messing up. It was more like my aunt who started to act strange. She's my uncle's wife. She was cool at first, but then she began making all these long-ass-distance calls to Mexico. I don't think she wanted to pay for their share of the bills."

"What's up with that?"

"Man, I remember her arguing about it to my mother. All I know for sure is that my father got my uncle a job at the place where he worked, and one day they both got into a fight. Because of that, my father left his job. I don't know why he didn't ask my uncle to leave instead. He was getting paid really good there too. After that, things just kept going down. Dad got into an accident. Some drunk person hit him nasty coming off the expressway. He fucked up his back and couldn't collect insurance because he wasn't working. Everything happened all at once. And we didn't have any more savings to cover us because my father had used up a lot of money to get a *coyote* to get my uncle across from Mexico. Those people charge a lot, Carlos. Like two thousand dollars! Sometimes they don't even get you across. But, anyway, when he recovered, it was hard for him to find a job that would pay half of what he got at the other place. I don't know. It's like everybody was making a lot of money and then things went down the drain. Man, I told them they were going to lose the house!"

"Are you pissed off at your parents, Lou?"

"Nah, they just made bad decisions. I'm not going to cry about it. It's over . . . Hey, so do you want to walk with me to the rectory?"

"Sure. Is that where you're suppose to meet Father Tom?"

"Yeah," taking the shirt off my head, "that's where the interrogation is gonna be at." A few water droplets dripped from the ends of my curly hair. "Hey, do you want to hear a cool story?"

"Sure."

"Well anyway, my dad told me this story a long time ago . . . You know that before the devil became the devil he was a good angel. Man, he wasn't even just a good angel. Lucifer was a powerful angel. One day he saw just how powerful he was. He was dipping hands in the water of this lake and when he pulled them out he saw the little drops of water turn into small angels. All the angels around him were amazed at how powerful he was. They even made him their leader. And at that moment he felt that he didn't need God. And that's when the war against God began." I began to walk up the stairs to my apartment. "When Lucifer thought that he was better than God. But do you know why God is really still more powerful than Lucifer?"

"Because God is God?"

"No, because God knew what Lucifer could do way before even Lucifer knew himself."

"Exactly. Because God is God."

"Hey," thinking through his statement, "that's right. I wonder if it really happened?"

"Lou, you think Father Tom's kind of weird?"

"I don't know. I hardly see him. The only times I do is at church when we're serving Mass or once in a while when he comes to school. Why?"

"Well, I feel bad for saying this, considering that he's done a lot more things for the parish than Father Malick ever did. But he kind of gives me the creeps."

"How come?"

"I don't know. It's a feeling I get from him. He invited a bunch of us who go to Quigley for a game of poker next Saturday."

"That's right. My brother was saying something about that to Mom."

"You don't think it's weird?"

"Naw. I think it'd be pretty cool. Maybe he's going to ask me if I'll go to the game too."

"Doubt it," patting my shoulder, "you'll still need to finish this year, Lou."

"That's fine, I don't have any money anyway."

"Besides you don't know how to play poker."

"Man, Carlos, what are you talking about? That's all we use to play at the old house in the summer. It was me, my dad, Israel, Jose, and my uncle. Sometimes we'd play until four in the morning. We use to get mad at Israel because he'd win like fifty bucks and leave to go to sleep. The fucker. Here, Carlos, let me get a shirt before it gets late."

"Okay," he ran up and opened the side door to the hallway stairs. "I'm going to tell Mom where I'll be. I'll meet you down here in five minutes."

"Cool."

"I stopped and turned to look at the street.

"What's wrong, Lou?"

"Nothing, man. You just have me thinking about what it would be like to go to Mexico."

"You should go sometime."

"I will. My ma just has to take care of our papers."

"That's right," Carlos said. "You and Jose weren't born here. Only Iz. Right?"

"Yeah. It sucks. And it's not like we haven't been living here for a long time. I wasn't six months old when they brought me. We still need green cards or something like that if we want to leave the United States and come back."

"Don't worry, Lou, something tells me everything will turn out right for you guys. Now go get your shirt."

"Okay."

The visit to the rectory was making me nervous. What if Father Tom wanted to know everything between Kim and me? Then what?

I told my cousin to leave if I wasn't out in fifteen minutes. I rang the doorbell. Seconds later, a loud buzzing sounded. Still, no one came out. Again the noise.

"Push the door," screamed Carlos. "You dorkus!"

"Oh." I grabbed the handle of the door and moved forward. Inside, I saw a small elderly woman standing a few feet away beneath another doorway. The ringing ended suddenly.

"Hi," her aged eyes glowed fiercely. "I thought you were never going to come in. You must be Louie?"

I nodded.

"My name is Frida," extending her hand to me. "I take care of things for Pastor around here," she hustled over to close the door behind me. "You know, I always see you at church. Boy, you must get tired of serving Mass?"

"Sometimes."

"I bet. Father's been expecting you. Just go right up the stairs." She walked over and opened a second door. "You'll find him on the second floor," holding her hand up. "There's no way you can get lost. I'm sure Father's playing music in his rooms. He's always putting on operas and musicals. That sort of junk," she laughed. "Follow what you hear."

"Frida, do you know what Father Tom wants?"

"No, dear. He didn't mention anything at breakfast. If it was something bad, I'm sure he would've made a fuss over it. He's not one to keep things to himself. Why?" waving her index finger at me. "Have you been a bad boy?"

"I don't think so."

"No, you look too sweet. Although you do have a mischievous look in your eye . . . Well, go on up. Father gets extremely impatient when things aren't done on time."

The staircase climb. The farther along, the stronger I could hear the keys of a piano being struck, crisp and sharp. I ended up in front of an open room and entered it, breathing in an alluring mixture of olive green, crimson, celadon, turquoise, and others. I stared at the multipatterned sofa and squinted. The melting collage reminded me of a favorite painting I had seen in some book at the library. The music heightened the new feelings.

"Make yourself comfortable in the den next door, Mr. Aguilera."

I turned to my right, startled. Never had I seen Father Tom like this before. In plainclothes.

"Are you okay?"

"Ummmm," indicating the throat, "you don't have the white collar and stuff."

"Because we're priests does not mean we're old stiffs. Please," showing me the way to the room next door, "make yourself at home." I walked past him to the other room. "Unfortunately, none of the rooms in the rectory are very spacious."

I dropped onto a firm sofa chair. "This room is bigger than the room my brother and I have in our apartment!"

"Father Mike's room is the largest one of them all. But the view he has is horrible. Who wants to see the parking lot and some brick siding? Now here," entering to indicate the window behind me, "I have something unique. Go on. Just be sure you pull the blinds up first. The last thing I need is some idiot thinking I'm some nosy old grandma."

I did as he asked and looked out the window. The first thing I saw was the rectory's front lawn and the grotto that stood next to our school. I could see the worried head of the stone-white statue of the Virgin Mother Mary, overlooking a neat file of red and white flowers at her base. Her hands were outstretched as if to say, "this is all I have left for you."

A group of children were gleefully riding back and forth on their bicycles in the street, trying pop-up wheelies and the like. Their howls were coupled with the familiar tune of an approaching ice cream truck. The louder the music, the louder their screams.

Higher up, the triangular roofs of the neighborhood houses, neatly resembling one other, rose to about the same level. It was the ends of the trees that had the privilege of disappearing into the sky, like fingers pointing away to the sun.

I edged closer to the window. Wow, peering up, I was always amazed at how there seemed to be a black heaven in between the bright blue sky.

"Rustic almost, but can you imagine how this was," interrupted the priest, "say, sixty years ago, in the days of the Roaring Twenties when everything was so young? Milkmen brought their bottled goods right to your doorstep. Things seemed more magical back then than they do today. Men would pull up in these huge wagons in front of your home in the morning and deliver these great big blocks of ice to whoever would buy. You see, they didn't have electrical refrigerators back then, so they had to keep things cold in an icebox. And they would use ice as a means to maintain the low temperature."

"Where would they get the ice?" I kept at the window.

"They had it stored in large warehouses."

"Yeah," turning to him, "but where did they really get it from if they couldn't make it?"

"Well, I think they took it off of Lake Michigan in the winter."

"Cool."

"Yes," Father Tom stared out. "It had to have been for it not to melt . . ."

I thought, that's not what I meant.

". . . The Twenties was an era when men like Capone ran the city. Nothing escaped their eyes. Jazz flourished. Speakeasies were the place to be. Flappers took care of their men. Everything was so wonderful. Now it's a bunch of thugs riding around in their cars playing trashy boom-box music." He shook his head. "Somehow this little neighborhood has managed to survive like an island in the ocean. Not bad . . . So, what do you think about my humble surroundings?"

"Ummm," turning to observe his collection of books and records sitting on top of the mantles opposite the sofa, "I've never seen a room like this before. It's pretty cool."

"Well, I'm happy you like the place," he sat down. "I wasn't too sure what you were thinking when you first came in. Did you know that your eyes lit up as soon as you saw the room? I was watching you the whole time."

"No way!"

"They did." He crossed his legs. "That says a lot about something. Doesn't it?"

"I don't know."

He put his hand on his chin and began to stroke his mustache. "Go on, keep looking around. Don't let me disturb you."

He kept to himself, providing me time to reflect on every detail of the room. There was a cartoon-like portrait above one of the mantles of two individuals sitting next to each other. Whoever had done it had taken a considerable amount of time, I thought. Clean thin black lines were finely pressed on a pristine white surface. The image appeared both calm and comical to me.

"It's an original Hirschfeld," he pointed out. "Sits nicely there, doesn't it?"

"Yeah. Who are they?"

"The two men? Stephen Sondheim and Hal Prince. Sondheim is a songwriter-composer and Prince is a director. They're big on Broadway."

"That's like in New York or something?"

Father Tom smiled. "You should have seen this place when Father Malick lived here."

"Why? Was everything messed up?"

"Well, for one, the place stank beyond belief. Piles—and I mean piles—of garbage were literally thrown all over the place. I found tons of newspapers dating back to the nineteen-seventies in this room. Old empty bottles of scotch and brandy were tucked inside the fireplace right next to where you're sitting."

I looked to where he was suggesting; there a pile of records was now neatly stacked.

"Holy cow, they had a fireplace here? Like with wood?"

"Sure, how do you think they used to heat these old places in the winter months before central heating came around?"

"Can you still use it?"

"The fireplace? God, no. It's too much of a hassle to take care of than it's worth. Besides, the insurance company wouldn't hear of it."

"Yeah . . . I guess the church and school did start to look cleaner when you came."

"Oh, you noticed. Good for you. I'm glad someone's on top of things around here. Did you know the old janitor, Chester, used to sit up there in the roof of the church and drink liquor every day? We filled over four large industrial garbage bags with empty bottles of cheap whisky one day."

"Really?"

"Really. Except those days are over for him. He's history."

"Yep. I remember you coming into the lunchroom last year—your face was all red—telling the teachers . . . I never even drank a beer once. One of my uncles died because he was an alcoholic. My dad told me he was a smart man. That everyone in his town in Mexico respected him because he was so smart. I guess he had one weakness."

"We're all made of flesh, Mr. Aguilera."

"I guess."

He stood up, removing himself to a small wooden cabinet. He swung open its pair of doors, displaying an assortment of oddly shaped bottles with heavily decorated labels. There were also cans of soda and short round glasses.

"Would you care for something to drink? Coke or 7-Up maybe?"

"No, I'm cool."

"Are you sure?"

"Yeah. I'm not thirsty."

He pointed to a glass pitcher. "Water?"

"Okay," giving in for his sake.

He grabbed something shiny in his hands.

"What are those?"

"What? These?" holding them up. "Ice tongs. You use them to grab ice cubes. Haven't you ever seen them before?"

"No."

"Don't worry. I merely use them to be pretentious. If you want, I can use my hands. I've washed them."

"That's all right. I just didn't know what those things were."

"Here you go," handing me the ice water. "Now," serving himself one, "is there anything on your mind you want to talk about?" He sat down. "I hear you're having difficulties with Sister Odelle and Sister Therese, as well as Miss Barbara. They seem pretty concerned about your relationship with Miss McGregory. You must be doing something insane to get everyone so riled up."

"No. I'm not doing anything."

"Mr. Aguilera." Father Tom put the drink aside on the small table next to the sofa. "Why do you think you're here?"

"I don't know. I thought maybe it was because of what happened to Richard."

"No. That was some time ago. Don't get me wrong, the thing with Richard and Saúl was awful. Who would have guessed that Saúl would have thrown those chemicals into Richard's mouth?"

"It's good nothing happened," I grinned. "Right?"

"Of course. After we found out about the incident, we immediately called the chemical distributor in Philadelphia. Did you know that that particular mixture isn't even sold to elementary schools anymore? There's still an arsenal of things that need to be disposed of from your science room."

"Yeah," smiling deviously. "The teachers never let us touch anything that's in the metal cabinets."

"And with good reason," shaking his head. "Obviously Saúl saw things differently. People have died from less, you know."

"I'm sorry."

"Technically you weren't at fault. But from what Miss Barbara said, you apparently orchestrated the entire episode. She said you had been egging Saúl on all day. Something about his haircut?"

"Yeah, his aunt really messed it up. But I only made fun of him because he was making fun of me all year and he wouldn't stop."

"So you waited until the most vulnerable moment to strike. When there was no way that he could argue with you. A bit vengeful and calculating on your part."

"I just gave him what he gave me all year. Except I gave it to him in one day. I didn't know he would do that to Richard."

"Unfortunately, you'll learn that it's usually the smaller ones who receive the wrath of the wrongdoers."

"Man, but I wouldn't have done it if I knew what he was going to do to Richard."

"There's a lot of what-ifs in this world. I'm only glad nothing serious came of it. God, what a hassle. But that's not the real reason why you're here. Is it?"

"I don't know."

"You do understand that whatever you say will be held in strict confidence. Let's pretend this is, say, Confession. You are aware that a priest is not permitted to divulge anything he hears in Confession."

"But you're not wearing your priest clothes."

"And you think that because I'm not wearing my 'priest clothes,' as you put it, that I'm incapable of performing my duties as a priest?"

I turned away, distracted.

"What's wrong?"

"Nothing, I was looking at your sofas. Whoever upholstered them did a pretty good job."

He let out a broad smile. "Really? Now how exactly do you know what good upholstery is?"

"Ummm," feeling the quality of the texture on the sofa chair, "my father's an upholsterer. I've looked through this big sample book at home. He showed me the difference between the expensive material and the less expensive material. They used okay stuff on this."

"What about something that isn't either/or? How can you tell its value?"

"Well, you kind of know after a while. I don't really know how to explain it, but it's something you just know after looking at different material over and over again. Sooner or later you figure out what's made good and what's not. It's like the same thing when I go buy comic books."

"Right."

I purposely worked the room again, hoping he would forget to say anything more about the "Confession."

"Why don't we go back into the living room," he said, standing up. "I don't imagine you took the appropriate time in getting fully adjusted. I'll give you the grand tour."

As we went through the ceremony, I found the most interesting items were on a simple shelf with a light stain varnish. Glass doors displayed a set of carefully arranged glasses. The collection included a number of odd shapes and colors. One of them was tinted blue at its rim, stem, and base.

"So, which one do you like best?"

I singled out the one with the blue tint.

"My eccentric martini glass? Interesting."

I smiled and nodded.

"Blue must be your favorite color?"

I smirked. "No, I don't have a favorite color. All colors are pretty cool. Everyone in school thinks I'm weird because I don't have a favorite one. Why should I?"

"I don't think that's *weird* in any way," pausing briefly. "In fact, it's very good that someone at your age reaches out for different things, especially in a place like this where things may seem so mundane. I imagine that's why you're not embarrassed to wear your hair in that fashion."

I brought my hands to my head and felt my way through the chaotic webs of hair. "It's just the way it is," shrugging my shoulders. "I don't care what people think anyway. It's my hair. But I still didn't do it to look like anything."

"I bet the kids in school bother you for it. People like Saúl."

"People are always going to be saying stupid stuff about you." I went back to the martini glass. "Where'd you get it?"

"I found it while on vacation in Italy."

"You went to Italy?"

"Yes, I went in '78."

"1978? Wow. I've never even been out of Chicago. I mean, I've been to Wisconsin Dells. But only once."

Father Tom's face broke into a passive chuckle. "Oh, Mr. Aguilera, I'm sure you'll see more of the world. You're what? Only thirteen right now? Don't worry, your time will come."

"But, Father, I already see everything I want to see anyway."

"How is that?"

"With all the books I read. They tell you about things that you don't ever even think about. My mom bought us a whole bunch of books once when we were little. About twenty-five of them. I read them all a whole bunch of times already. They show you all these different places and how people are in these different places."

"You enjoy reading?"

"Hell, yeah!"

"But how do you know that what the authors write is even true?"

"Man, I just know what looks like the truth."

"But the truth may be the grandest lie."

"I guess. But my brother Jose says that there's no one who can tell you the whole truth anyway. That there's no such thing."

"And do you believe him?"

"Why would my own brother lie to me?" I was insulted by his question.

"You really do like it?" quickly changing topic.

"The martini glass? Yeah. I've never seen one in my whole life like that."

"Mr. Aguilera. Are you aware of the number of times you keep saying 'yeah'?"

"I mean yes."

"Well, just be careful it doesn't become an incurable habit. Whenever you adopt slang into your vocabulary, it gives someone the impression that you're uneducated. You don't want people to think that. Come on, let's go back into the den."

"I don't think it matters what you say."

"What?" turning to frown. "That's silly."

"For real, people are always taking things wrong anyway. Why even change the way you talk?"

"So there's some bridge of communication between men. How else can we escape acting like the fools on the Tower of Babel?"

"People still don't listen no matter what. Who cares what you say?"

We stared quietly at each other.

"Do you have a lot of friends, Mr. Aguilera?"

"Kind of. Not real good friends."

He bent his head in approval. "Does your mother allow you to go out with them?"

"She didn't at first but now she does."

"What made her change her mind?"

"My grandma. I guess she saw how bored we were."

"We? That's as in you and your two brothers?"

"Yep. How did you know?"

"I'm the Pastor. I'm supposed to know every little thing about you guys . . . The three of you get along?"

"We fight sometimes. But I think everyone fights with their brothers and sisters."

"Yes, I agree. I have two sisters myself."

"No brothers?"

"None. Now, who do you spend most of your time with? Your friends or brothers?

"I guess I used to spend a lot of time with my brothers."

"Why?"

"Because, my friends didn't want to do what I wanted to do. They didn't get that I got tired of doing only what they wanted to do. Like I remember once we tried to go play basketball with them and they only wanted to use their basketball. And everybody argued because they wanted to use their own basketball. It was so stupid. I don't understand why they couldn't just use one for one game and the other for the next. Anyway, only my brothers and my cousins and I used to go out because we lived so far away from school and no one wanted to come out to our house."

"How do you know that? What if their parents just didn't allow them to travel that far?"

"Nah, they were just lazy. All they want to do is watch TV."

"You think people are selfish?"

"Yeah."

"And what sort of things do you want to do?" his tone now filled with curiosity.

"It's like when me, my brothers, and my cousins go out. We go everywhere on our bikes. We don't plan it or anything. But none of my friends really want to go far, just mostly stay at home. They don't even want to go to the park. I don't know why. I like doing things with people."

"So what wouldn't be boring for you?"

"Going real far and seeing other things. Like when we go to downtown on our bikes."

"You consider *that* to be fun?" seeming utterly surprised by my answer. "Aren't you worried about getting hit by a car or, even worse, having your bike stolen?"

"Why?" grinning, remembering the countless times the people on the streets had asked us this question. "If I can get hit by a car downtown or going to downtown, why can't I get hit on the street in front of my house where cars pass by too? . . . No one's going to steal the bikes anyway. They're banana seat bikes."

"I suppose you're right in some sense. Still, one may argue that you place yourself in greater jeopardy the moment you begin venturing farther away from home, especially with the type of vehicle you're using."

"Ummm . . . nothing's ever happened to us."

"Still, the peril is there."

"Yeah, but at home I feel trapped. Like I'm dying in some weird way. Except when I'm doing something cool. Like listening to good music. I like to do that. It doesn't make me feel lazy. I hate that."

"I see your point." He left his place and went over to the cabinet. "I imagine the temptations of a large city like Chicago are too hard to resist for a young person like yourself. I found myself in the same situation when I was fifteen and going to the high school seminary downtown. With all the crazy things that were happening in my era, I'm surprised my generation even made it. I see you've finished your drink. Want the same or something else?"

"I'll have a Coke. Thanks."

"So," pouring the can of soda, "the three of you are pretty tight?"

"Not like before. I think my older brother Jose likes hanging out with his older friends more."

"I'm sure it's the girls who keep him occupied. They'll do that, you know."

"Nah. I don't think so. Not Jose."

"Mr. Aguilera . . ."

"Father, can you call me Luis? I don't like it when the teachers call me Mr. Aguilera."

"Very well then. Luis. Let's get right to business. When are you going to tell me what's been going on between you and Miss McGregory? Or did you think I would forget?"

And this was what is was all about, I thought. Why wouldn't they leave it alone? There were so many things *they* didn't do right.

"Miss Kim and I aren't doing anything wrong!"

"*I . . . did . . . not . . . say . . . that.* Did I? Luis, are you screwing Miss Kim?"

Why was he so upset?

"Yes," I whispered, "we make love."

"Make love? I believe the appropriate terminology for sexual intercourse between a thirteen-year-old boy and a twenty-six-year-old woman is child molestation! Do you have any idea what the consequences are if anyone finds out about this? Have the two of you even realized that you've placed the entire school's reputation in jeopardy? Well? Answer me!"

I rested my eyes on the glass in my hand. The sloshing water opened me to a new realization. I was shaking.

"How long?"

"It's been some time."

"How long?"

"I don't know. Not long."

Father Tom rolled his eyes. "What were you thinking?"

"I know a lot of people can get into trouble but I'm not going to tell!"

"Listen, obviously you're a bit more clever than your average boy of thirteen, but you're underestimating what may result from this whole affair. What am I supposed to do with the people breathing down my back? What about Sister Odelle? She hasn't been very happy about your constant visits with Miss McGregory. Believe me, they're beyond having suspicions about what's been going on between you two. You're not even discreet about the whole thing! I never used to even see you walk into the parking lot from here. Now, you take leisurely strolls in broad daylight. Don't you think anyone's going to care? Well?"

"No one cares what I feel. Why should I?"

He lowered his chin and placed his arm at the back of his head. "I'm surprised your mother and father haven't come over to the rectory to talk to me. Do they know?"

"I don't think so."

"You don't think so?"

"Look, Father, I'm graduating after this year, so you won't have to worry about this."

"That's a few months away, Mr. Aguilera. What do you expect me to tell Sister Odelle when she asks me how our meeting went?" I felt my eyes dip. "Either you end your actions with Miss Kim, or a suspension may be on the horizon for you, young man . . . I don't expect Sister Odelle will allow you to continue your education here so long as there is no further cooperation from you."

I felt my energy drain.

"Considering this is your last year here at St. Peter's, I don't believe you'll want to blow it. Well, Mr. Aguilera, what are we going to do?"

"Why should I be suspended?" my temper flared. "I didn't do anything bad! I know what I'm doing doesn't look normal to anyone but I can't help how I feel for her."

"Well, you're going to have to if you don't want to be suspended."

"Look, I'm going to tell my mom everything and then we'll see what happens."

"You're making this very impossible, Mr. Aguilera."

"I don't like it when people try to hurt me."

"No one's trying to hurt you, Luis."

"Then why do you keep telling me you're going to punish me? Man, that's not cool!"

Silence.

"Luis, let's do one thing. Promise me you're going to keep this low. You've already caused enough grief, especially for Sister Therese . . ." Me, I thought. Me? ". . . She's had enough to deal with. She comes to your defense on a number of occasions and generally boasts of your good character. For some reason, that woman has a great love for you."

"Yeah," I smiled, "she made me kneel in front of her the other day in front of her class because I was being mean. She said I needed to be humbled. I didn't mind she made me do it. I'll do anything for her."

"And why is that?"

"Because, she's cool to me and gives me respect. She always believes in me. She says I can do anything. No one else says that to me here. And she says what she wants to say and doesn't leave the good or bad things out to make you happy."

"Well, you better make sure she knows how much you appreciate her."

"See, you don't even understand! She already knows that. It's like we don't have to say anything to each other 'cause we know what the other one is feeling."

"Thinking," Father Tom said.

"No," I replied, "feeling. It's different. Just like yeah and yes."

He let out a grunt. "She's sick, you know."

82

"Are you serious?"

"Yes. She's getting enough stress from Odelle as it is. It's bad enough they're thinking of shutting down the school."

"Are you kidding?"

"No. Your dealings with Miss Kim are only a minute part of the mess that I have to deal with right now. That's another reason why this situation with her has to come to a halt. Understand?"

"I didn't know Sister was getting in trouble."

"There's a lot of things you still don't grasp, Mr. Aguilera. I'm sure you'll figure them out eventually. Now, what are you going to do?"

"I guess I'll be cool. I don't want to get Sister in trouble. But I'm not going to stop seeing Miss Kim. I just won't do it around school."

"I don't know about that."

"I promise."

"You promise?"

"Yes."

"And your promise is good?"

"I don't play around with that. I'm telling you the truth."

"Good." He left the sofa. "See, now that wasn't too bad, was it?"

"Are you going to tell Sister Odelle about me and Miss Kim?"

"Of course not. And I know you won't either."

"I'm not stupid."

"No one said you were. Well, look at that," indicating the clock, "we've spent a long time cooped up in this room. I imagine you're hungry?"

"Yeah. Oh man, I mean yes."

"That's all right. You'll learn. Let's go downstairs to the kitchen and make ourselves something to eat."

I stood up.

"I better not hear any more complaints from Odelle or the next time I get you in here I won't be so nice," giving me a quick pat on the shoulder.

"Father, what are you going to tell Sister Odelle?"

"Obviously not what you told me."

"Frida, what do you know about this pint-sized criminal?"

"Oh, Father," she held me from underneath my arm. "I remember seeing him and his brothers come to the six o'clock in the winter all bundled up in their cute little snow suits to serve Mass." She turned to me. "That older man? He was your grandpa?"

"Yeah. But he's dead now."

"Oh, I'm sorry to hear that. He knew very good English, Father. Everyone in church thought he was a very kind man."

"Really? Good for him. Now, Frida, tomorrow we're going to . . ."

My thoughts coasted away at the mention of Ventura. At the memory of the old man peeling an orange. His large blue-collar fingers, the fingers of a steelworker, gently rubbing off the thin white layer of the fruit's second skin.

He divided the orange into two halves, handing me one half and still giving me a bite of his, encouraging me to take as much as I needed. And you? He pulled out another orange from the pocket of his sweatshirt. He asked that I wait, so he wouldn't have to eat alone.

". . . Luis?" Frida asked, "do you have a job?"

"No. They say I'm not old enough to work but I work all the time."

"What do you think, Father?"

"What Frida is leading to is that we usually hire highschoolers to work in the rectory on weekends and whenever she's gone for the day. The kids answer phones and take messages. It's easy money, even though we just got rid of four or five knuckleheads."

"Why? What happened?"

"The imbeciles. They were stealing booze from the cellar."

"And having who knows what kinds of parties right here on Friday nights," added Frida.

"I found empty beer cans inside two or three garbage bags," Father Tom continued. "The morons didn't even have enough sense to hide their crimes and throw it in the alley. God, what gall."

"What a bunch of dorks."

"What can you do? Like I always say, if you're going to do something wrong, do it right . . . Actually, working here wouldn't be bad for you. You can always bring your homework and do it right in the office."

"Cool."

"So you'll think about it?"

"Yeah, I'll take it. I've been thinking about getting a job for a while. When can I start?"

"Hold your horses. Let's go to the kitchen and discuss your future over a meal. One thing's for sure, you'll always be fed."

"Father Tom."

"Yes, Luis."

"You have any white bread or wheat bread?"

"To answer your question, we only have rye bread. Would you like some of that?"

"I've never tasted it," watching him hold the loaf in his hands. "Does it taste like wheat?"

"Try it," dropping it on the kitchen table, "I think you'll like it."

"What if I don't?"

"Then you don't eat it." He set out a pair of plates.

"No, I'll eat it."

"Even if you don't like it? That's odd."

"Yeah. I feel bad if I let food go to waste. When I was younger I use to throw up my vegetables all the time."

"Can we be a bit less graphic?"

"Yeah, well, like I was saying, I didn't like the way they tasted but then I started seeing a whole bunch of stuff on TV that showed all the people that were poor all over the world. That made me think I shouldn't be so picky."

"I'm sure your parents had something to do with it as well."

"Yeah, my mom wouldn't leave me alone until I ate everything. The cool thing was whenever my mom turned around, I gave whatever I didn't want to my older brother."

"Here," Father Tom sat me down at the table, "allow me." He opened the refrigerator's steel door and began taking out a multitude of ingredients. "Can you trust the Padre with your food?"

"Yeah."

"Mr. Aguilera?"

"*Yes*, I can."

"Much better. Really, how do you expect to command respect from the people around you if you're unable to communicate yourself properly? For example, the way you handled yourself with Frida was good. You were courteous but not the big ham. Where did you learn to act that way? That's some good savvy."

"My mom always told me to be polite."

"Yes, everyone's mother teaches their children proper behavior. But how do you get it down so well? I could have sworn you were an alderman trying to score a vote."

"I don't know."

"It doesn't matter. What you need now is refinement. Which high school are you planning to go to?"

"I don't know. I haven't checked it out yet."

"Have you considered the seminary system?"

"You mean Quigley?"

"South. Not North."

"There's two of them?"

"Yes."

"Wow," I watched him. "What's there?"

"Well, for one, their liberal arts education is exceptional. Better than most places. At least it was when I used to attend."

"You use to go to Quigley South?"

"No. I went to North. That campus is right around the corner from Water Tower. Near the chi-chi shopping district. But I hear Q South is as good a place. Students there are drawn from all sorts of backgrounds. You're not just going to get one type of crowd there, you know. The world's changing, Luis," spreading a roast-colored mustard, "you'll need that sort of diversity to help you deal with the knuckleheads in life."

"But it's all guys in there."

"Come on," shaking his head. "you're only going to be in there for a few hours a day. You can spend the rest of your afternoon hunting down girls."

"No, it's not that. I just think that it's kind of weird that the school only has boys in it."

"It's a seminary! The whole point is to produce priests, not to have a meeting ground where exchanging telephone numbers between guys and chicks is the primary function."

"But what if I don't want to become a priest? Will they still let me in?"

"If you do decide to enter come next year, don't tell them you're not interested in becoming a priest. Give them what they want to hear. *Tell* them you're seriously considering priesthood. I'll even write a letter for you. If nothing comes of it, at least you've secured yourself a solid education. What are you going to do? Go to a public school and get yourself lost in the shuffle? Worse, get yourself killed in a public school like Kelly?"

"Actually, I was thinking about getting in to St. Ignatius."

"Are your grades that good?"

"I haven't had a C in anything since second grade. That's when they told my mother I had a learning disability. Since then, I've had nothing but B's and A's, mostly A's though. Oh, but maybe I did get one C in math in fifth grade."

"Fine. But Ignatius is tough. You can't pull whatever it is that you did here to get your grades up."

"You don't think I can do it?" insulted by his accusation. "What, you think I cheat?"

"The question is do you really want to go there and have your parent's finances scammed by a bunch of Jesuit stiffs? They're such prudes."

"What do you mean Jesuits?"

"What!" Father Tom cried. "You don't think the whole Roman Catholic Church consists of only one kind of clergy, do you?"

"Aren't all priests and nuns the same?"

"No, Luis. They're not. There's different orders in the Church. There's Franciscans, Jesuits, Benedictine monks. The list goes on. As for nuns, well our school has none. They're Sisters. Felician Sisters as a matter of fact. Didn't they already teach you this in school?"

"Sort of. What makes them different from each other anyway? Don't they all believe in Jesus and that other stuff?"

"It's not that simple, Luis. Some of the missionary orders require that you take a vow of poverty. Some dedicate themselves to a life of prayer and seclusion. You have heard of monasteries?"

"Yeah. That's where some of those priests go and pray by themselves in those big costumes like Father Peter, right? Father, did you take a vow of poverty when you became a priest?"

"Nooo," he squealed, "that's not exactly my lifestyle."

"I can tell."

"Oh can you?"

"Yeah, you have a lot of cool things in your room. Is that how come you didn't take that vow of poverty?"

"Well, Luis, people have different views of what God wants

from us. Why do you think Miss Barbara insists on having a children's choir?"

"I don't know. Why?"

"Because her beliefs are rooted in that type of ministry. She doesn't make the boys and girls sing because she's some old witch. She makes you guys sing because she believes it's a way in which you can get closer to God and hopefully inspire others who hear you guys get close to God as well. She may have her bad days, but overall she's harmless."

"Yeah, but she's suppose to be the teacher. Sometimes she's mean without any reason. And she's into all this weird stuff. Like how she believes that the group KISS stands for 'Knights in Satan's Service.' She's strange."

"And you're not? I'm sure you've given your parents a hard time. Remember, Luis, each of us is a sinner from birth. And there's no doubt in my mind that we'll sin from now on until the day we're dead. But our faith teaches us to forgive and to continue trying despite our imperfect human nature." He grinned. "And the great thing about our Church is the opportunity to repent, even at the last minute, for everything we've done."

"Yeah," feeling disappointed by the words he spoke. "I guess that's the way people want it. So you think I should go to Quigley South."

"Where else, Luis? There's no better school for you. Besides, isn't your brother Jose there?"

"Uh-huh."

"There you go. You'll have someone close to you who's already gone through the system. That way, you'll be ahead of the game."

But, I thought, I never saw any of this as a game.

"Look, take your time. You still have plenty of time before you make any concrete decision. If you go to Quigley, it may change your life forever. Who knows, we may even pull some strings and make you a priest or bishop some day. That's the wonderful thing about Chicago."

"I'll think about it. But I'm not promising anything."

"Here," handing me a plate, "eat your sandwich."

I took a bite, feeling some taste missing.

6

*L*ouie, what are you doing here?"

I jerked my head up. Sister Therese was looking down at me from the top of the stairs. She held her hands behind her back in her customary way. Her wooden crucifix dangled against the dark brown uniform.

"I'm helping Miss Kim with some stuff."

"What kind of stuff?" Her long rectangular face drew cross.

"Oh," feeling awkward, "ummm, just putting things up on the boards and cleaning the classroom," resuming my climb at a slower pace.

"Does your mother realize you're here?"

I pulled up close to her. "Yeah, she does. I told her I was coming to see Miss Kim."

"Then you wouldn't mind if we give her a call?"

We started to walk toward the principal's office.

"I think we need to have a serious discussion, Luis."

"About what?"

"I think you know what it is we have to talk about."

We reached the office. Sister began searching for a key. Once she found it, she opened the door and we both went in.

"Louie, I've noticed that you've been spending an extraordinary amount of time with Miss Kim, ever since she's arrived here. At first, I thought it would pass. But I've known you for quite some time now and I know you're different than the others. I was hoping Miss Barbara would take care of it, considering she was your primary teacher last year. But she didn't . . . You know, it's not rare to develop a strong relationship with someone older. It happens quite often. Isn't that the case with God? But things here seem to be way out of control. When summer came around and I continued finding you here, day after day, I came to the conclusion that there was something seriously wrong. Why would a boy of thirteen stay indoors at school when he could be outside playing with his friends?"

"I don't have any real friends."

She sighed. "But you do remember me talking to you about it at the beginning of July?"

"Yeah."

"Well," she continued, "I haven't seen you curb your visits with her. That's why I asked Father Tom to speak to you a couple of weeks ago. Obviously, that hasn't helped either. Sister Odelle has informed me that for the last two weeks you've been with her every day she's been here."

"That's not true! I go home too!"

She gave another long peaceful sigh.

"Louie, I don't believe it's healthy for you to keep seeing her so much, however much of your time you spend at home. I don't see any reason why she's unable to attend to her own duties without the aid of anyone else. And I'm not about to ask what's really going on. But whatever it is, think about what you're doing. Think of the consequences. For your own good, stop this nonsense."

"Sister?"

"Yes."

"I already told you my mom knows where I am. If you want, you can call her right now."

I felt a warm hand fall gently over my shoulder.

"The reason I want you to stop seeing Miss Kim has nothing to do with what I want, what Sister Odelle wants, or even what Miss Barbara wants. They have their own agendas at heart. No, this has to do with what's best for you. I know it's hard for you to let go of something you really want. The attention must be marvelous at your age. But this isn't something you need. Remember the difference. There's a reason for it. Sometimes people do things at an age when they're too inexperienced to know their limits. Emotions are only part of life. Not the whole thing. Slow down. Look at the big picture. There's time for everything. I'm saying all of this because I really do love you. I've been teaching for over thirty years now and there's nothing else in the world I would rather do. I think of each of my students as one of my own. It pains me to see you stray so far. Miss Kim should know better."

I picked up my head, looking right into her eyes. She stared right back into mine. She must have seen the red in my eyes because she grabbed a tissue from the principal's desk.

"Remember, you need to do what you feel is right but don't forget to use your head. Here, wipe your eyes. And don't be so damn melodramatic."

"Yes, Sister. Thank you."

"Now go home. Go play."

"Can I first go upstairs to tell Miss Kim I won't be able to see her anymore?"

"I suppose," she was reluctant, "but make it quick. And this had better be the last time."

"Thank you, Sister, it'll take only five minutes."

"I'll be counting."

"I know."

As I left, I looked back. She had taken off her glasses and was now massaging her temples. I could tell she was growing weary, that this supernova was reaching her limits.

"Kim, I just finished talking to Sister. She says I can't come to school to see you anymore."

"What? Hold on, you're not making sense," speeding nervously over to the classroom door and closing it. "Now, what's going on?"

"Like I said, I was with Sister Therese and she asked me not to come up here anymore. Don't worry, I didn't tell her anything about us."

"God, for a minute I thought she had found out. Geez! You're sure she didn't say anything that would give you the impression she knew?"

"Positive. What I don't understand is why they don't say anything to you?"

"Wait a minute. Who is they?"

"Everybody."

"Luis! You're being vague again. You see, now that's what I mean about you not telling me everything. You have to let me know about these things! Otherwise, I'm left in the dark with no way of knowing what's going on. *You* expect me to tell you everything about my life!"

"Sorry. It's not that I forgot. I just didn't want to lose you over stupid shit. Don't worry, nothing's going to happen. I took care of it."

"Ahhh! I don't like the sound of that."

"I did, Kim. We just won't see each other here anymore. We'll have to meet somewhere else. Why don't you just pick me up two blocks away from here? Or maybe you can pick me up at the park."

"Great, that's all I need. Some parent or student from school seeing me pick you up off the street."

"Like the last time," I mumbled, remembering the sight of my mother's friend walking along the edge of the park with her son. Kim and I had been in the backseat of the car for sometime, completely naked, when she had passed us. I had come up for air and at that instant our eyes met. And still, knowing full well what was going on, we both grinned at each other. From me, a devilish smile of mischief.

"Louie, maybe it's best we don't go out anymore so much."

"Man," I said angrily, "that's why I didn't want to say anything to you. I knew you wouldn't want to go out with me anymore! I thought you said you loved me?"

She rushed over. "No, baby, I didn't mean that. I meant that maybe you and I should let things settle down."

"Listen, Kim, if you want to break up with me, why don't you just say it right now because I really don't know what else you want me to do. You know I want you."

"I know, honey, but what are we going to do?"

"Like I said. Just pick me up a few blocks away from the school. I'll keep telling my mom that I'm going to school. How's she going to check?"

"God, you have it all figured out. My little demon."

"I told you I know how to take care of things. I knew this was going to happen. I had to come up with something."

"Always waiting for the crisis, huh? Okay. Well, there doesn't seem to be much else we can do. I just wish you were already eighteen! That way we wouldn't have to hide from anyone. We could even get married like we talked about. We could tell them all to screw off and leave us alone."

"I know. I'll be eighteen soon."

"Oh right, in another five years."

"Look, nothing's going to happen," caressing her cheek with my thumb. "We're just going to have to be more careful."

"Are you sure no one knows?"

I kept my eyes on her. "Trust me."

"Come here, my little Latin lover."

"Not right now. I have to go back downstairs. I promised Sister Therese I wouldn't stay up here for too long."

"See, already they're interfering with us. You've never said no to me."

"You don't understand. It has to be done right. Or we won't get to see each other anymore."

"You and your elaborate planning."

"I'll see you later."

"Call me at home tonight at exactly eight o'clock. I'll make sure to answer."

I frowned. "Yeah right, what if your parents pick up the phone like the other night?"

"Don't worry. You played it off pretty well that day."

"Yeah, but I really hate lying like that. It's bad enough I don't even tell my mom everything that's going on."

"I'll make sure they don't answer."

"We'll see. I'll see you later then."

"I hope so."

I left the room, frustrated and disgusted with these lies. As much as she understood me, I felt it wasn't enough. There were no mysteries in this adult life. No revelations. Only malicious deception. Wasted time.

These people seemed to have their lives led by the judgments of others, denying themselves freedom. Why? What I knew was that I felt ever more thirsty now than before. But for what?

I thought about the hunger as well.

7

*T*he wet bristles resounded from the gangway of the apartment house. They crashed in a wild but orderly fashion. My mother was cleaning the outdoor stairs on the side of the house.

"Lazy ass motherfuckers," thinking of the other tenants who lived here, "*they* fucking making the mess. Why don't *they* take care of it?"

I was consoled by the living-room stereo. The song playing was from a band called *Los Tigres del Norte.* Tigers of the North.

The lively sounds of the high-pitched accordion filtered out to the street. It interested me to hear the many similarities this style of music had with Polish polkas. The only major difference was that the Spanish lyrics weren't as cheerful.

When my father's favorite song ended, I went back into the house to rewind the tape. Outside once more, I sat myself back on the front steps and listened to it again. I wanted to know every word.

Aquí estoy establecido	Here I am established
en los Estados Unidos.	in the United States.
Diéz años pasaron ya	Ten years have passed since
En que crucé de mojado.	I crossed as a wetback.
Papeles no he arreglado.	Papers haven't been fixed.
Sigo siendo un ilegal.	I continue being illegal.

Tengo mi esposa y mis hijos	I have my wife and my children
que me los traje muy chicos	whom I brought very young
y se han olvidado ya.	and who have since forgotten.
De mi México querido.	My dear Mexico.
El que yó nunca me olvido	The one I never forget
y no puedo regresar.	and can never return.

Chorus:

¿De que me sirve el dinero,	Of what use is money,
si estoy como prisionero	if I am like a prisoner
dentro de esta gran nación?	within this great nation?
Cuando me acuerdo hasta lloro.	When I remember, I even cry.
Y aunque la jaula sea de oro,	And even if the cage is of gold,
no deja de ser prisión.	it does not stop being a prison.

"Escúchame hijo. Te gustaría que regresemos a vivir a México?"
"Listen to me, son. Would you like us to return to live in Mexico?"
*"Whatcha talkin' about, Dad (the boy says)? I don't want to go
back to Mexico. No way, Dad."*

Mis hijos no hablan conmigo.	My children don't speak with me.
Otro idioma han aprendido	Another language they've learned
y olvidaron el Español.	and forgotten Spanish.
Piensan como Americanos.	They think like Americans.
Niegan que son Mexicanos,	Negate that they're Mexicans,
aunque tengan mi color.	although they have my color.
De mi trabajo a mi casa	From my work to my home,
yo no se lo que me pasa,	I don't know what's happening
aunque soy hombre de hogar.	even though I am a family man.
Casí no salgo a la calle,	Hardly go out on the streets,
pues tengo miedo que me hallen	I'm afraid they'll find me
y me puedan deportar.	and they could deport me.

Chorus:

¿De que me sirve el dinero,	Of what use is money,
si estoy como prisionero	if I am like a prisoner
dentro de esta gran nación?	within this great nation?

Cuando me acuerdo hasta lloro.	When I remember, I even cry.
Y aunque la jaula sea de oro,	And even if the cage is of gold,
no deja de ser prisión.	it does not stop being a prison.

I lay motionless on my back. Poor Dad. Is this how you feel?

The cleaning stopped. My mother called. I didn't answer. Instead, I waited for her to repeat herself. Her looking for me always felt right. This time she appeared near the gate leading into the gangway.

"Y ahora que tienes?"

"Nothing's wrong," turning to her. "Qué quieres que tenga?"

"Es que te veo muy desilusionado."

"I'm not sad."

"De verdád? Qué tienes? Porqué no sigues llendo con la Señorita Kim?"

I shook my head. Last year we were arguing over my visits with Miss Kim, I told myself. Now she was wondering why I had stopped seeing her. I couldn't understand.

"No tienes que trabajar si no quieres," she said.

"No es el trabajo, Ma. I want to work . . . I need to work . . . A mi me gusta trabajar con el Padre Tom. Cuando salga de 8th grade en June, I'm going to work there, Ma, until I don't want to."

"Me da gusto que le caístes bien al Padre Tom," she said proudly. "Me alegro que estás allí en la iglesia y no afuera en las calles haciendo travesuras."

"I'm too old to be playing outside, Ma. I have to make money to buy stuff."

"Donde están tus hermanos?"

My brothers? "No sé," answering. "Maybe se fueron con Gustavo and Carlos. Oyé, Ma?"

"Dime Flaco."

"Can I go downtown?"

"Y que vas a hacer allá?" a concerned expression on her face.

There was a store I wanted to see, I told her. It was by the "Loop."

"Y todavía te recuerdas donde está esa tienda?"

Of course I remembered where it was, I said. I'd been out shopping with her so many times. How could I forget?

"Y que venden en esta tienda que quieres ir?"

I told her it was a music store. That Rudy had told me about it."

"En qué te vás a ir?"

I let out a smile. Her asking how I would get there meant I was already being granted permission to go. I told her I would take my brother's bike.

"Hay loco?"

No, I responded. I wasn't crazy.

"Sabes qué? Mejor te voy a dar dinero para que te puedas ir en el autobus. Te vas por todo la Ashland y te subes en el tren de la 18. Entendistes?"

"Si," accepting her decision to take the bus instead. "I know how to get there on the bus too, Ma."

"Tienes dinero por si acaso quieres comprar algo?"

"No," hoping she would give me money. "Me prestas? Después te pago cuando el Padre me pague."

"No que no," she pulled out a five-dollar bill. "Ya vez. Aunque tienes un trabajo, todavía me necesitas."

"I'm always going to need you, Ma," taking her money.

"No, ojalá que venga un día en que tú tengas para ti mismo y para tus hijos y no me necesites."

I hadn't thought about that. About the responsibility of having my own children. Why have them? They were just a lot of trouble, I thought. I should know. I knew how reckless I was.

"Yo no quiero tener hijos! Not me! Never."

"Pues quizás sea mejor que no los tengas. Alcabo, de que te sirven? Sino solamente para darte lata."

"Right, Ma. You know I'll go crazy with kids."

"Entonces, ya vete antes que llegue tú padre. Ya sabes que no le gusta que estén en la calle como vagos."

"Dad doesn't care if I go by myself . . . Ma?"

"Dime Flaco."

"Cuando se pelean mi pa y tú. No es por mí?"

"No," reassuring me I wasn't the cause of my parents' woes.

"Con la perdida de la casa, se ha puesto más difícil entre él y yó."

"I know. I miss the house too, Ma. We use to be happy there."

"Pero ustedes no tienen nada que ver con eso. Ni tu, ni Isi, ni José. Esas son cosas entre tú padre y yo. Por qué? No me digas que por eso estás triste?"

"I don't know," glancing out across the street. "Everything's messed up, Ma. Sometimes pienso que es mi culpa."

I saw leaves already beginning to change color. From now on, I thought, night would come faster. The streets would inevitably turn barren. Of course, no one wanted to be out in the cold, in that supposed misery. Except maybe me. And so I asked God for a long and harsh winter, for peaceful solace.

I turned to the person who had been watching me all the while. An innocent smile on her face.

You try to hide so many things.

The arguments with Dad.

His words.

Pain.

God, sometimes I want to just cut off my ears so I won't have to hear his offensive words, the impositions.

Remember the day when you threatened to leave the house after squabbling with him? Remember the look in your eyes? I do. I felt lost too. Like the time I couldn't find you in the supermarket, thinking I had been abandoned. Or the time I banished myself to the basement, the lights completely turned off, my self-punishment for the wrong I did that day.

The loneliness can sometimes be cruel too, I thought.

I took hold of her hand. The first time I saw someone die was with you. We had gotten off the city bus. A few steps later, the collision. Two cars. Two men. The elder remained in his car. The young one left his place and walked onto the black pavement. He covered his bloody face, as if it would stop the spilling. He wailed, hmmm, like a man who was about to die.

You tried to take us away from it. But I wanted to see. I was determined to know what it was about. Like other times, I had felt it coming before it occurred. I wasn't even scared. Maybe it was because it wasn't me.

The older man was taken out of the car and laid out on the street, a single cut on his head. How? Why was he the one not moving? Wasn't it supposed to be the other way around? What about all that blood? Why wasn't it the guy with all that blood? Hmmm. His cries seem ridiculous to me now as they did then.

But you worried as to how it would affect us. He was old, you explained to us. Probably heart attack. The other one, the drunk, he would be punished. Not by men, you said.

But wasn't it supposed to be the other way?

No, you answered.

No one here but God knows.

Stop thinking about it.

You'll have nightmares.

You'll keep us all up. As you always do.

I laid my head on her lap and curled into a ball. Even in my dreams, you try to protect me, I thought. Unfortunately, that's where you can't follow. I wish you could and were right next to me when I felt that thing over my body. That pressing sensation. The loss of air. It weighs so much. Am I crazy to think I've wrestled with the Devil? With God? With something that respects me and sees something in me that it wants? Needs?

And what about the other times? Those were real too. I felt myself flying, surrounded by best friends. Yes, I did. Why did they go? What did I do to make it all go away? How can I bring it back?

I looked up and threw her a soft punch. Do you hope? You must. Even after all these years, you have hope in him and this thing called love. For us, you say. Never for me. Man, I wish you were a little more selfish. But then it wouldn't be you. Would it?

How we need each other, I thought, burying my head deep into her lap once more. So why do we hurt each other so?

"Hay, Flaco," making knots in my hair, "pase lo que pase, nunca dejes de sonreír."

"Don't worry, Ma, I'm never going to stop smiling."

"Si tú papá nos quiere dejar. Los cuatro le vamos a seguir duro. Porque así son mis tres hijos, duros como su madre."

I wanted to tell her she was the one who made us strong. But I couldn't. The words had left my heart all too fast and I was still much too slow to grab on to them. So then why is it so easy to say the mean things?

"Ma, si un día te quieres separar de pa, yo no me voy a enojar."

"Ojalá que no venga ese día. Pero se viene, yo sé que te tengo a tí, a Israel, y a José."

"You're always going to have us, Ma."

"Oyé, dime la verdad Flaco. No te has enfadado de la casa donde vivimos ahora?"

Tired of where we lived? "No, I'm not tired of this place like Jose. Por qué? Recuerda que tú me dijistes que hay gente en México que quisiera tener lo que nosotros tenemos. Mira Lupe, vez que bonita es la ventana de flores. Y mira esa cara que esta arriba de la ventana, abajo del apartamento de mi tía."

I pointed to the face that overlooked the stained glass window above our unit in the brownstone apartment. It was staring out into the air, ignoring all. I admired it. It doesn't mind being there, I told her. It doesn't care that it's in the rain or snow. It's just happy to exist. So why shouldn't we be happy, I said, repeating the message she had once taught me.

I went on to explain to her that it was the face of a saint. Don Victor, our landlord, had mentioned to me it had been placed there to give good fortune to those who lived in the apartments.

"Hay no," she exclaimed. "La cara se vé como el diablo."

The devil? "No way, Ma! Es un saint!"

"De veras?"

"Yes!"

"Bueno," with skepticism. "Hay, pero todavía se vé muy feo."

I shook my head in confusion. Nothing I could say would convince her otherwise. She wanted to think what she wanted to think. She had taught me not to take that away from anyone by not teaching me the lesson herself.

"Oyé, por favor ya vete Flaco," she said, "porque se te va hacer tarde. Si algo te pasa, me llamas. Oístes?"

If something happened to me, how was I going to call her? I laughed.

"Sangrón," she smiled. "Síguele mendigo. A tí siempre te ha gustado llevarte con la gente mayor."

"Yeah," trotting down the stairs. "Bye, Ma. I love you."

"I love you too."

The first thing I did was to stop, close my eyes, and pretend to eat the air in front of me. I grabbed a bite of the damp, raw odor of the tunnels. Down my throat and out through my nostrils. The smell of the underground subway station, a consistent reality. The humid grime made me feel alive.

What I didn't understand was why everyone was in such a hurry to leave this place. There they went, passing each other in the most reserved manner. And even though everyone dressed differently, I concluded they all had one thing in common. They were void of any energy for anything besides their immediate wants.

Moments later, I pushed against the turnstiles and flew up the stairs into the commotion of State Street. The world below became buried by horns blaring from the cars passing along the streets perpendicular to the main avenue. Only public transportation was permitted on State. Fleets of green limousines came from opposite directions.

I glided in between a group of pedestrians and walked for about a block south, jumping from one side of the sidewalk to the other, imagining this place to be a cold metal valley, my wilderness.

Before I could even see the store, I heard it. The pulsing sound of house music was coming from about twenty feet away. I reached the window and took a look at the display. Up close, it didn't appear as strange as it did from far away. Album covers, concert posters, and fliers littered the storefront. Not done on purpose, I thought. This mess was very real.

The red neon light wasn't as mysterious as it had been the first time I saw it from across the street. No matter, the music played and this new place awakened an incredibly good mood in me.

A large rectangular black and white advertisement hung above the store. It read *Loop Records*. I opened the door. The pounding engulfed me. I stopped to admire whatever song I was listening to. I began to nod in sync with the beat.

The cashier's counter, directly to my left, was raised a few feet off the floor. The attendant smiled. I said hello and let him know my name.

"Can I look?"

"Sure, bro'. That's why we're here . . . By the way, I'm Gabe. If you need anything, let me know and I'll hook you up."

The store was dimly lit and extremely narrow from front to back. There were records everywhere. In racks. In shelves. Basically anywhere that there was space to put them in. There were even records hanging on the walls like prized trophies. Those came in a variety of colors.

"Wow. Cool."

A few young men, some flipping rapidly through the records, looked up. Heartfelt smiles.

"Hey, Luigi," Gabriel snickered, "since this is your first time here, don't worry about buying me out!"

The strangers laughed. I looked back and noticed Gabriel standing in front of three machines that lay across the counter. He had on a pair of headphones that looked like giant earmuffs.

Of the three pieces of gear, two were impressive silver-gray turntables, unlike anything I had ever seen. They were separated by a smaller and narrower black machine. But why did they need two turntables instead of one? I went to take a closer look.

"Don't worry, *Gabe*," a stream of small colored lights on top of the black machine bounced back and forth with each hard beat, "I don't think I have enough money on me to buy even one record."

"Damn, bro', a little late on that comeback," pulling the headphones off. "Like my mixer?"

"Yeah."

"You must. You've been staring at it like a motherfucker." Gabriel moved his hand slowly across the machine, pushing a black switch to one side. The song that was originally playing ended and a new song came on. The change a smooth transition.

"So that's how they do it."

"Do what?"

"Mix."

"You've never seen this before, bro'?"

"No. I've never even been in a place like this."

"Are you for real? You know what a record is, don't you?"

"Yeah. I know what a record is. Duh. I've just never been to a record store. You've seen a lot of kids but you've never been to my school?"

"Straight. Just don't get all crazy about it. Remember, you're the one popping a cherry here. It's straps that you did it here and not somewhere else," he smiled.

"There's other stores like this?"

"Hells yeah, bro'! Not a lot, but there is. There's one about three blocks from here on Plymouth Court. They sell a lot of import stuff. Shit I don't sell. I carry mostly Chicago labels. Domestics. *DJ International.* If you do swing over by *Importes,* say what's up to Derrick for me. Make sure he hooks you up."

I stayed on for about four hours, feeling my way around the place. I pulled out records for Gabriel to play. What I enjoyed most was seeing him mix them together. He seemed to appreciate every second.

"Damn, bro', you okay?"

"Yeah, it just looks so fucking cool."

"Maybe you should get yourself some equipment."

"I don't think I have enough money."

"You can always get something cheaper than Technics, you know. You don't have to get expensive tables when you're first starting out."

"I guess."

"Check it out. Since you're pretty cool and you don't have too much bread, I'm going to give you a couple of promos I just got in. Keep 'em, bro'. They're bad."

"Then why do I want them for?"

"No, bro', I mean they're straight. There's some tunes in there for you."

"Oh . . . Thanks."

"Of course," handing me a couple of unsealed records with plain white labels from a milk crate. "Next time you come in, bring in a tape with the mixes you like and I'll see what I can spot you."

"That's cool, but I still won't have too much to spend."

"Chill, bro', we'll work something out. I know what it's about. Especially when you're poor. Hey listen, it looks kind of dark outside. How are you getting home?"

"I'm taking the train and then a bus."

"How far do you live anyway?"

"I live on 36th and Wood."

"So why are you taking the bus and train for? You can get to your crib by taking the Archer Avenue bus straight to Wood and walking maybe five or six blocks until you reach 36th."

"I didn't know that."

"Sure, just be sure you pick up the 62 bus here on State. I'm telling you, it'll save you time. And then get off at Wood. You can't miss it. There's a gasoline station across the street from the stop."

"Yeah, I know what you're talking about. I use to live right around there. Actually, I use to play catch across the street. A long time ago."

"Word?"

"Yeah. Hey, is it cool if I come over tomorrow to hang out?"

"That's straight. Just don't expect any more freebies tomorrow. I'm all out of promos until next week."

"That's cool," making my way out.

I walked over to the bus stop. As I waited, I saw the city lights begin to fire up. I hugged the record. My first one.

8

*H*ey, Gabriel," digging into my skin-tight corduroys, "I have a tape with a mix on it. I bought it at a flea market last year. I wanna see if you have something on it."

"Okay, let me ring this guy up and we'll check it out."

I watched as his customer bought a stack of records. I counted thirty. The bill came out to one hundred and twenty-nine dollars and sixty cents. A lot of money, I thought.

"Now let's see what you're carrying, little man," finishing the transaction.

"Are you sure?" feeling that I was wasting his time.

He played the tape.

"It's house. We got it."

My heart started beating fast. "You have it?"

"It's called *The Harder They Come,*" stopping to turn the tape's direction. "It's the record with the gray label over on the house side."

I swung around to the direction he was pointing.

"That sucker's old, Luigi, but it's a jam. I'm surprised you're into it. It came out in '82 and they still keep playing it. Hopefully, they won't kill it. Let me think . . . I think I saw an original twelve-inch in there somewhere . . . Yeah, it's under the same *Streetwise* label as the second prints. If you got time, knock yourself out trying to find it."

"You think it's worth it?"

"*Bro'*, it's up to you to make that kind of call. Are you looking for anything else? I heard some high energy on the other side."

"Naw, not right now," walking over to the records. "I want this record first."

The next hour I spent searching. Nothing.

"Try underneath the shelves!" Gabriel finally cried, "Maybe you'll get lucky!"

Fifteen minutes later, I found the record. Picking it up, I took a look at the label. What did they mean by "a cappella version," "radio version," and "extended house mix version"? I went over to Gabriel and desperately asked him to play it.

"Damn, bro', easy!" he ran one end of the record cover across his leg swiftly and pulled the record out of a white sleeve jacket. "It's the right one. I'm surprised you even found this baby." He dropped the record on the turntable and placed the needle over it. A sharp crash of thunder. And then the sweeping sounds of a synthesizer.

"Good intro, huh?"

"I never heard that before."

"There's a lot of good shit they don't play on the white-boy station. Fuck all that. Even the white boys here will tell you." He cranked the volume up. "Damn! This is a fucking jam! Listen to this raw bitch sing his heart out."

> Well they tell me of a pie up in the sky . . .
> Waiting for me when I die . . .
> But between the day you're born and when you die,
> you see they never seem to hear your cries.
> But as sure as the sun will shine,
> I'm gonna get my share now—what's mine.
>
> And then the harder they come,
> the harder they fall.
> One and all . . .
> I say the harder they come,
> the harder they fall.
> One and all . . .
>
> Well the old past souls are trying to keep me down—
> they're trying to keep me down.

Trying to drive me on the ground.
And then they think that they have got the battle won—
then maybe God—

I say forgive them, Lord, they know not what they've done.
And as sure as the sun will shine,
I'm gonna get my share now—what's mine.

And then the harder they come,
the harder they fall . . .

"Bro'," lowering the volume, "I think this is the part you had on the tape."

. . . And I'll keep on fighting for the things I want—
for the things I want.
'Cause I know that when you're dead you're gone.
And I rather be a free man in the grave—
a free man in the grave—
than living as a puppet or a slave.

And as sure as the sun will shine,
I'm gonna get my share now; what's mine.
And then the harder they come . . .

"What do you think?" He waved his hand as if to say so-so. "Too vocally?"

"I'll take it."

He smiled, took out another record from behind the counter, and produced a clean blend.

"That's dope, brother." A young man with headphones looked straight at me. "Where'd you get that record?"

"Over there," pointing to the bottom shelves. "It's the last original. But there's reprints over by the house music. The name's *The Harder They Come.*"

"I remember the first time I heard it. About three years ago. I was barely eighteen. Thanks, chief. I won't even ask you to sell me the one you got. I saw how long it took you to find it. Nice. Real nice."

"Thanks."

Gabriel leaned over. "Chill, bro', pretty soon you're going to go after my job. You also better watch out with some of these fellas in here. They like it the other way."

"What do you mean?"

"Some of them are gay, bro'. You know. They aren't into girls."

"Really?"

"Ask 'em. What I know is that that motherfucker was a tall ass chicken hawk. He was on the prowl big-time for you."

"Fuck that. That's not me. I mean, I don't care what he does, but I'm not into that."

"Chill, Luigi. Remember, you never have to do what someone else wants you to do. You pick the tunes. So, how'd you scrounge up the pennies to pay for this?"

"My mom gave me some money yesterday."

"Holding out on me, huh?"

"Man, I also have a job."

"Aren't you a little young, bro', to have *a job?*"

"Nope, I work in a church for a priest."

"You better watch out for those priests."

"Huh?"

"Come on, bro', you don't think it's kind of strange that any-one would keep themselves away from having sex for the rest of their life? It's unnatural. I bet you they fuck around. If they don't, I bet they're probably repressed motherfuckers with the weirdest shit on their minds. One on one is cool, but when you ain't even one that's not cool. It's like I don't mind some twenty-year-old messing with a nineteen-year-old, but going after a fourteen-year-old, when the kid don't know jack . . . that's not straight. Watch your back."

"Thanks, Gabe. I'm going home now so I can get to work."

"All right, it comes out to four dollars and thirty-one cents with tax. Need a bag?"

"Naw, I'll put it in my schoolbag."

"Luigi," Gabriel handed me the record and shook my hand. "Your first twelve-inch. Enjoy it. Don't scratch it. It's mint. And remember what I told you. Come back whenever. We'll talk some more."

"Cool."

"Take your time. I'm not going anywhere. Maybe after I get to know you more I'll even let you jam up here."

"For real?"

"Why not? You look like you know what's up."

The changes were intense. A thick, forbidding steel door replaced the aluminum screen door at the front. Is this what made
them feel secure? But then why live in a place that didn't make
you feel safe?

I leaned over the back gate. What irritated me as well was
that the new owners had converted the entire backyard into a
vegetable garden. I remembered my mother's patch being only a
modest component. I was angry they had torn down everything.

The pool.

The shed.

Most of the things I remembered that made us happy were
gone.

Sliding my eyes left, I noticed something else missing. The
pine tree was a stump now. I wondered if they would one day do
the same with the young tree planted on the front lawn.

I shut my eyes to the changing memories.

We were away, welcoming in the new year, when they ran-
sacked our home. I had walked in, despite my mother's objec-
tion, behind the gun-toting officer. Ah, the extent of greed. Our
radios, television sets, jewelry, furniture. So many things taken
away. They even stole two Mickey Mouse watches my parents
had bought Israel and me.

Strange, I never really understood what we had until that day.

The circumstances indicated to me that it was a well-
planned act, with people involved who knew us. When we went
back out, I looked around to see which neighbors had dropped
by and which hadn't. I reminded myself of the times when I
had done something wrong. I tended to hide rather than face
the horror of my actions. Weren't the missing doing the same?
Hiding.

And as for those who had stood by and allowed the crime to
pass, they were just as responsible, I concluded.

Fools. The imbeciles had done something even worse that
day. They had switched a piece of my faith for a bit of human
mistrust. And all for what?

"Fucking bastards."

I leaned back rapidly, threw my head up to the night air, and clung fiercely to the top rail of the aluminum gate, causing things to creak. I thought about the new chain-link fence erected around the front yard. Keep away, it said. This is mine. Maybe this *was* needed to maintain peace. Hmmm, feeling something wrong in that. So then, which way?

"So how's it feel?"

"Huh?"

"I asked *How does it feel?* Now that you're about to be fired."

"Aw, Father," looking at the clock on the wall, "I'm only five minutes late. I barely got back from downtown."

"Already spending your unearned millions on frivolous items? Why don't you invest in a watch instead?"

"A watch?" grabbing my naked wrist. "I don't need one."

"Seems like you do."

"Naw, I can tell what time it is inside my head."

"What are you? Some broad with a biological clock ticking?"

"Maybe . . . Damn, Father! How come you always keep cutting up on people? Your jokes aren't even getting better."

"Neither is your paycheck," he went for my schoolbag. "So," opening it, "what did you get me?"

"I got a record. Want to see?"

"Really? What's the name of the album?"

"It's only one song. *The Harder They Come.*"

"Sounds pornographic. Is that that stupid music you keep hearing kids blast from their cars?"

"It's not stupid! It's house."

"Whatever."

"Man, no one's telling you to listen to it if you don't like it!"

"Touchy, touchy . . . Listen, I don't mean to break up your party but let me just tell you I'll be heading over to say the five o'clock Mass in forty minutes. Make sure you come in during Communion to get the donations. Don't leave the bag sitting in the sacristy like you did before. Bring it inside. We've been noticing the amount of loose change drop over the past few weeks."

"So what do you want me to do with the bag?"

"Leave it under Frida's desk so they can count it on Monday."

I began to sit on Frida's chair.

"Don't make yourself comfortable just yet, Louie. Come over to the kitchen. Talk to me, dude. You can have some of the stew I made earlier today."

We went through the dining room and whisked into the kitchen.

"I bet you didn't even get anything to eat while you were out shopping?"

"No, I didn't have any money left."

"How could you when you were spending it all on that junk?" He grabbed a medium-sized pot from the refrigerator and placed it on the stove, turning on the gas pilot. "So what do you think we should do about your eighth-grade graduation trip?"

"I don't know. Where can we go?

"Enchanted Forest."

"No way!"

"I'm kidding," lighting the flame.

"Yeah, that place is nasty!"

"You boys didn't have a problem with it a few years ago when we would take you out on your altar-boy trips."

"That was a long time ago, Father."

"Okay then, realistically, I was thinking about taking a group of you and maybe some of the other lower classes to see an operetta at the Civic Opera House. We'd be going to see Puccini's *La Boheme*."

"Is it good?"

"Why would I take you if it wasn't?" He grabbed a wooden spoon from a drawer. "One thing. It's in Italian."

"Cool. So how are we suppose to understand it?"

"Knucklehead," dipping the spoon into the pot, "there's a screen with English subtitles right above the stage."

"Are the words big enough?"

"Why? Are you having problems with your eyes?"

"A little."

"Louie?"

"What, Father?"

"What did I say about taking care of yourself?"

"I know. I just don't have enough money to go to the eye doctor."

"But you have enough to spend on trash," he stirred.

"It's not *trash!* I need it. Music makes me feel good. Ever since I was a little. Besides, I don't believe in doctors. My body can take care of itself."

"You would be the one to say something like that. But getting back to the trip. Well?"

"It's cool, but I don't know about the rest."

"Screw them!" He set two green bowls and the silverware on the kitchen table. "If it was up to those dingbats, they'd be going to an amusement park all the time."

"Hey, I like them too! They got rollercoasters."

"What's so freaking great about rollercoasters?"

"Man, they're bad. They go up and down just like seesaws. Didn't you ever like them when you were little?"

"Sure, but I'm an adult now."

"So? That's you. I'm always going to like them."

"Well then, you can pay for you and your friends to go to one. I still think an excursion to the Opera House would be a more rewarding experience. They might not appreciate it now, but later on I guarantee it. I can see it now. A busload of South Side Polish and Mexican kids going to see Puccini's *La Boheme*. What a riot. Well?"

"You're paying the bill."

"And just think," serving the food, "you might end up throwing away that record you just bought and start collecting something reasonable."

"Hey, I've seen some of the old tapes and records you got. They don't look too awesome."

"I bought them when I was young."

"So what the fuck do you think I am? And, anyway, you haven't heard what I got."

"All right, you got me on that."

"Oh wow," twirling my finger in the air, "first time."

"Come on, let's eat before it gets cold."

After finishing, Father Tom stood up and grabbed his black jacket. He inspected it for lint.

"Father?"

"Now what?"

"Can I use the turntable upstairs in your room to listen to the record?"

"Go ahead," putting on his black coat. "But if you bust it, guess who's paying? It's an expensive piece of machinery." He opened the kitchen door. "Lou, if you're going to be listening to music, keep it low. And don't forget about running over to church."

"Yep. I won't. I never forget."

"Grab a beer if you want. Just don't overdo it."

"Thanks, Father."

"Jesus, you feel like my son," turning off the light and closing the door.

9

*Y*ou're all going to be graduating in a little over a month from now. I asked Sister Therese to bring you all to church so we can go over a few steps to prepare you properly . . . Since there's only thirteen of you—eight girls and five boys—there'll be one pair made up of two girls and one girl left without a partner. The rest of you will pair up, one girl for each boy, and walk down the middle aisle like you did for Confirmation . . . Does everyone understand? If everything goes the way I want it to go, we should be out of here before school lets out."

"Everything seems to be going right so far," Miss Barbara said an hour later. "I'll tell you what. Since everyone here looks like they're ready to drop dead, let's wake up with a pop quiz. Does anyone remember how many apostles there were?"

"Twelve," Jennifer answered hastily.

"No way, man," I argued. "There was like thirteen apostles. After Judas hung himself on the tree, another Judas guy took his place."

"That's good, Louie," Miss Barbara said. "Now why don't you remind the rest of your classmates why Judas hung himself."

"He hung himself because he was sad and felt bad. He thought he did something wrong."

"What wrong did he commit?"

"He betrayed Jesus for some silver coins."

"But I don't think that among the thirteen of you, we have a betrayer," she grinned. "Do we?"

"Maybe," I retorted. "Maybe I'm Judas."

"Mr. Aguilera," tilting her head down, "you're beginning to talk gibberish."

"No, you told us a long time ago that each time we sin we betray Jesus and that we're all like one of the thorns on Jesus' head. So then everyone is Judas because we each betray Jesus every time we sin."

"Well, I think that's the smartest thing you've said all year. So then you see," looking out at everyone, "that's why we try to abolish the evil Judas in each of us. Because as Louie pointed out . . ."

"But," I interrupted, "I don't think we should try to stop from being Judas. I think Judas was on earth for a reason, Miss Barbara. Like, I think without Judas, Jesus couldn't have been Jesus. I think Jesus loved Judas the most because he had to do the hardest job and they both knew it. I bet it was their secret or something. Judas had to be who he was and stuff. He had to give over the thing he loved the most too. Man, I think that's hard. I mean, think about it. He could of made more money. Right? Greedy people know that. He knew that. He just wanted to get something over with right away. I don't think he did anything wrong. He did what he had to do."

"Mr. Aguilera, you can sit down now. I think we've all had quite enough of your interpretation . . . What did you say?"

"I just told Charlie I can't wait until I'm out of this place."

"Yes," frowning, "well, you'll soon have your wish."

"Thank God," I said under my breath. "You guys don't even know what's up. You only think you do. And you want people to think you do."

So no one can say shit to you, I thought.

10

*S*o what were you doing, bro'?"

"Nothing," still not recognizing who was on the other end of the line. "Why?" pulling the telephone cord into the living room.

"Just asking . . . How's Quigley?"

"Straight," realizing it was my friend Rudy. I hadn't seen him since midsummer.

"You're not thinking of becoming a priest, are you?"

"Maybe."

"Phony! Why didn't you pick Rita instead?"

"What am I going to do there? I don't know anybody there. At least I have Jose at Quigley."

"What about us? You know us!"

"Oh yeah, I didn't think about you and Lou."

"Shit, bro', and your mother told us you were smart."

"Hey, I can't have everything going on in my head or else I'll go nuts like that one scientist guy."

"Who?"

"Einstein, bro'. Didn't you ever see how his hair's all fucked up, flying in the air? Tell me he wasn't crazy."

"But that's the way you look."

"Well, I'm like him then."

"Shut up, bro'. Now you're just talking garbage."

"Hey, you're the one still listening!"

"Whatever. Stop interrupting, nerd. You still haven't given me a real reason why you're at Quigley. Rita's way better."

"Of course, why are you going to dis on your own school? That's stupid. So what's up? Did you call to talk about schools? Don't you got anything important to say?"

"Shut up, jerk. I called to see how you were doing and ask you something. Has Jose told you anything about what him and I talked about?"

"Nope."

"Well, my brother Lou and I were wondering if you and your brother wanted to check out a party tonight. There's these guys from around the neighborhood that are starting something called a party crew and they asked us if we knew anybody who wanted to join. We thought of you two."

"So what are we suppose to do in this crew thing?"

"This 'crew thing' is called the Ultimate Party Crew. And all you have to do is hang out with them whenever they have parties."

"It's all guys?"

"See, it's like a college fraternity, but not really."

"A what?"

"Come on, bro'. You know what a college is, don't you?"

"Yeah, asshole. I know what a college is. I just don't know what a fraternity is."

"Nerd! A fraternity is like a club that only guys can join."

"Oh."

"Pay attention and learn," Rudy continued. "The UPCs are like a fraternity in some ways but they aren't in others. They're not associated with any college, Greek system, or anything like that. It's just a bunch of friends from the neighborhood who'll join mostly. We're going to throw house parties. If we get enough guys, we'll probably be able to play football games against other crews at McKinley Park or Harrison Park in the winter. It's not a gang, so don't worry about getting into trouble or having to represent like a gangbanger. If you get in, you'll probably get your own jacket with the name of the party crew and its design on the back of it. They just made it up. Lou and me already put an order in for ours."

"But I thought you said you weren't in the crew yet?"

"Technically, we're not UPCs. But we know some of the boys from playing basketball with them in front of the crib at Barrett's.

We've known them since we were real little, like you guys. And like I said, jerk, all you have to do is just hang out and that's it. Do you get it now?"

"Sort of. It's kind of strange. Don't you think?"

"What's strange about it?"

"It sounds kinda good and kinda weird."

"That's because you live out there where the white boys live. Party crews have been around since I was in grammar school."

"Yeah, I think my second cousin was in LT."

"Latin Taste? That's straight. They're one of the originals. But anyway, we're going to have a house party tonight around 47th Street—close to your crib. So how about it, Priest?"

"What did you call me?"

"Priest," he chuckled. "You're going to become one, aren't you?"

"Shut up . . . Anyway, I want to go but I don't know if Jose will come or if my mother will let us. Why don't you ask your mother to talk to my mother?"

"Actually," he laughed, "I called to see if you could ask your mother to talk to my mother."

"Man, what the fuck?"

"Look, just say to your mother that our mother already said yes and we'll do the same. They'll figure it out."

"Okay, but who and who is going with us?"

"Well, it'll be my brother Lou, you, your brother Jose—if he goes—and me. Someone will pick us up from here and we'll head over to pick you guys up. You still live on 33rd and Wood?"

"Naw, bro' . . . I thought you knew?"

"Sorry. I completely forgot. I remember my mother saying something to us about you guys losing the house. It must feel shitty."

"Yeah," I said sadly, "I'm over it."

"Cheer up, Priest. If we get to go out, we'll hook your ugly ass up with some girl. That'll make you happy."

"Hey, so what about Mickey and Israel? Aren't we going to invite them?"

"Fuck no, bro'. Lou and I already talked about it. Mick's too young. He's barely in seventh-grade. Isn't your brother in the same year too?"

"Yep. Israel won't even be graduating until next year."

"Don't worry, bro', once we're in, we'll get them in when they become freshmen."

"That's cool. I guess you're right, though. They're still kind of young to hang out like that."

"Besides, Priest, the UPCs that we know right now are way older than them. Some of them graduated or are gonna be graduating from high school. A couple dropped out of school. I don't think your mom or my mom would want Iz or Mick hanging out with guys that old. I don't even know what the boys are going to say about you."

"Hey," thinking of those he was describing. They seemed far removed from who I was. "Are you sure they're cool?"

"Fuck, yeah. They hang. But I'll bet you a million bucks that you'll probably be the youngest one there."

"That's what I mean. You think they won't mind?"

"See, that's why I didn't want to say anything to you. They might not let you in because of that. If anyone asks, tell them you're a sophomore."

"Man, Jose's only one year older than me!"

"Yeah, but I don't think they'll care with Jose. Even though he's one year older, he's pretty built. The last time I saw you, you looked like you weighed a feather."

"Shit, if they say anything to me, I'll make them let me in."

"You're not making anyone do anything, nerd. Be cool and chill. Can you do that?"

"I guess."

"Okay then. Look, I got to let you go so that Lou and I can get our shit straight. Don't forget to ask your brother Jose about it and don't forget about your mother. Remember, Priest."

"I heard you already! Hey, Rudy, what kind of music are they going to have?"

"House music and high energy. Is that cool with you?"

"Fuck, yeah!"

"Later then."

"Yeah. Later."

Our mother wasn't very happy about us not knowing where we were going. What we told her was that we would be at something called a house party and that they would be playing the music I liked to listen to at night.

After persistent negotiation, she gave us an okay. As before, my father gave her complete responsibility for anything that happened to us.

At around five, I went upstairs to my aunt's apartment to see if Carlos would join. I needed him there. He had been helping me out ever since I had broken up with Miss Kim.

"So then what, Carlos? You know you want to go."

"No, Lou," stretching out on his bed like a cat, "I'm happy right here."

"But it'll be cool."

"Thanks for asking but you go ahead. Tell me how it went when you come back."

"No, man," leaning against the doorway. "I can't go by myself. If you don't go, I won't go. You know I need you there. You're my radar. Without you I won't meet any girls."

"Shut up, Lou, you're going with your brother Jose anyway."

"Aw, he's going to be busy with all his older friends."

"So what am I suppose to tell mom?"

"Tell her that you're going with us," resting on Carlos's bed. "You know she'll let you go if my mom talks to her."

"My aunt already said that it was okay for you two to go?"

"Yesss! Why would I come up to tell you about this if I didn't have it all straightened out?"

"So what exactly is this?"

"It's a house party, Carlos. You know the same as me. You remember Rudy?"

"That's Alicia's son?"

"Right. He called me up to tell me about this group called the Ultimate Party Crew."

"What if the party is something like the kind of parties we use to go to at St. Peter's."

"No way! Those were by the school! I don't think that's the way it's going to be tonight. These people are doing it on their own."

"Lou, you have the weirdest thing about getting yourself mixed up in shit. So how do you think it's going to go?"

"I don't know. I don't think it'll be mothers serving punch and shit. And there won't be any little kids running around. It should be better than that."

Carlos sat up in his bed. "You really want to go to this thing, don't you?"

"I'm tired of getting stuck at home all day doing nothing. I want to do something crazy. Stuff we never did."

"Oh boy," scratching his chin, "Lou's getting that itch . . . Okay, I'll go, but you have to ask my mom because I don't want her to flip."

"Cool, I'll go downstairs right now and have Mom call her."

"No. You're going to stay right here and tell her yourself. If you want, call your mother but first tell my mother. Okay?"

"All right. Tía!" I yelled from the room, "puede ir Carlos a una fiesta."

"A donde?"

"A una fiesta. Mire, usted llámele a mi mamá y ella le va a explicar todo."

"Real smooth, Lou, throw it all on your mom." Carlos flung his hands to his head. "Now we'll just have to see what your mother tells my mother."

"She'll know what to tell her."

I could hear Carlos's mother grab the phone and dial a number. She hung up quickly.

"I wonder what happened?"

"I bet she's coming up to talk to her."

A knock on the door.

"See."

"Estos están locos," was the first thing my mother told my aunt as she entered.

"See, they think we're nuts," Carlos whispered.

"Que quieren ir a una fiesta." My aunt sat down at the kitchen table. "Como vez?"

"Vamos a dejarlos ir," said my mother. "Alcabo, no van a ir solos. Los dos hijos de Alicia también van a ir. Que no crees que se enfadan estar en la casa?"

"Y que opina el señor de la casa," my aunt stood up, offering my mother some fruit.

"Nada," my mother took a piece of melon and some strawberries. "Ya sabes que él ya no se quiere meter con ellos . . ."

"See," I said to Carlos, "your mother's going to let you go. They already forgot about us and are talking about my dad."

"So, Lou, what are you going to wear tonight to this thing?"

"Man, I have no fucking idea. I didn't think about that. I guess I'll put on a pair of black corduroys and my black school shoes. That's the only thing I got. What about you?"

"I'm in the same boat as you. Do you think we'll need money?"

"I think so. Take ten bucks just in case. Man, I hope our mothers give us more."

"Okay, Lou, I'll ask my mom for some dough after she's finished talking to your mom. How are we going to get there?"

"They'll come pick us up." I slapped the palm of his hand.

"Do they know about me?"

"Not really. But they're looking for more people to join so why should they have a problem with you coming?"

"Right."

"Don't worry, Carlos. I'll give them a call right now to ask them when they're leaving and tell them that you're coming."

"I'm not worried, Screwie Louie, this is all you."

"Trust me. Tonight we're going to have fun."

"I just hope we don't get shot."

"What are you talking about, Carlos?"

"You said it was around 47th. There's some crazy people out there, Lou."

"We'll see. I don't think anything will happen. We're not doing anything wrong."

"Still, some people don't give a shit. You see how it's getting around here?"

"I guess."

"Hey, Lou? Are you nervous because of tonight?"

"Yeah, man, I am."

Nine-thirty. I peeked through the curtains. The three cars were still double-parked in front. It had been a few minutes since they last honked.

Rudy was waiting outside of the cars with some of his friends. They were all wearing skin-tight corduroys. I felt mine, finding them loose everywhere.

Rudy's brother Luis came over to the porch with someone at his side. I went over to open the door.

"Lou!" stepping up. "Haven't seen you in a while."

"I know, Lou. It's been a long time. Here, I want you to meet Smurf."

"What's up?" Smurf greeted me by jerking his nose up. "Shit, at least it'll be easy to remember names."

Lou looked over to my mother. "Buenas noches, señora."

"Buenas noches, Luis. Están contentos de que van a ir a una fiesta?"

"Sí," Luis said.

Smurf stroked his thin black mustache and nodded in agreement, adding the party was going to be good and that he would take care of me personally.

"Okay, bro'," Lou interjected, "that's enough bullshit. We'll be waiting outside for you and your brother."

"Cool." I closed the door, but not before they bid farewell to my mother.

"Y a que hora van a regresar?" my mother asked.

I told her that we'd be back by two.

"No. Se vienen mas temprano! Y no quiero que vengas tomado."

I went to the kitchen, searching for a last bite in the refrigerator.

"Siquiera me llaman para decirme que están bien?"

"Sure, Mom," I told her. "We'll call you! Come on, Jose, they're waiting for us outside."

"All right!" he yelled from the bathroom. "I have one more thing to do. Why don't you go out and tell them to hold on. And remember to go upstairs and get Carlos."

"Do you need me to get you something from your room?"

"What room? You know I sleep on the living-room floor."

"I know. I was just joking with you. God, can't you take a joke?"

"Shut up."

I left the apartment, yelling a quick good-bye to my father. He was watching the boxing match on television. Something we used to do together, I thought.

I gave my mother a kiss on the cheek.

"Que no vengas tomado."

"Right, Ma. I won't drink."

I stepped outside.

"Hurry up, nerd!"

The muffled yell came from the back of the blue car.

"Wait!" I screamed. "I have to go get my cousin!"

Ten minutes later, our anxious caravan was on its way. Once on 47th Street, our group slowed down in search of the right street. Turning south on Paulina, we headed five houses down and saw what we were looking for.

There was a two-story home with swirling red emergency lights coming through the windows of the second floor. Young men and women were walking up and down the long front stairs. The girls were far better dressed than the boys. They looked back to see who we were, watching the police car that was also stationed in front.

"Shit, I hope it didn't get raided by the cops," Rudy said.

He brought the black-tinted window down and asked someone who was coming over to our car what had happened.

"Nothing, bro'," said the young man. "They only wanted to see that we weren't gangbangers. We told them who we were and they told us just to keep it quiet. There's been trouble with the Saints around here. They've been shooting it out with the Latin Souls for the past week. I think they killed one of their boys or something so now they're at war. Fucking gangbangers. Always fucking it up."

"How is it in there, Ruben?" asked Rudy. "Is it dope?"

"It's bad. It's barely ten and we already finished a keg. We sent Juan and Izzy to get another one. They should be back soon. So are you guys going to sit around in a car all night and hold each other's hands or are you coming in?"

"Are there fine girls in there or what?"

"Man, relax, Rudy, there's fifis in there," Ruben said. "They look straight. But I'm telling you, the place is starting to get packed so you and your boys better come in already. Are these the new guys?"

"Yep. Jose, Luis, Carlos. This is Ruben."

"Hey, that one looks a little young," Ruben turned to me. "Rudy, you sure you didn't steal him from a day-care center? He still looks like he's breast-feeding."

"Shut up," Rudy laughed.

"No, seriously. What's his name? Spanky?"

"He's the Priest."

Everyone began to laugh.

"The what?" cried Ruben.

"The Priest," repeated Rudy. "Him and his brother Jose go to a seminary."

"Then what the fuck are they doing here?" Ruben smiled. "Shouldn't they be in Church praying for us?"

"Stop talking so much shit," Rudy barked. "And get the fuck out of the way before I tell Smurf to drive over you!"

"Smurf," Ruben looked over to him. "You're going to take orders from this bitch?"

"Shhhiiiiitttt, what they don't know is that they're the ones who are going to fill up my car, or else I'm going to leave their stupid asses here. Let's see how the Saints take care of them."

The contest of words kept cutting back and forth. No one was spared the humiliating bombardment.

"Pretty cool," I whispered to Carlos.

"I just want to see how it is inside," he remarked. "It looks wild."

"I know. That too."

The loud music drowned our words. We squeezed slowly through the tightly packed mass of dancers, making our way to the back of the apartment. Strangers' bodies were constantly touching. Everyone seemed to be having a good time. No matter how close you were in contact with someone, there was a sense of respect for the other.

"What do you think, bro'?" Rudy backed up against the wall. "Pretty straight?"

"Yeah!" leaning against the wall. "This is bad! What do you think, Carlos?"

"Lou, I'm just taking it all in! I don't think I've ever seen so many people crammed in like sardines!"

"Man, don't tell me it doesn't beat those parties at St. Peter's!" I said. "I mean, all they did there was break-dance every once in a while! And they couldn't even really battle!"

"Right . . . At first, I wasn't too sure about this whole thing, but now I'm glad you asked me to come!"

"Listen," Rudy interrupted, "you little girls want something to drink?"

"Sure," turning to him. "What do they have?"

"Beer, bro'. That's it! They said that the keg would be over by the kitchen! Let's go see who's over there!"

"Carlos! You want to get some beer?"

"I'm with you, Lou," stroking the back of my head with the palm of his hand. "Lead the way."

We found just as many people waiting in the kitchen in front of an aluminum keg. Someone in a fifties-style sky-blue jacket was dispensing beer from a handheld nozzle. The three of us took our place in line. When it was our turn, the young man recognized Rudy.

"Rudy! What's up, chief? So you brought your boys."

"Yep," handing him his cup. "These are two of the guys I was talking to you about, Serg. This is the Priest and his cousin Carlos. The Priest's brother is out in the living room chillin' like a villain."

"Priest?" Sergio exclaimed. "Oh shit!"

"Yep," Rudy stated. "He goes to Quigley."

"So you guys want to be UPCs?"

"Yeah," I pulled past Carlos. "I want to."

Carlos stepped back. "I just came to see what it was like. My cuz here dragged me out of bed . . . I was wondering, do you always have this many people at your parties?"

"Kind of," Sergio replied. "We barely started the party crew. One day we'll do a hall party. There's only about twelve of us now but we have eight more guys ready to turn, including Rudy and his brother Luis. You guys will probably be able to make the next group that gets in. We'll see. How old are you, Priest?"

"Fourteen."

"Shit. You're young. Well, we'll see what happens after tonight. Rudy, why didn't you tell me?"

"Who the fuck cares? If he's down, he's down. It's not like we're recruiting for a gang. Anyway," he smiled, "I bet you he's twice as smart as your dumb ass. This little motherfucker has a brain."

"Are you good in school?" Sergio asked.

"I get all A's and B's in school."

"Good, bro'. You keep educating yourself or else you're going to end up like Moneybags over there!" He singled out someone standing in the corner of the room near the kitchen sink.

"What the fuck, bro'!" putting his cup down. "Why you talking shit like that?"

The older-looking fellow with short black hair came over to us. He was wearing black baggy trousers and a gray sweater, and was sporting a goatee.

"Don't listen to Sergio," Moneybags said. "Little fucking poser can't even add two plus two on a calculator. Fucking wannabe, talking about education like he knows. It doesn't take shit to pour beer."

"Damn," Rudy laughed, "that's jive."

"Hey," I asked. "Why do they call you Moneybags?"

"I'll tell you why," Sergio took the cup from me. "Look at him. This bum's a fucking millionaire. The reason why he's got holes in his pocket isn't because he doesn't have money to buy new clothes. It's because he's got so much fucking change from all the pennies he collects on the streets."

"Damn!" Rudy cried. "What a dud. You're going to take that, Moneybags?"

"Shit, you know I don't mess with little boys, Rudy." Moneybags felt his goatee. "Especially from jive motherfuckers that try to grow a mustache but all they get is peach fuzz! Shit looks like his ma's pussy." Everyone roared. "Calm the fuck down! Don't you see we're going to scare the minors? Look at 'em. They think we're all serious and shit. They're going to think we're wack too."

"Wack?" someone yelled. "Someone tell Moneybags that break dancing's old. We don't use wack anymore."

"You watch, bro'," Moneybags said. "That shit is going to come back. Shit's always coming back."

"Is that why you're wearing your old Ponys? . . ."

"Come on," Rudy whispered, "let's go before they start cutting up on us."

"I know."

We went back to the living room where everyone was still dancing. A dj was in a corner of the room, playing his mix. Someone next to him grabbed a microphone and brought the music to a halt.

"All right! Check it out! Up next, we have Raphael 'Ito' García from the Ultimate Party Crew! And he's going to jack up the house! Yeah, boyeee! We have another keg on its way." A loud hurrah spread through the room. "No way are the UPCs going to keep this party dry."

Another hurrah.

"You were listening to the sounds of Orlando," continued the mc. "I'm your host for the night, Cool Dan, from the Ultimate Party Crew. The freshest party crew in Chi-town. That's why we're ultimate! Take it away, Ito!"

The static crackling sounds of an old record played. Less than five seconds passed before a flow of clean beats pounded from the two four-foot speakers that were stacked on top of each other. A stream of melodious record scratching occurred.

"Who the fuck is that?"

"That's Ito," Rudy told me. "He scratches pretty good, huh, bro'?"

"Yeah, and look how everyone dances when he mixes."

"Yep. That motherfucker is throwing down big-time."

"Who's that?" I pointed to a girl with long jet-black hair, dancing with Rudy's brother.

"The fine girl dancing with Lou? That's Norma. She's pretty cool, dog. Her family's from Mexico City. They live in Pilsen now, by our crib."

"Yeah, she looks old and young at the same time. I wonder if she's going out with anyone."

"Check it out. I'm going back to get another beer. Are you coming?"

"No. I'm going to stay right here and check this Norma girl out."

"Okay, but can you hold on to my jacket? I'm starting to roast in it."

"Yeah, hand it over."

"Thanks, bro'."

"Don't worry about it. Carlos, you want to give me your sweater?"

"No, that's okay, Lou," folding it over his arm.

"Hey, Carlos, can you bring me back another beer? I'm almost finished with this one."

"Sure."

As they left, a woozy, blissful feeling began to empty me. A few minutes and Rudy's brother came over.

"Are you straight, Lou? I see they have you holding the coats."

"It's Rudy's," opening my eyes. "Man, this party is bad. So who's the fine girl you're dancing with?"

"Norma? You know her from St. Vitus, don't you? Even your mom knows her. Her and her sisters are in a youth group with us there. I'm surprised you haven't seen her in church."

"Naw, I've never seen her."

"Well, let me introduce you to her."

"Now? Nah, maybe next time."

"What's wrong, Lou? Oh, fuck, don't get like that. What's she gonna do? She's only a girl."

"Yeah, but she looks soooo fine. I think I really like her. Look at her. Look at the way she is. She's like a little kid in a beautiful body."

"Chill, Priest. You're drunk. You barely saw her and you're acting like you're all in love. Here, let me introduce you to her." He pulled me by the sleeve of my jacket and called out her name. She came forward. "Norma, I want you to meet an old friend of mine. This is Luis. The Priest. His brother's Jose."

I took her hand, maintaining my grip for as long as I could. She didn't pull away.

"Wow, you and your older brother don't look the same. You're little."

I looked away.

"Don't worry. You're cute in a different way."

I turned to her again. "Aren't you hot in your coat from dancing?"

"Maybe. Why?"

"Let me take it. I don't care."

She smiled and handed me the red jacket.

"Here, Lou, while you're at it why don't you take mine too." Luis handed me his. "Thanks."

I grabbed everything and went to a corner. When Rudy and Carlos returned, I quickly gorged my second cup of beer. Carlos proceeded to give me his.

After I had a few more, the partygoers seemed to melt together to form a reddish-brown sea. The ocean was filled with slow, oscillating plankton. I felt relaxed, unshaken by the visual phenomena.

It aroused in me a pleasant thought, a photographic image of a jigsaw we had worked on with my father a few years back. The picture on the puzzle box displayed a rustic mill, centered within the serene setting of a thick forest in a would-be autumn. I imagined someone toiling in there, in that dark lonely haven, making sure things were taken care of.

During the nights we labored over that project, we positioned ourselves on the floor around the puzzle, found our place, and prostrated before it. One handed the other a piece whenever it seemed necessary for his side of the work. We focused. In this wordless environment, we understood the other's needs and intentions. There was a harmony.

And here it was again. Moving us in this dark red world.

I loosened my grip on the cup, wiped my eyes, and began to slip back into the music. Happily raising my arms, I dropped my friends' belongings on a nearby chair and drifted into the sea, latching on to whoever or whatever was near. This is the way things should be, I felt. Life once again familiar.

II

*T*he attendant threw the red flag at his feet.

"Shit . . ."

How idiotic we must seem, I thought, looking away toward the hotels, to those lounging in the open-air bars sipping their tropical cocktails. Him, down there, screaming orders for me to let go of the rope and I, up here, purposely tugging on the wrong rope.

"Holy cow . . . ," admiring the enormous extent of the ocean below and behind me.

The former flag-bearer's steady shelling of Spanish increased.

What! If anyone would be hurt, I reasoned, it would be me. What was he complaining about?

I recalled my airplane ride from Chicago, and how the American city from up high presented itself as neatly contained and ordered. So different it seemed from afar, so distinct from the chaotic mess that I found it to be below. I laughed at my change in view, knowing full well that it was distance that was creating both illusions.

I remembered recognizing Archer Avenue from the rest of the streets. It was a prominent renegade, cutting at a forty-five degree angle to the crisscross pattern of the rest of the South Side, straight through the neighborhoods of Brighton Park, McKinley Park, Bridgeport, Chinatown, and so on. Archer, our passageway to downtown.

I began to descend.

How different Mexico City was, I thought. Arriving at night, my first impression of the metropolis was of a gargantuan web of miniature streetlights, drawing you in from all sides.

The customs agent had proudly declared twenty million inhabitants. Don't get lost, he grinned.

Hmmm, a different order existed here, I told myself as I looked over a city map displaying an archaic pattern of streets veering in multiple directions and ending quite abruptly. The discontinuity intrigued me so. Life here had spread in a wild, uncompromising fashion. But there was some sort of order. There had to be, I reasoned, as I searched for an uncle I had never met. How else could things go on, I asked myself once we were in his car, riding toward the higher ground where he lived.

Hmmm. This Mexican beach appeared to be a synthetic combination of two distinct worlds.

"Oh maannn!"

I was beginning to rapidly near the dark blue scales of the ocean. I looked up.

"Oh shit!"

The red and white parasail had collapsed unto itself.

"Oh shit!"

I slipped through the air. Right before I went in, I closed my eyes, took a semi-long breath, and thought about my uncle Cosme. I worried that he would be angry if they found me dead.

As I broke into the water I tried to stand still. In some comic book I once read that this would be the best way to fall into water from a great distance without breaking your neck.

I opened my eyes. Saltwater! Aghhh. Even worse was the surrounding darkness where my unanswerable questions lived. I shut my eyes. Too late. The claustrophobic sensation had already reached me. What would it do if I just curled up and told it to go away? Would it work? I decided to pray.

Suddenly, a new calm arose inside, asking me to eliminate any of my needless chatter. I fumbled across my chest, searching for the metal clips attached to the ropes that were meant to keep me safe. They were currently condemning me to death. I remembered there were three. The first two seemed easy. I let out some air and began to work on the third.

I was having a hard time with it when the strong dragging sensation came.

Direction? None.

No up. No down.

Just a magnificent pull.

But where was I going? Where was this hand taking me? It felt like a hand. A gigantic hand holding me in its palm, spinning me round and round.

I don't want to die, I thought. Not like this. Not anymore! Please, let me live. I'm sorry. Please.

When I finally reached the surface, I was greeted by a cussing boat crew. My escapade would cost them hours of pay, they shouted. They went on about the time it would take to dry the fabric.

On the way back, I sat shivering and humiliated but also wondering what really was keeping me alive. Why was I so fortunate?

daytime

1987—1990

12

"So you never told me a lot about Mexico, Lou, except what happened on the beach."

"Oh, Mexico was awesome, Carlos. The first place I stayed at was the capital. I got there around two in the morning. Man, there was still traffic. My uncle Cosme told me that was because Mexico City's the most populated city in the world, and that people are working there all the time. While he was driving to his house, he also said people lived in these big 'colonias,' like little cities within the city."

"Yep." My cousin sat beside me on the apartment stairs and took off his sandals, lightly tapping them on the steps to remove whatever dirt they may have had. "What about Cosmos's? Was it weird? I know he's your uncle and all but it's not like you guys really know him or any of your mom's other family, except for the ones who came here to Chicago when you guys were little."

"I know," staring at his brown sandals, "I thought about that. My uncle's straight. He reminds me of my grandpa when he was alive. He's got the same kind of eyes, except I think they're green and not blue like Ventura's. But their noses look the same. He's a big motherfucker too, just like my grandpa. Even bigger than Jose."

"No way!"

"For real, Carlos. And he also talks to me real nice. Like how my grandfather use to. He wears nice clothes all the time—so does his wife. They're both civil engineers and own their own company. Man, I fell in love with my aunt Chepina."

"Who's that?"

"That's what everyone calls my uncle's wife."

"Why? What's so special about her?"

"Well, for one thing, she's really fucking beautiful. Did you ever notice how a lot of women when they get married or have kids cut their hair?"

"Yeah," bobbing his head.

"Well, she's not like that. She's got long brown hair that goes way below her shoulders. Her face looks totally different from other people's faces too. She sometimes looks old and tough and other times she looks so young. Like a little kid. And the way she acts is also different from other ladies I know. It's like she knows what she wants and she isn't going to settle for anything less. If I ever get married, I hope I find someone smart like her."

"Someone who can take care of you on two different levels?"

"Right. Yeah, that's what I want."

"So what else did you do while you were there, Lou?"

"They took me to a whole bunch of places. We went to those two beaches, Mazatlan and Acapulco. When we went to Mazatlan, they showed me some land they were renting from the government. Dude, they're trying to fucking cultivate shrimp there! I wouldn't even have thought of doing that. They dug these big ditches with these big Caterpillars they have out there and were filling them up with saltwater and regular water. They said they needed the right combination for the shrimp to live. Those cats are cool."

"Are you serious?"

"Hell, yeah! That's why I liked them so much. They don't sit around and wait for their dreams to come. They try to make them happen themselves. Realize your dreams, my uncle Cosmos said, don't just forget them. The other thing I really liked about them was how they didn't really ignore their two kids the whole time I was there. Their shit's balanced, bro'. The way it should be. Oh, and that's another thing. Older people treat people like you and me who are around the same age differently. Even the kids act differently."

"What do you mean?"

"I don't know. It's like they don't know what's up. It's like they act like real kids, all innocent and shit."

"So what else did you do, Lou?"

"I went to where I was born. To Irapuato, Guanajuato. Hey, Carlos, you didn't tell me they grew strawberries there."

"You wouldn't expect it, would you?"

"No way! They're like everywhere. My aunt said they export them to places like England and Ireland."

"I wouldn't doubt it."

"Yeah. Irapuato is just like you told me it was, Carlos. Dusty and smaller than Chicago."

"Did they take you to Guanajuato?"

"Isn't that the name of the state I was in?"

"Uh-huh, but there's also a city called Guanajuato."

"Guanajuato, Guanajuato? No. Why? What's over there?"

"That's supposedly the birthplace of the Mexican revolution, Lou. They say some priest mustered the people together there. I think the city of Guanajuato use to be either a French colony or Spanish. I know it's got great colonial architecture. You would have loved it, Lou. Especially the cobblestone streets and the old churches that are falling apart. The place looks like it's stuck in the time it was built, except for the cars and tourists you see around there."

"Are the churches like the ones here?"

"No way. All the buildings there are ancient . . . Wow, I can't believe they didn't take you there. You missed out on the mummies."

"What mummies?"

"They got this museum where there's a collection, like over eighty of them."

"Cool. Do they let you touch them?"

"No way, they're behind glass."

"Man, now I'm pissed I didn't get to go to Guanajuato. I'll go next time."

"Even if you have to go by yourself?"

"Yeah, well that's kinda how I went this time anyway. I didn't go on the plane with Mom or anyone else. Trust me, dude, I walked the streets alone out there too . . . Oh, before I forget. When I was in Acapulco, I went on an Argentinean battleship with our cousin Rosendo."

"How the fuck did that happen?"

"Him and I met some girls at a disco. There were like eight of them. Some sailors were trying to pick them up and invited them to hang out on their boat. I was dancing with one of them and she asked me what I thought about her and her friends getting on the ship. I told her I had heard bad things happened on those navy ships. After that, a couple of them still wanted to go. So it ended up that they wouldn't go unless we went with them. You should have seen Rosendo. He was freaking out and being a big baby. I told him to chill. If anything funny happened, we'd leave right away, I said. He kept saying something was going to happen to us. What a jinx, bro'! What's the worst thing they could do, I told him. Throw us overboard?"

"So was it cool?"

"Hell, yeah. But I think the only guys that weren't sailors were me and Rosendo. I was so buzzed it didn't matter. I just kept drinking."

"And the sailors were cool with you?"

"Some of them gave us dirty looks, that's it. But then the ship started moving. Fuck, I didn't realize it until Rosendo told me what was up. I didn't believe him either and then it finally hit me. Man, I started shitting in my pants."

"Holy fuck! How long did it go for?"

"I can't remember," shaking my head. "All I know is the girls started freaking out. I tried to be calm so they would think that things were going to be cool. When we finally touched land, I was happy like you couldn't believe."

"So how was Rosendo on the vacation?"

"He was all right."

"I'm asking because I know your family and his have had problems before."

"Man, Carlos, the way I see it, whatever happened between my parents and his is between those two. But I still don't like Rosendo's mom. She's mean. And the dad's the same way. They're always talking smack about my parents and the way they raise us. Like they're way better than us. But anyway, I don't know what happened five or ten years ago. How am I suppose to judge shit I didn't actually see for myself? People are always changing things around to make them look like they didn't do shit anyway. I don't think all people do it on purpose. But some do. Other people just don't see the wrong stuff they do. But I bet you if everyone in the world put themselves in someone else's shoes, things wouldn't be so fucked-up. People have to start thinking about their shit."

"Lou, I know exactly what you're saying," feeling his face with his hand.

His and Jose's acne had grown worse over the past few years. I knew the way people stared at them, the mean words they would say. And not even to their face. I really wanted those idiots dead or to have something really bad happen to them, I told myself. I hope I'm never ignorant like that. What if I was?

"I mean," breaking thought, "I love my parents, but that doesn't mean they're not human. We all make mistakes."

"So you don't think some people are better than others?"

"Yes and no. It's hard to say. All I know is I respect someone more if they fuck up all the time and don't know what they're doing than someone who fucks up once in a while but knows exactly the shit they're doing. But even the people who don't know are fucked-up. Just in a different way. I can't explain it. Like something's not letting them see things around them."

"So, dude, you really liked Mexico?"

"It was cool. I even went horseback riding for the first time. Met an awesome girl named Gisela. She's German and has been living in Mexico all her life. We went to this one valley near Mexico City where you can rent a horse for as long as you want. I told them to give me the biggest one they had. They gave me their newest one. The owner called him Satanás."

"Satanás!" Carlos started to roll with laughter. "Fucking Lou, do you know what that name means in English?"

"Yep. It means Satan. Demon riding Satan. Get it?"

"Right, the UPCs call you Demon."

"Yeah, and don't forget Priest," smiling. "Anyway the people taking care of the horse asked me if I had ever ridden before. I told them I did because I knew they wouldn't let me on if I told 'em the truth. I even made up some story of growing up in Texas on some ranch."

"Lou," holding a closed fist to his mouth and turning a deep red, "you've never even been in Texas!"

"Shhh!" nudging him. "I know. But I wasn't going to get on some little horse and have some guy take me with a rope. That would've been stupid."

"Yeah. It would've sucked."

"Anyway, when I pulled out the money my aunt gave me, they let me have a horse right away. Money talks, bro'."

"No shit. Don't you wish we had some of it?"

"Kinda. Anyway, so I got right on top of this horse, just like they do in the movies. Man, that baby was beautiful. It was a dark brown color and had a black mane. It trotted like for a few feet and then took off. Pow! I don't know what I did, but it just zoomed right through the trail. Shit, bro', I could hear him breathing hard like a motherfucker! I then took him into a forest. I thought he would slow down. But he didn't. He went even faster. Crazy style. It's like he knew what I really wanted. I think I held on to his neck more than to the reins. I swear, Carlos, Satanás knew me. I felt so strong on top of that fucker. I'm positive he knew. I swear to God he was laughing a couple of times too. I could feel it. All I did was keep talking to him, telling him he was the shit but that I was strong too. And he got crazier. After we got out of the forest, we went down a hill. Now that was fucking wild. It felt like I was going to fall off. Man, it was steep!"

"I'm surprised you didn't fall off and break your neck."

"Man, Carlos, I tried to stop Santanás, but when I pulled back, that fucker rose on his back two legs. That's when I really almost fell. Fuck that! I wasn't going to let him drop me. It's like when I almost drowned out there. I just let the ocean do whatever it wanted to do to me. I didn't fight it. What for? Cosme told me you can't fight the ocean. He said there's something about some things that make them way bigger than you, me, and everyone else in this world. But it's like I already knew that. Even before he told me. Just now I know how to say it."

"He thinks like that?"

"Yep, some of the other people are fucked-up, though."

"What do you mean?"

"Well the people in Mexico are cool—kinda. It's like they're in some time warp or something. They're really old-fashioned."

"Do you think they're naive?"

"Uhhh, it's like they believe all the things they see on television and in newspapers. You should see how they think."

"It's the same here, Lou."

"I guess, but they ask real weird questions."

"Like what?"

"Well, they kept asking me about black people. They think all black people here are on welfare and that all of them own guns and are in gangs and stuff."

"You're joking?"

"No way, dude. They're really ignorant about it. The funny thing is they think they're being told the truth."

"Hey, at least they ask. Some people just believe what their parents or what the news tells them. Pssst, they don't go beyond that."

"Yep, but when I told them why they were wrong, they acted really surprised."

"What did you tell them?"

"I told them it wasn't all like that. I think they thought I was lying when I told them how many gangbangers here are Mexican. They looked at me like I was crazy or insulting them. I don't get it. How can people be so ignorant and not see what's out there? It's right in front of their faces."

"I don't know, Lou. That's just the way it is. We all think we're so smart. I'm just happy I have you to check my shit with. It feels great to be on a wave with someone."

"I know, but people better start thinking and getting things straight or else all this shit is going to blow up."

"Think so?"

"Fuck, yeah. Man, I feel the tension building up all the time. You know they're starting the 'wars' at Quigley, don't you?"

"Lou, you know I like to keep to myself."

"Well, everyone's in their own little group. It started out like a game but I bet you people are going to end up hurting each other. For real. I mean people don't just care about sticking with each other; they want to get other people out of the way too. That's stupid."

143

"Quigley's own civil war."

"Yep."

"Who you with, Lou?"

"Me?" I cringed. "I'm neutral. Fuck these little cliques. I don't need backup for anything. If I can't take care of my own shit, then I might as well be nobody."

"Good man." Carlos slapped his hand on my back. "That's the one thing I've always liked about you, Lou. No matter what you're into, you're still in your own world."

"Sometimes," I smiled. "I don't know."

"No, Lou, seriously. Listen to me. Even with the UPCs, you still keep the crazy part of you going. Just the other day I told myself, Self, now there goes someone who's all together. The bomb would drop and he'd still be all in one piece." He made a sudden gesture of pulling an imaginary microphone from the air in front of him and holding it in front of my face. "Tell me, how do you do it, Lou?"

"Shit, I don't know," playing along. "I just am who I am. I do what I want to do. I guess I'm God."

"Hey, it works for you."

"It works for everybody. But seriously. I think it's the way you look at yourself that does it. If you believe in yourself, that's all you need. Don't you notice how it's only when people talk shit about you all the time that you can't do anything? It's like they make you nervous or embarrassed. I say people are either going to be with you or against you. Man, don't even pay attention to those jive motherfuckers that talk shit. They don't see how everyone's a little crazy at some point in life. Fuck 'em."

"But, dude," putting the imaginary microphone away. "You don't have the acne problem that your brother Jose and me have. You don't know what it's like to be looked at like a freak. Some people don't even look us in the eyes."

"Yeah," lowering my eyes, "I know. But don't let those jagoffs get you down, bro'. They're nothing in this world."

"No, Lou, they're here and there's a whole bunch of them. Don't tell me you don't look at us and think how bad it looks."

"I don't. I never even saw it until people started saying shit about it at school. I still don't care. I just tell them to shut up. They

144

know if they say anything around me they're going to get their asses beat. And if they kick my ass, I'll keep coming at them."

"But Lou! That doesn't stop them from thinking like that. One day, they're going to have children and they're going to teach them to think in the same way."

"I'll beat their asses too!" feeling agitated. "I'll fucking kill 'em all if I have to."

"Then you're going to have to kill the whole world, Lou, including yourself, because I think everyone thinks like this at some point in their life. Didn't you just say that some people don't know when they're doing something bad? Remember? Lou, listen to yourself. Sometimes you'll be happy and not care what other people think. And sometimes you'll be angry and sad and pissed at everyone. Dude, I don't know where you get it from, but it's weird. Like I don't know you."

I said nothing. Instead, I stretched my naked back on the cool concrete surface of our porch. Why couldn't people just be different? More considerate? Father Tom warned me things were going to get complicated in the years to come. But I had no idea things would get this difficult. I closed my eyes. Carlos was right; I had forgotten my own words. And that troubled me.

I needed to remember. The whole bullshit starts with one person fucking up, I thought.

"So how's everything with the UPCs?"

I turned on my side.

"Where did that come from?"

"It's just you and I haven't hung out like we use to, Lou," drumming his hands on his lap. "Things haven't been the same."

"What are you talking about?" I picked myself up and let out a yawn. "We live right downstairs from you. You know anytime we go out you can come."

"I know, but hanging out with the UPCs is just not my thing. I mean, it's okay. Remember the first party we went to on 47th Street? That was insane. People were falling all over each other, making out right on the dance floor. I've never seen anything like it. We were in a totally different world."

I nodded.

"Lou, before that day, I never got into house music like you. I remember you telling me about how you use to lie on the living-room floor on the weekends at your old home and just listen to it all night. I never understood how you could do that and not sleep. But that day, when we went to the house party, all I had to do was listen and I knew how great it was. It all felt too good to be real. You know what I mean?"

"That's why I became UPC."

"Lou, you became a UPC for other reasons. The music you found yourself. It has nothing to do with being UPC. Maybe you also just really enjoy watching other people have fun too."

"Yeah, I do . . . Hey, Carlos, what time is it, dude?"

My cousin checked his watch. "Damn, Lou, you know how long we've been out here?"

"About three hours and fifteen minutes."

"That's good, Lou. You're off by about five minutes."

"Thanks. I haven't had a watch since they stole our Mickey Mouse watches when we were little kids."

"That's right, you told me about that. They really cleaned you guys out. Did they ever catch anybody?"

"Are you kidding? The cops got there and left. They said they'd be back to get fingerprints but they never came. We're lucky we had insurance on most of the stuff. Still, that shit was so fucking jive. To take our shit on New Year's. Come on, you know it was someone from around there. The shit was done too well . . . Man, now I'm getting depressed. Let's do something crazy tonight, Carlos."

"Like what?"

"I don't know. Maybe we can drink."

"All right, let's get drunk." Carlos wiped the back of his shorts and lunged onto the cement pavement from the top of the stairs.

"Yeah, but with what? I don't have anything in the crib that'll get us even buzzed. There's not one beer in the fridge. My dad doesn't drink except for every once in a while when he goes out. And he hasn't done that in years. I tell him to get out of the house. But no, does he listen to me? Nope. Man, I wish they would get divorced or something. I keep telling that to my mom. I wish we were at the old house too. There at least we could go to the basement to cool off."

"Except when you were burning down the house."

"What? Oh yeah . . . on my God!"

"You guys were nuts. Tying a string from one side of the basement wall to the other and then hanging a plastic mask on the string so that you could pull it with another string. What the fuck!"

"Shit, everything was going great."

"Except when you set the mask on fire."

"We just wanted to have a cool haunted house. I didn't know that the Darth Vader mask was going to go up like that. I'm happy nothing happened . . . Hey, remember when Jose made a bow and arrow and shot it at Iz?"

"I don't know what the fuck was going through his head. Jose was always crazy about weapons. Maybe it was all those ninja and Bruce Lee movies he watched. I remember the time when he bought a whole mess of Chinese stars, the ones they sell at la gara. That crazy asshole, he thought he was a ninja or something and asked me to stand underneath a tree. 'Come on, Carlos,' he said, 'it won't hurt. Just don't move. Come on, Carlos, let me practice.' And that bastard was serious."

"Yeah, we bought a lot of cool shit at the flea market like that . . . Oh," pounding excitedly against my knee, "do you remember when I threw the rock at him in the alley?"

"How can I forget?" my cousin rolled his eyes. "Instead of hitting him, you got me in the mouth."

"Sorry . . . Hey, I can't believe you fainted."

"Yeah, well. I remember you screaming 'kill me' in Spanish— 'mátenme'—over and over to your mom."

"I felt bad, Carlos. I wanted to die when I saw you faint."

"It's all right. I knew you were aiming it at Jose."

"Yep," staring down. "Man, Carlos, we use to fight a lot—all three of us. And over any little thing. We'd fight hard, bro'. Use whatever was in the house to beat each other up. Man, we were fucked-up little kids."

"Lou, we were little."

"I guess . . . You know what it's like, Carlos, to have to hear your mother cry late at night? It's the nastiest feeling in the world. And it's not like my father hits her or anything. I've never seen him do that. He just uses words. But that's worse, I think, 'cause once you hear them they're always floating around inside of you. I feel bad for Ma. She's just got too big of a heart. Don't get me wrong, Carlos, I love my dad. He was always there for us when we were growing up. But he's hardly like that anymore. I don't know. Once in a while he'll talk about the things he use to talk about. He'll come outside at night and sit on the steps and smoke his cigarette, all by himself. And he'll just sit there, quiet, like he's thinking a million thoughts."

"Yeah," Carlos scratched the side of his head. "I don't remember too much about my dad."

"He died when you guys were little?"

"Yep."

"That's fucked-up, bro.' I don't know if I could handle that."

"I didn't really know him."

"But don't you get sad?"

"I feel more for my mom. She tries to hide it but it comes out from time to time."

"Yeah, but you know what?"

"What?"

"It kind of bothers me how some people think more of the people that are dead than the people who are alive."

"Lou, let's just not talk anymore about this. Pretty soon, you and I are going to be crying here and our moms are going to start asking questions. So are we going to get drunk or what? I think we have a bottle of something upstairs. We can drink it wherever you want."

"Let's see what it is first and then I'll tell you."

"Okay, then get your ass up so we can take care of business."

I grabbed the side rail and hoisted myself to my feet, staring across the street. Nicole, our neighbor's daughter, was outside. I waved hello.

"She's gorgeous. Isn't she, Lou? Why don't you ask her out?"

"Are you kidding? She won't go out with me. I'm fourteen. She's like twelve."

"But she looks good."

"You think so?"

"Look at her, Lou," my cousin continued. "I'm getting that strong wave from her bouncing right to you. You know I can pick 'em. Lou, I think it's time you think about getting a real girl. Something sweet and innocent, not like those UPC girls you have at the parties."

"María isn't a UPC girl. And Miss Kim wasn't UPC either."

"Come on, Lou, you can't compare that angel," pointing to Nicole, "with anyone else in your head. I'm telling you, Nicole's the girl."

As he went up the stairs, Carlos sang a tune. The name Nicole appeared in the song. I looked across the street again. She was taking care of her two younger brothers. I saw her glance over.

"We got a bottle of Jack Daniels," Carlos reappeared.

"Cool," semi-ignoring him.

"What did I tell you, Lou? Incredible. Look at the way she smiles at you. You can't keep your eyes off of her."

"She smiles like that with everyone," turning to look around at Carlos who was standing beneath the doorway.

"No, Lou. That, my dear cousin, is the special smile. And it's all for you."

"We'll see. Maybe I'll talk to her tomorrow."

"Oh Lou! Don't tell me you're scared. Not you. The Casanova. Jesus, you're beginning to blush. Holy shit! You're beginning to turn into a tomato."

"Mannnn, I'll go tomorrow."

"Sure, Lou. Why can't you go right now? I don't think her mom's even home. Her car's not in front of their house. Do it, Lou . . . Do it! Do it! Do it!"

"Okay, okay, okay. But you better help me out."

"Look, I'm not going to talk to her for you. She's going to think you're a kid. Just do your Louie thing."

"What Louie thing?"

"You know. That Louie thing you do."

"Jerk. I don't know what you're talking about."

I left. Carlos began clapping hysterically. When I reached Nicole, she asked me what it was all about. I told her that he was just trying to be funny.

"You boys aren't making some stupid bet to see who gets to kiss me or something, are you?"

"Ummm," beginning to perspire heavily. "No. He just didn't think I would come over to talk to you and ask you out."

"Is that what you came here for?"

"Yep. So do you want to go out with me or what?"

"But you don't even know me," she squeaked.

"Yeah, I do!" leaning against her green fence. "You live across the street from me. I see you every time you're outside. You seem nice."

"Is that what you're looking for? Someone nice?"

"Yeah," picking at the links, feeling my hands sweat, "But you also have to be smart. What am I going to do with someone who's dumb?"

"Is that how you really feel?"

"Yeah! So do you want to go out with me or what?"

"Let's talk about it tomorrow. Come over around eleven in the morning. My mom won't be home then. Okay?"

"That's cool. I'll see you tomorrow."

I left her and went back to Carlos.

"What did she say, Lou?"

"That she'll tell me tomorrow."

"Tell you what?"

"If she's going to go out with me or not."

"You asked her out?"

"Fuck, yeah. That's why I went over there. Right?"

"Fucking Lou," spreading his hands over his head. "I don't believe you. Now that takes some balls. I'm proud of you, son."

I grinned. "Now, hopefully, she'll say yes."

"She will, Lou. She will. I can feel it in my bones. Can't you?"

"I don't have your bones. But she was kind of friendly."

"Yeah, I saw you had her smiling the whole time."

"But it was so weird! Man, Carlos, I wonder if this is normal?"

"With you, screwie Louie, anything's normal."

"So you got Jack, huh?"

"Yes, sir. The only other bottle we had looked pretty corroded. I don't understand why Mom even keeps anything in the house. She doesn't drink. And I know Gus or my grandma doesn't drink."

"Maybe it's for guests," I said. "Hey, let's mix it with Coke and ice. That's the way Father Tom sometimes mixes stuff. It'll make it taste better."

"Sounds good. Where should we go?"

"The gangway. No one's going to see us there."

"And if our mothers find out?"

"They're not going to say anything. We'll just go take a walk or something."

"Okay, screwie Louie, let's head for them hills."

After drinking the bottle, we wandered around the streets, not caring what anyone would say.

By the end of the night, before the beginning of the day, we found ourselves in McKinley Park. In an open field, a parade of ducks crossed my path. The way I saw it, they were playing "follow the leader," displaying complete trust in the one in front. What struck me as interesting was seeing each individual duck act as leader at one point or another, helping the smaller one behind at all times, to the very end of the chain. I enjoyed that very much. But Carlos only laughed, commenting that there were no ducks at all. But who knew the truth? We were both still just drunk.

"Porqué vienes así?"

"Come on, Ma. Look," pointing to the living-room window, "the sun's already up. Leave me alone."

"No te voy a dejar en paz hasta que me digas por que vienes tán borracho!"

"Ma! Pleeease, leave me alone. I wanna go to sleep."

I started for my room. She placed herself in front of the doorway, blocking my path.

"Eso lo hubieras haber pensado antes de que hicistes lo que hicistes. A ver, dime. Porqué andas así?"

"'Cause I wanted to get drunk with Carlos, Ma. Why? What do you care? I always get drunk when I go out to the parties, anyway. I still go to work. I still go to school and get good grades! Why don't you go bother Dad or somebody else? You should complain to him. Or Jose. He never comes home! I haven't done nothing!"

"Mira Luis, tú te me vas a aplacar o le voy a decir a tú papá."

"Man, Maaa, you don't even know what I'm saying," letting out a curling laugh. "Go ahead and tell Dad! I don't give a fuck! Like he's going to tell me what's wrong and what's right."

"Qué? Qué me dijistes?"

"You mean why did I say the word 'fuck'? 'Cause I wanted to. That's why. Now come on, Ma, let me go to sleep."

"Nunca quiero que me digas esa maldición. Me óistes?"

"Ma, I didn't say it to you. It's not my fault you don't understand English. Come on," pushing her to the side, "get out of my way." She resisted. "You're starting to tick me off, Ma!"

Without thought, I shoved her back, causing her to fall and hit her head on the edge of the stereo cabinet. She began to weep. From our bedroom, Israel snarled at me to leave her alone.

"She's the one that started it," I yelled back.

I escaped to the bunk bed, hounded by unwanted anger. I wrapped the pillow around my head and tried desperately to go to sleep and ignore the arriving day. Maybe I could sleep it all away, I thought. No, I realized it would be right where I left it when I awoke.

Why couldn't I stop hurting?

13

*I*s anyone sitting here?"

The few who pulled themselves away from their plates looked up at me suspiciously. The others kept eating.

"Está bien, carnal," one of them said in Spanglish, "sit down."

I sat next to him. Running down the corners of the boy's protruding jawbones were a pair of thick sideburns. That, along with his spongy hair, made him appear as if he were wearing a helmet over his head.

"Órale culeros," turning to his companions, "don't you recognize him? Indio's little brother?"

"Get the fuck out of here!" someone at the end of the table yelled. "Chiva, this little bitch don't look anything like Jose."

"Dile, bro'," Chiva said to me. "Tell 'em whose brother you are."

"My brother's Jose. You guys call him Indio?"

"Sí, huey," Chiva grinned, "we gave him that name last year at a soccer game. Your broski didn't tell you?"

"Naw."

"Damn, bro'. And that's your carnal."

"My what?"

"Carnal. Brother. Tu hermano, huey! Shit," he continued, "Ese culero's so fucking dark. Like a fucking Indian from Mexico. But tall. He looks like one of those giant wooden statues you see in the cartoons. All we need to do is have him hold cigars in his hands. What the fuck do you guys feed him at home, bro'?"

"Everything."

"Looks like it. Fucking Mikey. Just like in the commercial. Eats everything. Your brother's fucking crazy too, carnal. He'll take on anybody."

"Fuck," someone remarked, "he better. Ese huey is bigger than all of us here put together. He's even bigger than most of the seniors and he's only a sophomore."

"Pinche, Eddy," Chiva motioned to a freckle-faced boy, who was shoveling food into his mouth. "Don't talk and eat at the same time, huey. I can see your food." He turned to me. "That shit looks disgusting, carnal. Verdad?"

"It don't matter to me, bro'. As long as it's not in my mouth."

"I guess your brother got everything you didn't get," Chiva said. "Even your skin is lighter. And what's up with those funky curls you have at the top of your head. Pinche, carnal, you look like Bozo the Clown."

Everyone at the table laughed and urged me to say something in response.

"Hey, at least it doesn't look as bad as those rabbit teeth you have with those big fucking lips trying to cover 'em."

"Eso, bro'!" Chiva cried. "Now I know you're Indio's little brother. You guys talk the same bullshit. Except you're still way smaller than him."

"That don't mean I can't take someone down," rubbing the back of his neck gently.

"Cool, bro'," Chiva hammered me lightly in my rib cage, "me dá gusto you ain't a pussy like some of the other motherfuckers around here. Now I can really see how you and Indio are related. You can hold down the fort with us whenever you want."

"Thanks."

"No big deal, carnal." Chiva looked at my food. "Shit sucks, doesn't it?"

"It's all right."

"You want your corn?"

I gave it to him.

"So you get this free or what?"

"Yeah."

"Too poor, huh? No te molestes, bro', we're all in the same boat here. You had free lunch in grammar school too?"

I agreed.

"Were you born in Mexico como tú culero brother Jose?"

"Yeah," attacking the one slice of turkey and potatoes. "I was born over there and they brought me over when I was like six months old."

"Damn, carnal, you must've been a good swimmer at six months to cross ese Río."

"Shit, I didn't have to cross that river. My mom and dad told me that when I was a baby they hired a couple to bring me over. And when they were bringing me, my parents were scared that something was going to happen to me."

"Something did happen, huey," Chiva joked. "They switched you for another wetback. That's why you don't look like your carnal."

"Hey, don't call me wetback. Whatever you do, don't call me that."

"Y porqué?"

"I hate that fucking name," putting food in my mouth.

"You better get use to it, carnal, because that's what all the white boys in this country call us."

"I'm never going to get use to any of that shit."

"Don't worry, bro'," someone interrupted, "I don't get it either. I bet you some of those assholes who say that shit don't even understand that some of their parents and grandparents crossed an entire ocean to get here. They're ignorant bitches. They don't think about anything else but themselves. Fuck, they think they're so special because their asses are white. Shit smells no matter who takes the dump."

"Mira, bro'," Chiva continued. "Look around. You think because you're in a seminary we're all here praying together. This shit isn't even a real seminary. Dale atención, carnal. The mayates are over there, hanging with their own homeys. The white boys stick with each other and even the nerds have their own clique. If Jesus is here, he's probably in the corner by himself, wondering why everyone's acting like such bitches. And this is suppose to be Quigley, bro'! They tell you in your freshman year this place is different. Shit, there's still people in here who use the words nigger and spic all the time."

"So what are you guys?" looking at the staring faces.

"Us? We're the braziers, bro'! And so are you. Look in the mirror, bitch. Can't you tell?"

I sat in silence.

"Stop getting sad about what I'm saying, bro'. Don't worry. Since you're Indio's broski, we got your back."

"Move, freshman!"

Feeling the edge of a plastic tray against my neck, I turned to see who gave the command.

Chiva confronted the intruder. "Leave the kid alone, Kazlowski. He's almost finished."

"I don't give a fuck," the stranger retorted. "He should know better than to sit in my spot."

"I'm not doing anything," pushing his tray away. "Leave me alone."

"It's my spot."

"I don't see a name on this seat or anything that says you own it."

"You got a problem, freshman?"

"No," getting up, "I think *you* got a problem."

"You want me to do something about it?" Kazlowski pressed forward.

"Take it easy, Kazlowski. He hasn't done shit to you. Mira culero, sit your blond ass down over there." Chiva suggested a corner seat across from us. "There's enough space for your he-man body on that side."

Kazlowski frowned. "I don't think so. I'm gonna take this seat right now."

"Hey, Kazlowski, ya cállate huey. Don't you know this is Jose's little brother?"

"I don't care. Fuck that crater-faced bitch! He can suck my dick!" He put his tray down and grabbed me from underneath my armpits.

"Hey, let go!"

He tugged for about a second and then released me when he spotted a teacher coming our way.

"You know what? I'm not even going to waste my lunchtime with this bitch." He leaned over. "I'll take care of your pussy ass later."

"Man, fuck you!"

"What did you say, freshman?"

"You heard me," I glared. "Are you fucking deaf?"

"You're lucky we're in school 'cause if not I'd kick your ass right now."

"Whatever."

As he left, I asked Chiva about him.

"Kazlowski? Es uno de los wrestlers, bro'. He's on the team. I can't wait to tell Indio what he said. The shit about the crater-face is going to piss him off."

"But Kazlowski's fucking huge."

"Shit," someone smirked. "Especially after all the fucking steroids he takes. Fucker looks like a balloon."

"He takes stuff to make himself big? Can you do that?"

"That's what some people say," someone else chided in. "But I hear your dick falls off or something."

"He didn't like you at all, bro'," Chiva said. "If he hassles you anymore, just tell Jose about it. I can't believe you told him to fuck off. Pinche huevos."

"What's my brother going to do?"

"He'll beat the fuck out of him. That's what. Trust me, carnal. Ese Kazlowski won't fuck with Indio. He knows better. I think the only motherfucker that Indio wouldn't take on is that fat-ass mayate over there by the rest of the spearchuckers. They call that cabrón Fat Albert or some shit like that. I can't wait to see him and your brother get it on."

"Do you think my brother would win?" looking over to the one he nicknamed Fat Albert. He was both taller and heavier than Jose.

"I don't know, bro'," Chiva said. "But it'd be a good fight. The only problem is Baby Huey over there doesn't fight."

"Maybe he fights in a different way."

"What other way is there?"

"A lot of other ways, bro'. Better ways."

"Pinche, cabrón, don't get freaky on me."

"Naw, I'm not getting freaky, bro'. I'm just telling you what I know."

"Oyé, carnal. I've been talking to you all this time and I never even asked your name."

"Luis," I said. "My boys call me Demon."

"Your boys? You're in UPC like Indio?"

"Yeah. Why?"

"Oh shit," leaning back, "that means you don't need us. You got your boys."

"I don't need anyone!"

"Cálmate, carnal. Eat the rest of your food before it gets cold."

But I couldn't relax. I couldn't just forget Kazlowski and other people like him. Frustrated, I finished and said good-bye to Chiva and his friends.

In class, I thought about the time when I was picked on by a bully. It happened whenever I walked home from elementary school. Eventually, I collected a vial of jalapeño juice from the canned ingredients my mother had at home. My very first weapon. My intention was to splash his eyes with it. I even put a few drops on my eyes to convince myself of its painful properties. But something put an end to my plans. The fact is I would never see the boy again. Something had made him disappear and end my chances for revenge. Why? I was so close to teaching him a lesson so he wouldn't hurt anyone else.

14

I still can't believe we're doing this!"

"Why?" pulling back on the curtain, allowing the night breeze to enter her bedroom window.

"You don't think it's nuts?"

"No," squirming in her arms. "All we do is talk and hold each other."

A faint whistle seeped from downstairs. Her older sister's television set. She undoubtedly knew what we had been doing for the last few weeks, I thought. Any time now I expected her to come upstairs and surprise us.

"What if when you get old you have a daughter? Don't tell me you wouldn't get mad if you found some boy hiding in her bed at night."

"Why? My clothes aren't off."

"You wouldn't get mad?" she repeated.

"No. I'd talk to both of them."

"You're only saying that because you're a boy."

"No, I'm saying that because I'm Louie. I mean, I use to get mad at things like that but not no more. It's like they went away."

"Sure."

I let go of her. "Seriously. Do you know the story of the Tower of Babel? It's in the Bible."

"Kind of."

"Well, the way I see it, it was about a bunch of dorks who got together to work on this big old tower that was suppose to reach God. When they finished it, they thought they were all big and bad. They even talked shit to God 'cause they thought they could get their shit together and be better."

"And what happened?"

"Well, when they were at the top, talking trash to the big person, they fucking looked at each other and tried talking to one another but couldn't."

"Why not?"

"'Cause, they fucked up," I laughed.

"Shhh."

"Okay, I'll be more quiet. Anyway, they were all proud and thought they were all right. They didn't once think about slowing their shit down or seeing what they were doing. If they would've just slowed down and talked to each other before they started, maybe they would've figured out that what they were doing was stupid. Come on, you can't be God here. It doesn't make sense. God's too big. Anyway, each of them only thought about their own shit and didn't care about anything else. That's what messed them up, I think."

"Cool, did that really happen?"

"It doesn't matter. I think that's what's happening to us. I think those stories in the Bible and all these old books are made up so we can figure out our own shit right now . . . You know what pisses me off?"

"What?"

"Well, the other day I was thinking about that show, the Great Space Coaster, and I remembered there was this guy, the guy who was speed-reading all the time. I think that's fucked-up 'cause if you think about it, a real writer doesn't just put words down for the fuck of it. I think a real writer puts every word in for a reason. And when you speed-read, people don't pick up the whole shit."

"Maybe some people don't have time to read every word."

"Then," frowning, "they shouldn't read whatever they're reading. Look, if I buy something that comes with instructions, why am I only going to read part of the instructions? My uncle Cosme in Mexico said that if I do something I should do it one-hundred percent and not do it halfway 'cause it'll fall apart."

"You're funny."

"Why?"

"Because. Where do you get all this stuff, you weirdo?"

"I don't know. Some from people. Some from myself. All I know is I use to watch people all the time and now I feel like I'm starting to step back and watch people watching people. You know, like I'm outside of myself. It feels cool."

"And when do you think it'll stop?"

"What?"

"You stepping back?"

"I don't know . . . Shit, I never thought about that . . . I'll have to think about that."

"You better. What if you disappear?"

I addressed the curtain once more.

"Louie?"

"What?"

"Do you think you'll ever get bored of me?"

"Oh, I already thought about that."

"And?"

"I only get bored with people if they stop growing. Then I let them go."

"But why?" sounding distressed.

"'Cause what if it's me who's not letting you get bigger? Or what good is it if I can't grow? I don't know, I just feel like I'm suppose to be a giant or something. What am I suppose to do? That's what I feel."

"Slow down."

"Yep," burying my face into her neck, "that's why I like you, Nicole, 'cause you're not boring. You make me think. I like people who make me think. I guess that means I kind of like everyone."

15

*O*ne.

With my right hand I let the locker panel fly.

Two.

I pulled out the fingers of my left hand before the edge of the narrow yellow door slammed on them. "Luis?"

Three.

Poof! The impact of the air from within the school locker slapped the front of my face softly. The reward of this game was to feel things pass in slow motion.

"Hey, Luis!"

I curled my fingers in midair and felt no pain. I thought about the time in grade school when I went for the back wheel of a friend's bicycle while he was riding it. I remembered the white line bubble across the inside of my fingers and turn red. How I made a fist and squeezed out as much blood as I could. Other people would have cried, I thought then. I had seen them do so for less. So I felt superior when I didn't.

"You're UPC?"

I turned to my classmate from religion class. His long straight jet-black hair, combed back, reached the top of his neck. It barely hid the single silver hoop-earring he wore on his left ear. There had been an argument in class about the meaning of that earring.

Was he gay? Was he in a gang? I didn't think he was in a gang. And I cared less that he might be a homosexual. In fact, I hadn't noticed the jewelry until it had been mentioned.

"Yeah, bro'. I'm UPC. Why? You got a problem with that?"

Was he a new waver? I was beginning to see them at a few of the house parties. He was always coming to school well-dressed, headphones on, listening to either industrial music, the Cure, the Smiths, or Depeche Mode.

"I just wanted to ask how I could join the UPCs. I keep hearing you're the shit."

"Man," giving my locker combo a twist, "not here, bro'. No one here knows jack shit."

"I'm not talking about the people from Quigley. I'm talking about the people who go to Juarez or Curie. Isn't Juarez where most of the UPCs are at anyway?"

"Who told you, bro'?" eyeing him cautiously, not because he was lying but because he was saying the truth.

So far, I had only thought of the UPCs as my boys from across Damen Bridge, from Pilsen. His observation had suddenly changed that view. I admired that.

"I have friends that go to Juarez. My cousin Tito is going to be UPC."

"I don't know him. Did he tell you we were the shit?"

"Not just him. I see it all over the place. I see the way girls stare at you when you get on the bus on 35th with your UPC jacket. They look up and down at you like you're all that. It's bad. Like the guys sometimes give you hard looks, but they don't say shit."

"Naw," giving an embarrassed smile. "For real?"

"Everyone knows you guys."

"So what do you think about our jackets?"

"They're fucking bad!"

"Why?"

"Because. The design on the back looks professional. The way those eyes are looking at you from the sky is sharp. They're funky, like they're saying we're everywhere. And the way you guys put the words ULTIMATE PARTY CREW in small print, not fat and nasty like how other party crews do—that's bad. You're not trying to be phony by having your name all over the place like how some other crews do."

"Yeah, well only posers do that. We don't need big signs to show who we are. Your name's Raphael?"

"My friends call me Ralphie, Ralph, or Tear."

"Yeah, bro', you said something in class about being a tagger. About how that's spiritual for you." I held out one of my books to him. "Let's see. Show me what's up. Tag something on the inside cover."

"Are you sure?"

"Don't worry about it. My book's way too clean right now anyway," opening it and flipping through the pages. "See, there's nothing in it. I haven't even put in my name. Man, people are gonna think I'm some kind of nerd," handing him the book. "Just don't tag on the pages I'm going to read. I wanna be able to do my homework, you know?"

"Okay," seeming anxious, "but I only tag Tear."

"That's straight."

I watched him take out a thick black marker from his schoolbag. His hand smoothly descended on the pristine white space. He seemed to be somewhere else and someone else.

Tear. The first two letters of the name were in small letters while the last two were in capital letters. The signature grew gradually from left to right, reminding me of a newspaper cartoon when a character would yell out a word. The first three letters were well connected with one another. The R, the most striking, stood nearly detached from the rest.

"Damn, dog, that's fucking straight. I especially like the way you put the copyright symbol at the end of your tag in the corner. That's bad!"

"That way no one can steal it."

"Shit, I've never seen anyone do it like that. Cool."

"Thanks," Raphael continued, "I did it to make it special."

"You tag good, Tear."

"I-I-I . . . I saw your name Luis was on the front of your jacket. Is that the only name you have?"

"Nah, my boys also call me Demon, Priest, or sometimes Peter Brady. Peter Brady's just a joke, though; the other two are what they mostly call me by. My ex-lady gave me Demon."

"So you tag Demon or Priest?"

"Naw, what I'm trying to tag is Phoenix and Apocalypse. But I can't get it. There's no one around my crib who can teach me. Just wannabe-taggers. I guess it don't matter anyway because we're not suppose to tag anything with the name UPC next to it. Some other crews do it, but it's against our rules."

"How come?"

"'Cause, we're not taggers. It's not that we think it's phony; it's just that if we wanted to do that we wouldn't call ourselves a party crew. You know? Anyway, if we do that, people will think we're gangbangers. None of us wants that reputation. Why do you think we tell anyone who wants to join that they can't throw up UPC in that way? If they do, we'll kick 'em out. I mean, the only times we throw up UPC is when we go to parties. We throw it up like this."

I lifted my hand and extended my thumb and index finger in parallel form, roughly displaying the shape of the letter U. I placed it over my chest, across my heart, and lightly pounded it a couple of times, feeling soothing pride rise.

"That's cool," Tear smiled.

"Yeah," lowering my hand. "It's better this way. Anyway, we just want to party, not start any shit. You know? Hey, have you ever tagged anything else?"

"I use to tag Fear."

"Fear and Tear. Isn't it like the same?"

"Everyone keeps saying that," looking away. "No one gets it."

"Gets what?" frowning. "I bet you they both look the same when you tag them."

"It's more than how things look that matter. Because two things look the same doesn't mean they're the same, are they?" Raphael waved hello.

I looked over to see what was drawing his attention. Students were beginning to converge in the hallway. I had come early, around seven, hoping to get a head start on tomorrow's homework. But now everyone was already here. I would just have to do my work at lunchtime, I told myself.

"Don't you think it's bad how the meaning of a word can change," continued Raphael, "when you replace one letter with another?"

"Yep. That shit's out there, bro'. Fuck, I use to think about shit like that all the time, bro'. Especially when I was real little." I looked down at the ground. "I still kinda do. Check it out, I remember I use to play this game outside. My mom use to think I was nuts," shaking my head. "Anyway, I would throw a penny behind me and believe I was the penny, floating and spinning in the air all crazy and shit. I thought where I would be if I was that penny. And then I closed my eyes, turned around, and walked until I thought I was there. When I reached down and opened my eyes, I found the penny exactly where I thought it would be. Cool, huh?"

"That's fucking bad."

"Yeah," shrugging my shoulders, "but I kind of stopped doing stuff like that because people kept making fun of me."

"I know what you're saying. But you shouldn't of stopped. The reason I changed Fear to Tear is because of the way people use to make me feel and how they make me feel now. Before I was scared, but now I'm not. I think I'm more sad than anything else. The closest thing I think of when I think about being sad is the tears that fall from someone's eyes. That's why I tag Tear. It lets people know what I'm about. I don't care if anyone disses it. It's my tag."

"Damn, dog, that's deep."

"I've been through a lot. You know?"

"Yeah. I just don't let things get to me no more. Whenever I feel like shit or think I have a problem, I just think of the people in this world who have it really fucking bad. I mean, look at the shit that happened to those people in World War II. They got killed nasty by that one dude Hitler. I even saw on some television show that their bones were made into soap. Crazy. And those motherfuckers who let it happen were pussy bitches too. Man, I know I have it way better. I'm not saying I have it easy, but I know my life is pretty cool so far. Fuck, at least I'm still alive. I mean, they use to make fun of me in first grade because I use to want to hug everybody—even the boys. I'm not gay or anything, bro'. I just . . . I don't know . . . I guess I really use to feel like this love was all around me. Weird, huh? Even the teachers thought I was strange. It wasn't my imagination either, bro'. You could feel it a mile away when someone thinks about you in that way. At least I can."

"So what did you do?"

"Well, one day I just decided to change."

"Just like that?"

"Yeah," snapping my fingers, "like that."

"How?"

"Well," looking him in the eye, "at first—don't tell anyone else in school—but when I was around twelve, I tried something stupid, like killing myself."

"Damn. Why?"

"I didn't think anybody cared. I still kinda don't. Even my dad stopped hanging out with me and my brothers after a while."

"He's still with you?"

"Oh yeah, he lives with us, but sometimes I feel like it's better if he left. They're always arguing about how where we're at right now is way too small for all of us. I guess people need space or something. I don't know why. It's all in your head anyway."

"So that's why you tried killing yourself?"

"Naw, we were still at our real house when that happened. Like I told you, I had a lot of problems with the people at my old school and in my neighborhood. And there was all the arguing between my parents. Man, it's like everyone's always arguing," I mumbled. "I guess I got real shitty from all of it."

"How'd you try to do it?"

"One night. Right before I went to sleep. I took a whole bottle of some aspirins, some cleaning stuff, and some other shit my mom had in the cabinet to clean stuff with."

"And nothing happened?"

"I guess not," chuckling. "I'm still here."

Tear stood still.

"Actually," continuing in a lower tone, "I barely got any sleep because of some thunderstorm that was going on outside that night. I know for sure in the morning I had a nasty-ass stomachache. I think I threw up only once."

"You're lucky you're still alive."

"I know. But what was really strange was when I took all that stuff, bro'. Man, I saw the weirdest fucking shit. It happened right after I finished praying about a hundred Hail Marys. It was like something began talking to me and telling me that everything was going to be cool in my life. That a lot of shit was going to happen to me later on but that nothing was going to really hurt me anymore. It's like as if God looked down at me and said that my ass was gonna stay down here for a reason. I wish the fucker would've told me what that reason was. Fuck!" I went for my scalp, digging deep into it. "How come I always have to figure shit out on my own? Fuck, it all looked so real, bro'! I'm not bullshitting you. I use to see a whole bunch of shit like that when I was small."

"I believe you."

"Thanks." I grabbed his shoulder. "After that, I promised myself in the morning when it was over that I would never let anybody get me down again. That I'd be happy no matter what. I guess I'm the same still, kind of, but not really. Sort of like you changing from Fear to Tear. So then I guess people stop doing their shit no matter what. Kind of."

Raphael smiled. "How come you're telling me all of this?"

"You seem cool, bro'. Anyway, you told me about your shit. Now we're even . . . Come on, it's getting late. Let's go hang out by the cafeteria. You can tell me why you want to be UPC."

"Is it hard to be a UPC?" Tear and I glided down the stairs toward the lunchroom.

"Naw," holding the door for him. "It depends. I mean, the first thing you need to do is find someone that'll get you in. Like my friend Rudy, he's the one that got me and my brother in."

"So then you can get me in?"

"Yeah, maybe. But you still have to hang out with us a lot before that happens. That's so we can make sure no one's got a problem with you. We also want to see you're not some wannabe who only wants a jacket."

"That's simple. I can do that."

"It's not that easy. We go out a lot. We even have daytimes during the school year. You think you can hang?"

"I hope so. But what happens after I do all that?"

"We vote on letting you in or not at one of our meetings."

"You have meetings?"

"Now we do. Especially since we're starting to get bigger."

"And if I do get in, do I get a 'v-in' as my initiation?"

"A what?"

"You know," Tear said, "Get beat up?"

"Fuck, no! I keep telling you, Tear, we ain't like other crews and we're not a gang either. That 'v-in' stuff doesn't make sense anyway. Beating up on your friends to see if they hang. It's all these new crews that are starting to do that stupid shit. What the fuck is that all about?"

"S-s-s-sorry, I was just checking . . . So how does it feel to be a UPC?"

"It's bad, bro'. You meet a shitload of cool people. Throw a lot of fucking house parties. You know . . . Do shit like that."

"How many UPCs are there?"

"Around thirty. I don't think we're going to let any more guys in for a while. We decided we don't want to grow too fast even though there's a lot of motherfuckers who want to join. Have you ever heard of that party crew called After Hours?"

"I think so."

"Well, there's about sixty of those motherfuckers waiting to turn UPC."

"Are you going to let them in?"

"In their dreams! That'll cause too much static for us."

"Why?"

"'Cause. Their crew has a mix of girls and boys. I mean, we don't have anything against girls, but if we become a mixed group, everything will get fucked up sooner or later."

"How come? I don't see anything wrong with it."

"Look, check it out, Tear. Let's imagine you're going out with someone and she, your lady, becomes UPC. One day you guys aren't straight anymore and you two decide to break up. What happens then? How are you going to have two people who can't stand each other in the same group? You know how it is when you break up with your lady. Anyway, we started out with just our boys and we don't even know these people. We'll see what happens. Maybe it'll change."

"So when did you turn UPC?"

"Right after I graduated from grammar school. There was only like thirteen or fifteen of them then. I'm the youngest one right now. We don't really have leaders but one of our main guys is this guy Dave. He ain't Mexican. He's got blond hair and blue eyes."

"So, I've seen Mexicans with blond hair and blue eyes."

"Oh, yeah, I know," arriving at the cafeteria, "but I know for sure Dave's not all Mexican. He doesn't even speak Spanish. He's half-Polish or something. I don't think he even wants to be leader, but everybody keeps gripping to him. All I know is that that motherfucker's got a billion ladies after his ass and that he's real cool. He's not stuck up or anything. He's real quiet and doesn't like pick sides."

"People keep saying how you guys are straight and don't have gangs backing your shit up."

"That's what a party crew's suppose to be," I quipped. "I guess a couple of crews don't know what it's all about. Like I hear some of the Latin Image are starting to chill with some of the D's from Pilsen. I guess it's because they live super close to each other. Still, I'm happy that shit hasn't happened to us, even though most of the UPCs live right where there's a lot of gangbangers too."

"I know, it's fucked-up."

"No shit," yawning. "It sucks."

"I live in Pilsen too."

"Pretty messed up, isn't it?"

"Especially in the summer."

"I know. I see those gangbangers on the corners all the time when we go out at night to parties just chillin'. Man, they think they're bad and then when it gets cold they're gone. We went to a house party that got raided once and outside the D's started throwing all these bottles at the cops. Man, five-o left right away. I bet they thought it was us. Me and some of my boys were walking down the street and all these bottles were flying over our heads. Man, it looked fucking bad. Like a waterfall."

Tear took a seat at one of the lunch tables. "Yeah, even though there's a police station half a block away from my house, they're always shooting around my block."

"Why, bro'? Who's around your crib?"

"There's a bunch of D's near my house."

"Pilsen is mostly D's, then?"

"And Counts. And Bishops. And Ambros. La Raza. Two-Ones. Everything."

"D's wear black and blue, right?"

"Around Pilsen they do. The problem is there's a guy who lives at the end of my block and his cousins are Kings. And whenever his cousins show up from 26th Street, they get into fights with the D's."

"You know, I don't understand how that shit works. I guess it's because I lived mostly in McKinley Park and every time I go to Pilsen I don't see it too much. I mean, they'll say 'what's up' to me just because they always see me hanging out with the boys. I think they know we're not like that."

Tear nodded. "So there's not too many gangbangers over where you live?"

"Not right now. There use to be a couple of gangs, like the POPES. But all those pussy motherfuckers are history now. I'm worried because some punk ass bitches are starting to come in. Little by little you hear some shit happening. Man, it's like they don't have anything better to do. It's weird."

"What?"

"How things go up and down all the time."

The morning bell rang and the students began to rush out of the cafeteria into the baby-blue hallway. I dropped my imitation black-leather bag on the floor and, kneeling on one leg, began opening its side pocket.

"Look, bro'," pulling a two-faced flier out of my schoolbag. "You want to hang with us? Well then, come out to this party this Friday. It's at Highlander's. The hall. Go. Next time we have a meeting I'll tell my boy Rudy about you."

Tear took the flier in his hand and began whispering to himself the list of dj's and performers who were going to attend.

"That dj from BMX is going to be there. Bad Boy Bill. He mixes good. But you gotta keep coming out with us every time, Tear. Or else they're going to think you're some little kid. I don't think they'll have problems with you, especially since you live close to everyone's cribs. Do you mix or battle?"

Tear looked away from the flier. "No, why?"

"Well, some of the UPCs mix and some dance at the parties. I could always tell them that you do something. That'd be better for you."

"What do you do?"

"I don't mix at parties, bro', but I'm going to buy my equipment soon. I'm buying a lot of records right now. Whenever we go out, I kinda battle. I dance all right, I guess. Some of my boys make fun of me, but they're the ones who hold up the walls anyway. I meet a lot of girls. I think they like it when you act crazy and shit. Me, I just like to party."

"What's your favorite kind of music?"

"Everything. I listen to house, high energy, new wave, rock, oldies. Whatever's bad, bro'. I don't like sticking to one kind. You're into mostly new wave?"

"How do you know?"

"Man, bro'," staring up and down at him, "look at how you're dressed."

He was wearing light tan, loose-fitting corduroys, a black pair of Doc Marten shoes, and a silky cream-white shirt. His pale white complexion added to his industrial look, giving him a ghost-like appearance.

"What? Does it look bad?"

"Naw, it's straight. I'm going to buy stuff like that later on but first I have to get my tables."

"What kind are you getting?"

"The turntables I want are the ones they use at clubs and parties. The mixer I'll get from the flea market because I don't have enough money."

"And speakers?"

"Aw, I'll probably use my dad's little radio. It jams."

"Damn. Still. All that is gonna c-c-cost you a lot. Are your parents going to buy them for you?"

"Shit, you wish. I work, bro'."

"Where?"

"At a church. Right now I'm looking for another job so I can pay for the tables and still buy records. I need to get a job on the weekends at night so I can play sports and keep working at the rectory. Right now I'm in soccer, but it's almost finished. I might join track. I think my little brother is going to pay for one of the turntables. I don't know where he's getting the money from, but he's getting it. Look, bro', I gotta go before the next bell rings. If you go," pointing to the flier, "we'll hook up there. Why don't you give me your number anyway?"

He started looking for paper when the final warning bell sounded.

"Here," taking out the book where he had originally tagged the name Tear, "put it next to your shit."

"Thanks," squiggling his telephone number rapidly. "So should I call you Luis, Priest, or Demon?"

"It don't matter to me. Just don't go around school dissing me."

"Okay. I'll see you at the party, Demon. I promise I'll go."

"We'll see. Have fun at homeroom," walking away. "Pay attention! You might learn something new today."

"Is that suppose to be good?"

"Sometimes it's cool. Sometimes it ain't." I placed a finger on my temple. "Shit can stay in your head forever, you know?"

Midnight. A quarter of a block away from home. Most of the city sounds had collapsed now. I saw a figure buried in darkness on our porch, away from lazy eyes.

An orange-red firefly emerged in front of this person, hovering for about three seconds and then dipping into obscurity. After two more appearances, it was hurled into the air, landing on the sidewalk below.

When I reached the steps, I crouched down, inspecting the now lifeless cigarette butt. I looked up from my stance. At him.

With knees bent upwards and arms resting against his sides, he had his back planted against a narrow wall that divided two doors, one to his left and one to his right. He reminded me of the stone Chac-Mool I saw in Mexico City.

He too was serene. Dreaming his memories. Many times I overheard him say how trapped he felt indoors. Tonight, as before, he would resolve to stay out here for as long as he could. As if time were the answer to life's dilemma.

Another cigarette was lit.

He sighed. A haze of cigarette smoke passed through his nostrils.

"Hey, dad."

A mild grunt.

I set my bag down on the sidewalk and began to practice a dance move I recently learned. A crowd had gathered around another boy and myself at the last party I had gone to. The cheers felt good. Next time I wanted to improve.

"O pues, cálmate."

I calmed down. Didn't I have enough with the weekends? he asked. I answered no and sat on the bottom steps.

So why was I out so late?

Work.

Why didn't I go in and sleep?

I wasn't tired.

Why did I go to parties?

To have fun. To get away.

Isn't that what you do, I thought, listening to his questions. Leave? Aren't you the one who says we aren't boys anymore? How at our age you were doing this and that? Why have you grown tired here? Of us?

"Dad . . . nothing."

What about the times when we worked with you in the basement until two or three in the morning? Helping you dismantle, cut, sew, stretch, staple away. Didn't that count? Why couldn't you just deal with the changes that came? Why are you so stubborn? If this is what it means to be a man, then I don't want to be a man.

I went in, without realizing my own faults.

After washing, I went to bed, remembering my recent trip to Mexico, to the Pyramid of the Sun.

That rich climb to the top. I saw others only make it halfway. I wondered about them. Were they just lazy? So why did they come in the first place?

Even those who had made it shouted to their family and friends below that there was nothing up high. No impressive magnificent structures, they said. No ornaments of gold nor anything else of that nature.

With that, some stopped and made their way back down. What was wrong with all of them? Wasn't this wonderful view worth the struggle?

I draped the blanket over my head.

Father Tom's drink was bringing me to a steady halt, barring me from piecing things together.

16

Juggler?" whispering to myself. "You think I'm a juggler, Carlos? That's one thing. I know that."

On the opposite side of the school corridor the six-thirty sun came at me through a set of large windows. Rows of yellow lockers, on both sides of the hall, moved the gold along. A warmth pressed against my bare skin.

I finished gathering my books and sat against the front of my locker, stretching my long thin legs toward a shaded part of the floor.

"Wow!" watching a yellow ball burst orange-red. "Good-bye, Sun," waving a hand, "I'll see you tomorrow . . . I know you can heeear meee . . . I can hear youuu-oooooh."

Two silhouettes approached from the other side of the hallway. Their cleats dangled around their necks. Without my glasses, it was hard to discern them.

"Hey, Ziggy!" partially recognizing one of them. "Which bus are you taking?"

"I'm taking the Western bus, Lou! What about you?"

"Me too! Are you almost ready?"

"Uh," shoving his soccer shoes into his sports bag, "yeah. But I'm not going to take a shower here, Lou. I'll wait 'til I get home. How 'bout you?"

"I need to get to work, Zig. I can't take a shower. Things like that aren't even an option."

"Geez, Lou," opening his locker. "What time do you work anyway?"

"I start at seven-thirty and go until ten."

"You think you'll make it?"

"I can't think. I have to."

"You do this every day?"

"Naw. Only Mondays, Wednesdays, Fridays, and Saturdays. Or whenever Father wants me to go in."

"Oh, that's right. You work at that church. What do you do there? Sit on your ass answering telephones?"

"Sometimes. But I clean the church on Saturdays."

"Shit, dude, when do you get to do your homework if you have to go to practice and work?"

"I do it on the bus or sometimes at work when I have time. Usually I do it really quick here in the morning. Homework's not hard anyway."

"That's 'cause you don't have any honors classes."

"No. I don't know why I didn't get any this year. My grades were really good in grammar school. I mean, the only bad grades I ever got were in first and second grade. After that I only had A's and B's. And I did pretty well on all the exams I took."

"Face it, Lou. Its because you're Mexican."

"Shut up, you . . . you stoner."

"Or maybe you didn't suck some priest's dick before you got in here."

"Shut the fuck up!" I smirked. "I bet you sucked someone's dick."

"No, Lou. I bent over and let the fucker in. That's the real ticket in getting what you want."

"You're such a fucking dork!"

"I'm just kidding. Anyway, you know we're all dorks here, Lou. What do they call us?"

"Quigley queers," I grabbed my bag and stood up.

"Even Don's a dork, Lou. Right, Don?"

"Sure, Zig," sounding annoyed, "whatever you say."

"Come on, Lou," Ziggy walked over to me. "Let's get out of here before our asses get tight like Don's."

"Mike!" Don whined loudly. "You're so immature."

"Geez," Ziggy turned in Don's direction. "I was only fooling around, Don. Don't get worked up over nothing! You don't see Lou having a cow when I mess with him."

"Is he all right?" Ziggy came over to where I was.

"Who cares? You know how much of a baby Don is, Lou. He's on his rag today or something. Come on, let's split."

We headed for the first-floor lobby. Two students were standing near the school's front glass doors, seeming to contemplate whether or not to leave. Kazlowski was one of them.

"So the little pussy freshmen are going home now," he said.

"Kazlowski," Ziggy said, "you walking marshmallow. Why don't you pick on someone your own size? Like a cow or something? I hear they give them the same shit you use."

"Hey, Ziegler," Kazlowski responded. "I think that garbage can over there is big enough for you! Why don't you be a good nerd and get in it? I mean it!"

"Ziggy," I whispered, "you know you don't have to get in."

"Are you kidding, Lou? If he tells you to do anything, Lou, you better do it."

"Fuck that."

"Okay, Lou," moving away from me. "Do what you want, but I'm getting in it before he starts getting pissy."

Ziggy jumped into an aluminum can.

"How about you, freshman?"

"I'm not playing, man."

"You look like you can fit in there with Mike."

"I'm not Mike."

"You look scared, freshman. What's the matter? You scared because you don't have your brazier friends here?"

"I'm not scared. I mean, even if you're two times bigger than me, I'm not gonna do what you want me to do! You're gonna have to fight me . . . Just remember, since this isn't fair, I won't be fair either next time."

"I don't know who the fuck you think you are, freshman, but you better watch what you say."

"Man, you better watch what you do!"

"I think he thinks we're serious," said his companion.

"I am serious," said Kazlowski. "I'm not going to let some

skinny ass spic talk shit to me. You should have heard him in the lunchroom a few weeks ago. He thought he was all tough. Someone has to put him in his place."

My place? Biting down hard.

"Leave him alone," his friend said. "He looks like he'll tell on us. How about getting him at the end of the year? That way, Mr. Greely won't suspend you or anything and you'll get what you want . . ."

". . . You better watch your back, you piece of shit."

They walked out.

"Lou," Ziggy climbed out, "I think he really wants to get you. What did you do to him before?"

"Nothing. I never did anything to him."

"I don't know, Lou. Are you sure you didn't say anything to him?"

"Naw," watching them get into their cars. "Supposedly I took away his seat. Big fucking deal. I don't know why people act like that. Like everything's theirs. I guess some people don't know when to grow up."

"You should talk, Lou. You're like that sometimes."

"Yeah, but that's only to people who are jerks."

"Well, you picked a big guy to fight with this time. I hope things don't get worse for you."

"They won't. For some weird reason, bro', things always kind of work out for me."

"Okay, 'bro'," Ziggy mocked.

"Shut up, Zig. You know what I mean."

"Lou, you're crazy."

"I'm only crazy when people are mean to me," opening the glass door. "Isn't that how come a lot of people get mad?"

"I don't know, Lou. I just play soccer."

"So how's Quigley?"

"Cool, Padre," shaking the rain-soaked UPC jacket.

"You seem depressed. Sure everything's fine?"

"I'm straight."

"Of course you are." He stepped away from me and went over to a window. "Weather's starting to get pretty horrible out there?"

"I like it."

"You would . . . Louie, why don't you have an umbrella?"

"'Cause I don't need one."

"Not when you're singing in the rain?"

"Yep," smiling, "just like in the movie."

The priest turned away from the window, looking comfortable in his jogging pants and Mets jersey. "What's wrong? I've never seen you this depressed. Everything going well at school and home?"

"Ah, it's okay."

A flashing light came. The lights dimmed.

"I don't know," going over to the room next door, "something happened at school but I really don't want to talk about it."

I turned on the fluorescent light and sat behind Frida's desk. "Father?"

"Yes, Louie."

"How come people are such assholes?"

"Pardon?"

He walked in.

"How come people bother people for no reason?"

"I don't know, Louie . . . Why? Are the shines giving you problems over there?"

"The who?"

"You know. The niggers. I hear there's a lot of them in Quigley nowadays."

I frowned. "Father, why do you use that word?"

"Oh, I'm sorry. Does it offend you?"

"Yeah. A lot. It's like you calling me a spic."

"I didn't mean anything wrong by it. If you want, I'll stop using it around you."

"That's not it," I protested. "Man, it's not just about not saying it!"

"I don't know why people are the way they are, Louie. Maybe they're having a bad day. You don't know. Lots of things can be going on in someone's head."

"Yeah, but I don't act like an asshole when I'm having a bad day. I get moody, but I don't hurt people. Why should people be such dicks like that?"

"What are you going to do about it, Louie? Fight everyone who doesn't agree with you? It doesn't work that way, dude. Believe me.

Sooner or later you'll burn yourself out. For what? For a bunch of idiots?"

"I don't think I'll burn out. If I believe in something so much, how can I?"

"Happens all the time."

"So what am I suppose to do? Ignore everybody?"

"Do whatever it is you feel is right. Just be aware that some people aren't going to accept your stand on certain issues. Sooner or later you're going to have to decide what you can and can't show to people. Dude, this world's all about being the perfect magician and performing illusions. You're going to have to learn how to tune things out."

"But it's like I can't," bowing my head and rubbing my eyes. "I guess I think about things too much."

Father Tom moved in. "Listen, Louie, I've been around long enough to know people will always be at odds with one another for the stupidest of things. The more you fight them, the more they want to fight you. Ignore them. So long as they're not taking away from your life and family, who cares?"

"I don't know," resting my head. "You know how you learn in biology how one disease affects other parts of the body? That's the way I sometimes think of things. I mean, my parents are having problems but it's not just affecting them. It's doing something to me and my brothers. I feel it. I don't know how to explain it. But I know it's bad. Ignoring stuff doesn't help with anything. I already tried."

"Louie," becoming impatient. "What do you want? To never again indulge in a peaceful moment?"

"It's better than lying to myself," moving my chin on top of my arm.

My eyes roamed through the surroundings. I daydreamed I was smaller than the items on the desk. That way I could hide and listen to people, know who was nice and who wasn't. Who my real friends were.

"You're still young, dude. You've had so many things happen to you in the past two years. Don't get me wrong; you have an edge on your peers. Use it to your advantage. Don't be foolish and waste it by fighting a corrupt system that'll always be there. Go with it. Stop ramming into walls. You have no time to be thinking about such trivial matters. Play your cards right and you'll get whatever you want."

"If that means I have to go along with bad things, then I won't do it. That's not who I am."

"You're too young to know who you are. I'm thirty-something and I still don't know who I am. Don't let silly little arguments of what's right and what's wrong distract you from reaching your goals. They're not worth it. Focus. Remember to get what's yours. Be tactful."

"I hate that!"

"What?"

"Tact. They don't teach it where I come from, Father."

"Oh and where is that?" The priest skimmed through his mailbox. "The planet Mars?"

"Maybe."

"Louie, stop being so silly."

"I'm just being who I am," wanting to tell him what I felt, what all my beliefs were. But I wouldn't.

I was too disappointed to see someone shut themselves off the way he did. To think that there was only one way to think. So easy. It was the way he saw the world that came between us, I felt. He would only ridicule me if I explained it to him. He would never believe there was any other way but his own. I was hoping he'd be different.

"Father?"

"Yes, Louie."

His voice softened, knowing I was changing the subject.

"Would it be okay if we had our meetings here?"

"You mean your UPC friends?"

"Yeah," sitting up in the chair and looking right at him. "Can we use the basement downstairs? I promise we won't mess it up."

"Go ahead," pointing a finger in my direction. "But you understand if something goes wrong, I'm holding you accountable."

"I know. Another thing?"

"For Christ's sake, dude! What am I, your father? What?"

"Me and my little brother want to buy a pair of turntables so we can learn how to mix. When I went to the store that sells them the other day I found out they're eight-hundred dollars for two."

"That's a hefty price for toys."

"Yeah, they said we can make monthly payments on them but that I need someone to sign for me."

"You mean," seeming horrified, "you need a cosigner and you want me."

"Uh-huh. I wanted to ask Mom or Dad, but I don't think they'll say yes. They'll probably say it's a waste of money."

"It sounds to me like it is. By the way, how's that business going?"

"My father? I don't know about him. My mother wants to get a job at a factory but my father doesn't want her to. He's too old-fashioned and shit. He says the guys there will be hitting on her left and right. I don't see why he can't trust her. He knows we'd be better off if she got a job. Anyway, it's not like she needs to be home taking care of us anymore. She really needs to get out and do something else besides stay home. I don't see why Dad doesn't let her get a job."

"You have to understand they come with different perspectives on life, Louie. They don't know any better."

"Yeah, but it's not their fault they're here."

"You're not saying anything to them, are you?"

"Sometimes. You know how I am.'

"Louie," he moaned. "How many times have I told you? You can't get too involved in their discussions. Let them work things out on their own. You stick to school and don't mess around with the counseling business. Or is school and work not enough for you anymore?"

"That's one of the reasons why I need the turntables. I want to do something else. I'm bored."

"Okay, I promise we'll go to the store. But is it really necessary to get *two* turntables?"

"Why am I gonna have just one? That's not the way it works."

"All right. I don't have time to argue about frivolous things with you. Now get back to doing your homework. I don't want to hear your mother blaming me for corrupting you."

"I'm already corrupt."

"I wouldn't doubt it, the way I take care of you. By the way, take out the dog before you leave. Run him around a bit. He hasn't been out all day."

"Sure."

"And remember to turn off the lights. I had to come down-stairs last night to turn them off."

"Sorry."

"Goodnight, Louie. I don't wish to be disturbed. If there are any calls, check with me first before sending them."

"Right."

"And quit answering my private line."

"I'm just playing."

"Well, I really don't find you impersonating me amusing."

"Aw, you don't like me being you, Father?" I teased.

"No. Now don't forget about the dog."

"No way, I love him too much."

"I can see. The way you caress him is enough to make me jealous."

"Goodnight, Father."

"Goodnight."

17

*Y*ou work now?" staring at his soup.

He was fishing at it with his spoon, as if he were trying to find some imperfection in the cook's work.

"Yes. All the time. We use to have a house and my mom would tell us to cut the grass and we would do it. I even got down on my knees with these big scissors and cut the edges of the grass. Right now I'm working at . . ."

The woman behind the cashier register had sent me to him. She had said he was the manager and in charge of hiring.

"That's okay," looking cross, "you work. What I want to know is, have you worked in restaurant? Some type of business that handles public?"

"The church. A lot of people go to church."

He kept quiet, glaring at the bowl below. I noticed a few streaks of gray hair amid his perfectly cemented black hair. Wrinkles crossed his forehead. I glanced out through the tinted window next to the booth, watching the multitude of cars lined in the diner's parking lot.

"How old are you?"

"Sixteen."

He jerked his head. "You sure?"

"Yes," lying, "I'm sure."

"Sit down. Hungry? You want something to eat?"

"Yes, please."

"I'll have Mary order you something. Is chicken and rice fine with you?"

"I eat it at home all the time," taking a seat across from him. I grabbed a napkin and wiped my glasses. I still couldn't understand why I had chosen these golden frames, and with a brown tint, no less.

"Are you illegal?" hailing for the waitress. "You know I get into trouble if you are illegal."

Because of his thick accent, I assumed he hadn't been born here in the United States.

"I'm not illegal. I use to be."

He kept quiet. The waitress arrived.

"Something else, Mr. Kolopanas?"

"Chicken and rice, Mary. And tell Pedro not to send it cold this time."

"What would you like to drink?" turning to me.

"Water."

"Trying to get a head start on keeping fit, hon'?"

I grinned.

"So, you want to work here?" Mr. Kolopanas waved her off. "I can only hire you as busboy. You have no skills! Can't cook. Too young to work tables or be cashier."

"That's okay, Mr. Kolopanas. I need the money."

"Why?"

"It costs money to get things."

"Of course. But what about other job you say you have? Eh? The one at church?"

"It's not enough for what I need."

"Your parents?"

"I don't want to ask them for anything anymore. I want to start standing on my own."

He gave a quirky smile. "Big words for something small like you. You like to work?"

"My parents taught me how to work. That's why we're here."

"Let me just say this. Being busboy is hard. You can work Saturdays and Sundays and do the other job too? There's no sitting around," waving his arms. "No playing."

"I don't play when I work. I play when it's time to play."

"Do you steal?"

"No! I'm Catholic."

"Okay," smiling, "then we see how good you are. You own pair of brown pants?"

"No."

"Black?"

"Yes."

"Good. Come over tomorrow afternoon, around three when less busy, and I have a yellow shirt for you. Don't be late or you never work here again. Understand?"

"Yes. Thank you very much. Do you need to see my permanent resident card? We just got them. I can bring it to you. My mom keeps it for me at home."

"No, no, no. I'll pay you in cash. I'll show you your responsibilities tomorrow."

After dinner, I thanked him once again and rose up from the booth. I held out my right hand to him and waited. He didn't seem to notice. When he finally took it, he shook it aggressively.

Outside, I remembered I had forgotten to ask him how much I was going to get paid. I wasn't too worried, though. The place appeared busy enough. If they made good money, I thought, they would take good care of me.

The walk home was pleasant. I felt the strange sensation that all movement was proceeding at my pace. Life would not be the same for me anymore, I thought. The independence I was always talking about to my mother was near.

I noticed a red and white sticker pasted on the side of a rusting metal fence. A costumed figure with a hood over his head was sitting atop a horse. The rider displayed a tight grip on the horse's ropes. The horse, drawn with tight angular lines, seemed ready to buckle out of control.

I took a closer look at the set of words underneath horse and rider.

Save Our Neighborhood
The Meeting For The First Saturday Of This Month Will Take
Place At The A.L.
MEMBERS ONLY

Nothing else. No phone number. No address. I turned away, confused, trying to decipher the content of that peculiar advertisement. Somewhere, in some book, I had seen something quite similar.

When I arrived at the apartment I told my mother about the new job. Her first look was of surprise. And then it turned into bewilderment. Finally, inquisitive delight.

She hurled questions. she mentioned how uncomfortable she felt with me working two jobs and going to school. She also worried because I hadn't asked how much I would be earning. But in the end she was happy for me. She said that meeting new people was what I needed to bring me out of my recent slump of boredom.

"Ojalá que ahora aprendas a ser un poco más responsable," she added. "Ya que no vas a tener el tiempo para estar jugando."

"Mom!" heading for the bathroom. "Siempre soy responsible. Always! I never liked to play anyway!"

"*Sure,*" she said.

"Yeah!" turning the faucet on. "Remember? Dad would take us to the store to buy toys? The only thing I got was those little soldiers. The green soldados, Ma! That's the only thing I ever wanted! Remember? Israel and Jose wanted the bigger toys. Especially Jose."

I walked out of the bathroom and looked at the clock on the kitchen wall. I had less than half an hour before my shift at church.

"Ma," sitting next to her, "I saw something funny today."

"Qué vistes?"

I described to her the sticker.

Don't pay any attention, she told me. It's something very bad. She said nothing more about it.

"Usted no mas se concentra en su nuevo trabajo y su escuela."

"Aw, Ma," I groaned. "You know I'm always going to be good at concentrating in school. It's easy."

"Camarón que se duerme," she said, "se lo lleva la corriente."

"First, I'm not a shrimp. Second, I'm not going to sleep and let some water drag me into the ocean. And, third, all this weird stuff you say is just stuff you got from Mexico. We live here in the USA . . . Nothing's ever going to happen to me, Ma, 'cause I'm bad."

18

Raphael was helping me cover the windows of the basement apartment with brown plastic bags. We didn't want any of the strobe light attracting attention.

"Don't worry, Tear, I'll take care of the place like it's my own."

"You don't think the cops will raid the party tonight?"

"Naw, the narcs won't bust it. One of the dj's mixing tonight is a Guess Boy. His uncle's a big-time narc at a police station around the block."

"What if people mess the place up?"

"What are they gonna fuck up? There's no furniture. The only thing is the floor and the walls. Besides, all the boys are going to be here. Chill. I promised your mom everything was going to be straight. I just hope people show up."

"You think a lot of people will come?"

"I don't know, bro'," tearing a piece of duct tape. "We invited the Chiefs, the Exotic Ladies, Sweet Sensation, After Hours, Guess Boys, and a shitload of other people. I think someone even invited some of the Two-Ones. And they're at war with us!"

"You think they'll come?"

"Nah."

"Demon, where are we going to put the keg?"

I looked around the living room and marched directly to the bathroom. "We'll put it in the tub. We can throw ice in there. That way it'll stay cold . . . Actually, I don't want any motherfucker going into the alley and taking a piss out there. I guess we can put it in the front room, in a garbage can or something."

"What time are they coming to set up the equipment?"

"They're coming at six or seven. By the way, Tear, do you have an extra cassette tape at your crib?"

"Why?"

"'Cause. I want to record this party. This shit is going to be bad and when I grow up I want my kids to know the kind of shit I use to do."

"That's fucking cool. I'll make sure to get some by tonight. Make me a copy?"

"Of course, bro'. Anything for one of my boys."

"So who's collecting money?"

"Rudy and Jose. No one's going to mess with them. Is that cool?"

"Yeah," Tear said quietly.

"Man, Tear. If you're so worried, we can always call it off. I don't want you to jinx this shit."

"I know. I already told you I would do it. I need the money anyway. Besides what are the boys going to say if we call it off? They might not let me in."

"Don't worry about that, bro'. We'll find another place to party. It's not like we can't go by the lake and hang out over there. We can also go over by the Whiteroads, by the factories and throw the football around."

Tear rubbed the back of his neck. "I-I-I'm just nervous because this is my first house party."

"Me too."

"Really?"

"Yeah, bro'. I don't want them to think I don't contribute. You know? You and me, we have a lot to prove because we're younger than them. Hopefully, tonight we'll do that."

"I hope so, Demon."

"Chill, bro'. This shit is gonna be dope."

I found him watching television.

"What time you wanna head out, Carlos?"

"Don't worry about me, Lou," he scratched his head. "If I go, I'll probably go later on with your brother Iz."

"You sure?"

From a mound on his living-room floor, he picked up a fresh glossy comic book. "Yep," he answered, turning onto his stomach.

As he held it in his hands, I thought about the cover and all the others like it. They were flamboyant pieces rendered with intricate detail and fluid imagination. Yet the stories themselves, I felt, lacked substance.

This imbalance was upsetting. I felt cheated, especially since issues that used to cost fifty cents were now nearing the two-dollar range. But we both continued to search for the precious stories that made it worthwhile.

There were days when we would sift through waste for hours at a time. But now it was more Carlos than I that collected. There wasn't enough time for this activity and for the other things I wanted to do.

"Lou," Carlos seemed mesmerized by the colors on the cover, "you go have a good time with your boys."

I thought of a favorite comic, titled *Lone Wolf and Cub*. It told the story of a masterless samurai and his young son. This ronin, a supposed outcast, was faithful to his honor, his word. From the little I knew of him, he also seemed an individual with many questions. This led me to believe that he was wise.

In one issue he asked himself whether it is possible to become one with Mu. Nothingness. I sensed that it was an important question to ask. I wondered what would lead one to ask such a question. What were the catalysts in life?

The story itself, unlike the full-color prints of other comics, was presented in black ink on white paper. What troubled me when I read it was feeling that something had been lost in its translation from Japanese. The English words, at times, didn't seem to flow with the scenes quite right. Hmmm, I too had felt that way sometimes with English and Spanish.

He turned to me. "If you see a beautiful girl, give her a kiss for me."

"My lady's gonna be there."

"Now who are you dating?"

"Oh, I'm seeing some girl I met at a party on 45th. You know what? I even invited Norma."

"I thought that was dead?"

"I keep telling her I made a mistake," stepping over the heap of comics. "I guess I really fucked up. Man," plopping down on the sofa, "I still can't figure it out. Why did I ask her older sister out? She's like five years older than me!"

"Face it, Lou. You're never going to be satisfied."

"I hope I'm not like that when I'm older . . . Hey, I still don't see why you don't want to join UPC. Some even ask about you still. They say, 'where's your cousin Carlos? Is he coming?'"

"You're just saying that to see if I'll go."

"Naw, Rudy and his brother Luis ask about you all the time. Why am I gonna lie? Huh?"

He rolled on his back. "So how's it going with Father Tom?"

"Ahhh . . . You know how he is. You saw the way he treated us when we worked with him in the summer. He's so fucking mean."

"Tell me about it, Lou. Remember when he asked us to clean the gutters on the rectory because he said the rain wasn't going down right?"

"Yeah," snickering, "we didn't know where the fuck to start."

"No shit. All he said was to figure it out. I think that's his favorite line—'figure it out.'"

"Man, Carlos, he always says crap like that. I'm so use to it by now."

"Jesus, when we got on top of the roof I thought one of us was going to fall off."

"Fuck, yeah," remembering proudly, "but we did it."

"That and a million other things, Lou. And for what? Five dollars an hour? It's crazy. I'll never work for that man again."

"I know what you're saying, bro'. He doesn't have to yell at us like we're dogs either."

"I still don't understand how you can put up with him."

"Aw, he doesn't yell too much at me."

"That's 'cause you're his favorite, screwie Louie."

"Maybe . . . You know, he gave me two-hundred dollars to spend on the prom I went to with my ex-lady. I told him the other day, 'If you're straight with me, I'll be straight with you. If you're not, I'll find something that'll fuck you up ten times worse!'"

"Geesh, I'm surprised you're still working there."

"Fuck, why shouldn't I be? He knows I'm responsible. I mean, he even told me he's going to let me drive his car when I get my license. He's all right."

"I don't know, Lou. I didn't want to say anything because I know you and him get along pretty well, but there's something fucked-up about him. You know how your brother Jose is always doing something crazy. That guy's non-stop action. Well anyway, we sneaked into Father Tom's room the last time we were there and found all these porns in his closet right on top of his safe. There was six or seven tapes. A priest, Lou! A fucking priest!"

"Man, Carlos, I don't understand how people get excited over something that isn't real. I mean, a picture isn't the same as a real live person."

"Yep, it seemed pretty fake to me too."

"Yeah. Wouldn't you rather have a warm person next to you, holding you, giving you the real thing, instead of watching two people do it? I don't know, maybe we're just strange, Carlos. The only time I liked watching that stuff was when we were little and we would see Benny Hill at night. That show was fuckin' funny. And they always had these girls with big tits bending over and stuff. Man, I wonder if it did anything to our heads?"

"How about it."

Another roll and Carlos began to arrange the comic books in neat stacks.

"Come on, Carlos, you should come."

"You don't need me there, Lou. Your boys are going to be there."

"It's not the same. I need my radar."

He laughed. "Lou, I could never figure out why you don't think girls check you out. You and Jose. Remember that one married lady at the mall? Rose?"

"Yeah. She was beautiful."

"Right! You almost walked past her without giving her a smile. You big ninny."

"But I didn't," pointing a finger to him, "because of you. I thought you were pulling my leg when you said she was checking me out."

"No, Lou. Her eyes were right on you the whole time. Her sadness was absolutely, positively, unbearable. I'm telling you, she looked so lonely. But as soon as you walked by her, she let out this big fucking smile. I can't believe how much time we lost arguing about whether or not you should go up to her."

"I know," staring off. "If you hadn't called me all those shitty names, I don't think I would have done anything. And she wasn't just physically attractive either, Carlos. She was so fucking sweet."

"Tell that to her husband."

"Seriously. What a fucking idiot! I went to see her the next day, you know."

"I remember."

"She was so upset. After she finished work, she gave me a ride to the train station. We sat in the car for a while and talked about her husband and how he fights with her all the time. She showed me pictures of her two kids. I think she just needed someone to really listen to her. You know? Like that one lady I talked to in seventh grade by the park. The one that was crying like crazy."

"Tell me the truth. Why did you go to her?"

"'Cause, she was hurting. All she needed was someone to listen to her. I think that's what everyone needs. People look for all these great things and forget about the little shit, Carlos. About communicating and shit."

"Lou, did you get that from that Dianetics book you bought awhile back?"

"No," laughing. "I bought it, but I never even read it."

"It's too bad Rose was married," Carlos went back.

"I know. But I think my mom would've flipped if she had seen me with her. She told me she was twenty-nine. God, I hope my wife looks like that when she's twenty-nine!"

"No kidding. But you at least kissed her!"

"Yeah. And it wasn't one of those kinds of kisses where our mouths were open. It was just a kiss on the lips. But, man, it felt so unreal!" I cuddled over the armrest. "So much love in it. Poor baby . . . I just wanted to hold her all day and not say a word."

"See, Lou. Why don't you go out for someone like that?"

"I don't think I'm ready, Carlos. That kind of stuff is for people who want to get married. I'm still young."

"Tell me you wouldn't have married Rose if she had divorced that one dude and asked you to marry her?"

"Man, Carlos. You know I would've."

I got up from the sofa and went over to the window. A police siren sounded nearby.

"Come on, Carlos," turning around, "you have to go tonight. You know I'm throwing it with Tear, Jose, and Rudy."

"That's right . . . Okay, I'll go. Besides, it's not like I have anything else to do tonight. I'll see if your brother Iz wants to go . . . Hey, Lou, I want to ask you. Do you and Iz talk anymore?"

"Not really. I've been kind of busy."

"Well, he's always talking about how he misses the good old days. He's always saying about how we use to ride around when we were little on our bikes, checking out anything we could find. Maybe that's who you should get to join the UPCs."

"Nah, he's still too little. Maybe next year."

"But what if the UPCs aren't around then?"

"They're always going to be around. Forever, bro'."

"Right, Lou. That's what you think now."

"All right! All right! All right! I'm your host tonight, 'Cool' Dan of the Ultimate Party Crew. Up next! We have the youngest and freshest dj around! Only thirteen years old. Arthur 'The Applejack' from Chicago's Mystic Sounds and After Hours Crew!"

The dj placed two records on the turntables. The needle dropped. The static crackling of old vinyl came over the speakers.

"Well, I was listening to the radio, kinda half-asleep," said a man's voice.

"Yes, Mr. Willis. And what did you hear?" the would-be reporter asked.

"I heard a hissing sound . . . And bingo! Knocked me right out of the chair. Like this . . ."

A funky bass line and a flow of beats followed. I remained captivated, not by the music, but by the dj's cleverness. I had recognized Welles's "War of the Worlds." He had used the radio version as a beginning to his mix. I had heard it in the library.

"Hey, Tear, did you hear that dope ass beginning! That motherfucker's cold."

"I heard," frantically popping his head out the door. "Look, two narcs pulled up outside."

I walked past him. In contrast to the grimy stuffiness of the

195

house party, the night air was a relief. Behind me, I heard people talking loudly at the rear of the house. The boys, I thought, elbowing each other as usual.

"Are you the one throwing this party, son?" the officer at the front of the house asked Rudy. I remained in the shadows of the gangway, pretending to tie my shoes.

"Yes, officer. It's a birthday party for one of my boys."

"One of your boys? You don't look like the type mixed up in a gang."

"I'm not," Rudy replied. "It's for the UPCs . . . It's a party crew."

"I know who you are, son." He looked at his partner. "That's one of those party crews around here, Martinez. They're good kids. Don't really bother no one. Some of them just look a little bigger than the others. Right, son?"

"Yeah," Rudy answered shyly.

"Uh-huh. For some reason, I didn't think a gang would be stupid enough to hold a party a block away from the station. Son, do me a favor. Make sure you know who you're letting in. You don't want the wrong crowd in there. Things get ugly pretty quick."

"Thanks, officer. I'll make sure whoever's at the door knows that. Would you like a beer or something?"

"Not while I'm on duty," he laughed. "But I know that a young strong fellow like yourself doesn't drink. Or do you, son?"

"I just had one beer tonight. I drank it because it was my friend's birthday. That's all."

"Well maybe when you turn twenty-one, I'll take you up on that offer. How much liquor do you have in there anyway?"

"Just a keg. We wanted to keep it small."

The officer turned to his partner. "Come on, Martinez. Nothing's happening here tonight."

"Have a good night."

"Around this neighborhood? We'll be so lucky."

I headed toward Rudy. The officers sat in a blue-and-white patrol car. An unmarked Chevrolet Caprice stopped next to them. After a quick exchange, both cars left.

"What did they want, Rudy?"

"Nothin', Demon. They're just checking us out to make sure this wasn't a gang party. The one I was talking to was real cool."

"I know. I didn't come up because I thought they would say something about my age."

"Good, Demon," he sniffed at me. "Have you been drinking, bro'?"

"Yeah. Why?"

"'Cause I can smell your shit from a mile away. So how is it?"

"It's fucking bad. It's packed. We're almost running out of beer too."

"Fuck it, bro'. If people want more, they're going to have to go get it themselves. How's the tapper?"

"Cool. Remind me at the end of the night to get it because my friend Jesse wants it back by Monday."

"Did he show up?"

"Yeah. He's that guy with the heavy eyebrows who always combs his hair back perfectly. Why?"

"Isn't he a King?"

"I don't think he's a King, but him and his brother know a lot of them. Why? What's up?"

"You know the D's around here don't like Kings at all," he said. "I think him coming wasn't a good idea. They're always capping at them."

"How do you know?"

"'Cause I live here, bro'. Don't you know that People and Folks don't get along?"

"Sort of."

"Ah, poor Demon. Poor little Quigley boy."

"Seriously, Cubby. Tell me."

"Chill, cabrón, I'll tell you. Later. Let's go back in."

Halfway to the entrance of the basement apartment. "Luis!" Tear appeared to us in a frenzied state. "A fight! Stop them! They're going to fuck up my mom's place! Come on! Hurry!"

Rudy and I bolted into the apartment. They had turned off the music. I saw bodies pushed together, moving as a collective mass from one area of the room to another. "Cool" Dan was trying to bring the situation under control.

"Okay!" his voice came over the speaker. "Everyone relax! We're here to have a good time! Two-Ones just take a chill pill. Everyone back to their neutral corners!"

But "Cool" Dan's words were drowned in the ensuing madness. Rudy, Jose, and I dove into the middle of the human pit.

Rudy grabbed two of the main fighters and pulled them apart, pushing them in opposite directions. Jose did the same. And then a crash came from the living room. Everyone stopped and turned to see what had happened.

"Holy shit!" someone yelled. "They just picked up that motherfucker and threw him out. They threw that bitch out of the fucking window! Damn! Did you see that shit, bro'? That looked fucking nasty! Who the fuck was it anyway?"

"It was a Two-One!" Art, an acquaintance from school, answered. He was smiling, holding a cup of beer in his hand. "Fuck it. They were the ones who started it."

"Fuck you, Art!" someone else screamed, "I saw you turn off the light in there! I bet you even landed the first hit! You fucking asshole. Everywhere you go, you always have to start shit."

"Fucking Art," realizing how the situation had developed. "Man, what the fuck?'

"Party was getting boring," Art smirked. "Had to do something to cheer it up."

"Man, get the fuck out of here!"

"I was leaving anyway. You bunk ass motherfuckers don't have anymore beer!"

"Everyone's going to have to leave," "Cool" Dan announced over the speaker. "Of course the UPCs can stay, but everyone else has to go before the cops get here."

"The cops are already here!" I yelled. "They're right outside. I just finished talking to them."

Within minutes, the forty or so partygoers emptied out of the apartment.

"Hey, Ralph," after everyone had left. "What time do you have?"

"Twelve."

"Barely? Fuck! And this shit was going so good."

"I know. What do you want to do?"

"Hold on, bro'. Let me ask Rudy and Jose."

I went over to the two.

"So what should we do?"

"It's up to you, Demon. You think Tear wants to keep it going?"

"I think he'll keep it going. He's a little pissed about the broken window. How much money did we make so far?"

"Only about a hundred and fifty," Jose said. "But there's people outside waiting to come in. We can still make a little more."

"Yeah," Rudy interjected, "but we better tell them that we don't have any more beer."

"Fuck it. We'll let them in and see what happens. You don't think the Two-Ones are going to come back?"

"Naw," Rudy replied. "We wasted them. They might fuck with us later on, but not tonight."

"All right then, let's keep it going."

I went back to Tear and explained the situation to him.

"Well, the window's already broken so what can I do?" he asked.

"I'm sorry about what happened, man. I mean, it could have been worse. Don't worry, we already have the money to cover the window. Come on, let's just keep the party going. If you need me to talk to your mom tomorrow, I'll talk to her for you."

"She came over right now and wants to talk to you."

"No problem, I got it."

"Thanks."

"I just feel real bad about everything. You know?"

"Uh-huh."

"Look, at least this shit was bad. We could of had no one show up and then we would of looked like fucking idiots."

Tear smiled and turned to the door. "Yeah, it was bad. Wasn't it? Look, more people are already starting to show up."

"Yeah, fuck yeah. We'll clean up the mess when it's all over. Okay?"

"Okay."

"What's wrong, bro'?"

"Nothing," Tear said. "It's just that my brother got into a fight with one of the boys."

"Your baby brother George? But he's so little. That motherfucker comes up to my chest. Who the fuck was he throwing down with?"

"One of the boys. Whiteboy Tony."

"Aw, don't even sweat it. That woogie's always starting shit."

"Do you think the boys will say anything to me because of him?"

"Naw. Whatever happened is their own thing. Besides, everyone's gonna forget by tomorrow anyway. Trust me, it always happens."

His face, twisted out of shape, told me he was hiding something else.

"What's wrong, Tear?"

"It's not really what the UPCs are going to say that's worrying me. I just didn't like seeing my brother get so fucked up."

"Yeah, I bet he worries about you too. I think he kind of looks up to you. I was seeing how he was looking at you before the party started. He won't say it, but I bet he wants to be like you, Tear. That's the way kids are, bro'. It's fucking bad, ain't it? They're looking for answers and I guess they try to find them first with the people they know the most. And if they can't find it there, then they look everywhere else. I see that shit all the time. Just take a look around. Why do you think we're all here hanging out?"

"I don't know."

"'Cause," inching away, "some of us feel we don't have anything else, bro'. It's like they tell us at school, Tear. No one's an island." I poked my head out the broken window and waved hello to his mother. "Hey, I'm going to go talk to your mom and then tell Rudy and Jose to let people in. I guess we'll charge only two bucks because we don't have any more beer left. Okay?"

"Sure," Tear looked dismally at the living-room floor. The surface was littered with plastic cups. The stench of alcohol, mixed with dirt and sweat, was everywhere.

I looked at the shards of glass lying on the windowsill. The orange glow of the streetlight shimmered off their tops as I moved.

Suddenly, déjà vu. But only when I moved did that distant reality reach me.

"Cheer up, bro'," heading to our homemade dj booth. I motioned Rudy to turn off the lights. "It's not that fucked-up. When we look at it tomorrow in the morning, then it'll be fucked-up. I felt my buzz tapering off. "Tonight I want to get fucked-up."

"Oyé, qué no tienen verguenza?"

"No, Ma," feeling my head preparing to explode. "I'm not ashamed. At least we came home for breakfast."

"Porqué llegaron tan tarde?"

"We had to clean up the house," Jose replied. He turned to me. "Hey, are you going to take a shower?"

"Yeah," sliding into the bottom bunk bed. "You go first. I want to sleep right now."

"Ya no es hora de dormir," my mother objected.

"Oh, come on, Ma! Let me just sleep for an hour. It's Saturday anyway!"

"You should have thought about that last night."

Israel's voice came from above.

"I don't have the energy to argue with you today, bro'. So what did you do last night?"

"Why? What do you care? What did you do after the party?"

"We stayed and went out to Whiteroads."

"What's Whiteroads?"

"It's just a place where we hang out."

"Is it like Panther's Lair?"

"Kind of. There's factories there but there aren't any old buildings to play in. Hey, I thought you were going to stop by with Carlos last night?"

"I did, really quick, you just didn't see me. You were *busy*. I didn't want to disturb you . . . Hey, Louie, when are you guys going to let me be UPC?"

"When you get older."

"But you became UPC when you graduated from St. Peter's?"

"Yeah, Iz, but things are different now. They don't want kids in the group."

"I'm graduating."

"You don't understand, bro'. Look, we'll see what happens. Talk to me next year about it."

"Why don't you want me to be a UPC?"

"It's not that I don't want you to be a UPC. Man, things are changing."

"Uh-huh, sure."

"Come on, Iz. I'm tired. You understand."

"Man, whatever."

"Anyway," changing topic. "How does it feel to be in the last class to graduate from St. Peter's?"

"What?"

"Yeah, it might happen this year. That's what Father says."

"Oh man, I feel bad for the people who aren't going to graduate from there. Where are they going to go, Louie?"

"I don't know."

"That's not right. You know it won't be the same for them."

"I know. I feel bad for them too." I paused to take a long breath. "Stop talking all this shit."

"Why?"

"Because it gets me all sad." I turned on my back, bent my legs and pushed the wooden frame, bouncing my brother up and down.

"Quit it!"

"Hey, Iz, Mom told me you're gonna be the class valedictorian?"

"So?"

"She's pretty excited about it," I kept bouncing him.

"She hasn't told anyone? Quit it! Has she?"

"No. You know she's not like that," lifting the frame higher. "She's just happy you got it, bro'."

"She better be, one of us has to bring something home. You two had your chance at getting it and fucked up."

"Man," I brought my legs down. "We had to deal with some fucked-up circumstances. There was no way I was going to get something like that. I was a troublemaker. Remember? And I won't even get into what Jose use to do when he was there."

"Shit. Like I'm some fucking angel."

"No, but you got that little smile of yours that gets you out of trouble all the time, asshole."

"You're so stupid. You know what, Lou? You talk too much."

I pushed up hard. "Like you don't. Look, let me go to sleep."

"The day isn't suppose to be for sleeping."

"Well I'm a vampire, Iz. So leave me alone and go do . . . Fuuuuck!!!"

"I told you to stop, Lou!" The entire frame had dropped on top of me. "You never listen," I heard his muffled voice say. "You think it's funny?"

Actually, without thinking of what he was truly saying, I found the situation rather amusing.

"You have another job, Louie? Why? You already have this one. You must not be working too hard around here . . . And school?"

"Everybody keeps asking me about that. Man, people make it sound like it's hard or something."

"Louie!"

"Father! Seriously, I'll be fine with this new job. Anyway it's not that new. It's old news, Padre. Does the carpet in church need to be vacuumed today?"

"Same as always, Lou. Why?"

"No reason. I was just wondering."

"Say, we finally have that new sound system on the way. Compact disc and everything. Think about it, dude, pretty soon I'll have Gregorian chants coming out of the speakers right before Mass. The older Polish ladies are really going to dig it."

"What else are you going to do?"

"Well, once the remodeling in the sacristy is done, there won't be much money left to do anything else for a while. Still, not bad for a church on the South Side of Chicago that's almost a hundred years old. I think we'll be in pretty good shape come next year when the Archdiocese evaluates the joint. I can't imagine them closing us down."

"Why not?"

"Think about it, dude. Our weekly revenue for church offerings has skyrocketed well over a hundred percent since I arrived. Attendance at Mass is up. We had a great turnout at the summer festival and made a killing on that. Next year, I'm planning to have a friend from a local a.m. station cover the event on Sunday. Live."

"Wow."

"Oh yeah, if anything, the Archdiocese will probably shut the school down but I'm thinking it'll be for the best. We only had around a hundred and eighty kids enrolled in there this past year. For nine grades and a three-floor building, what a drag. What I really don't want is to have the other surrounding parishes consolidate their kids here. That'd be my worst nightmare, having to deal with a zoo like that. Right now I'm looking into what we could do with the school. I'm pulling some strings and seeing if I can rent the space out to the public schools. Connections, Louie, it's all about who you know, not what you know. Remember that."

"You think it'll happen?"

"Why not? Maybe not this year. But think about it. We only

have the best building in the entire neighborhood. The rest have gone to shit."

"Man, if you did it, you would make so much money. You don't think a lot of people are going to get pissed off if they close the school?"

"Screw them. The ones who complain are usually the ones who do little else but complain. When was the last time you've seen those people in here, Louie? The most they give at Christmas is ten or twenty bucks. If that. But when it comes to buying the gifts for their kids, they run off to the stores and dish out a couple of hundred. Now you tell me what sort of commitment they have? They know the world's not run on prayers. Speaking of which. Have you been keeping up with our payments on those turntables?"

"Yeah."

"With interest, they came out to be pretty expensive."

"I know. That's why I got this other job."

"And now you're thinking about getting rid of them, I bet."

"No, I really need them."

"Want. You really want them."

"No. I need them."

"Okay, Louie. I'm not going to argue with you. If you need them, you need them," he looked away at the clock on the wall. "By the way, before I forget, we might be missing Glennon tonight."

"Why?"

"He called in and told me he had to go to one of those cotillions your people put on. Ridiculous. Sometimes I think your people make any excuse just so they can have a party and forget their responsibilities."

"My people? Man, I don't have any people."

"Forget about it. What I'm asking you is if you would want to serve the five o'clock?"

"Aw, Father."

"Louie, you know I can't have any of the smaller servers hold the cross. They're liable to drop it."

"I don't know why you just don't get altar girls."

"Oh right, and have half of the people here die of heart attacks. Come on, Louie. You know better than that."

"Okay, I'll serve. But I'm not wearing those black and white vestments. They don't fit me anymore."

"Don't worry, I'll let you start wearing one of my own."

"Seriously?"

"Yes, I'm serious, but don't act like a clown in it. I want you on your best behavior whenever you wear it."

"Of course. I understand. Wow, that's a pretty big deal. Father, you got to start believing in me."

"Dude, sometimes I do. But sometimes you still have that childish bug in you."

"Yeah. Isn't it cool?"

"I worry about you, Louie. One of these days you're going to rub the wrong soul with it. And when that day comes, I can't imagine what'll happen to you."

"I can't wait."

"Arrogant. Arrogant, arrogant, arrogant. It's going to be your downfall."

"Sure, Father. Whatever you say."

"Well, getting back to the subject of money, which is your favorite subject. How would you like to serve at a party for Father O'Graley next week. You remember Father O'Graley, don't you?"

"He's that weird priest?"

"Eccentric . . ."

"He's still strange."

". . . Well, get this. He's having dinner on top of the roof of his rectory."

"That's fucking cool."

"Well, we'll see how it pans out. I'm thinking we can maybe get you a tux and have you serve like you did a couple of months ago at that dinner I had for my friends."

"What kind of people are going to be there?"

"It won't be stuffy old rich suburbanites like last time if that's what you're asking. It'll be a younger crowd, mostly foreign students who are interested in missionary work. O'Graley thinks you're quite a character. He talks to me a lot about you. I told him I'd provide the help. So what do you say, Lou? Easy money?"

"Yeah. As long as there's not going to be any assholes. The last time there was one married couple that kept treating me and Eddie like slaves. I hate it when people act like that. That's why I spilled some water on them."

"Did you really?"

"Yeah, I got them really late at night when they were drunk. That way, if they said anything, I could blame them and they wouldn't know what was the truth. Man, Father, they were getting on my nerves."

"I didn't even notice."

"Man, everyone was blasted, Father. Even you. But I think I woke 'em up," letting out a giant grin.

"Well, let's try not to go to those extremes next week."

"Don't worry. I'll take care of business. I'll just have to let the people at the other job know."

"Fifty bucks is fifty bucks."

"And I need them."

"Well, if you ever think about becoming a priest, you won't have a problem with that ever again. I can really help you out in that department."

"I don't know."

"What's there to know, dude?"

"Well, I've been teaching catechism at that church in Pilsen, you know, St. Vitus. I really like being there."

"Talk about a dead end. Word is that it's going to be one of the first places to go soon."

"Yeah, well even though I only have five kids to teach, I feel like I'm really helping them out. We don't even really talk about religion. They tell me more about all their problems at home, like I'm their older brother or something. I guess I'm not sure if I could do things the way you do them. I don't think it's in me."

"It is. You just need to work on it some more. You're already a character as it is. The only thing you need to do is to smooth out all the imperfections. With your Spanish background, there's no telling. You'd be the token bishop at the least. What else would you want to do with your life? Go to school and end up married by the time you're twenty-six with two kids? Come on. You see in your own house what that's all about. Trust me. I know what I'm talking about."

I wondered then why he never asked what I wanted to do. "I don't know. We'll see."

"You don't have to decide today. Just don't do anything stupid and get some chick pregnant. They're not worth it. I love you too much to see you hurt yourself in that way."

19

*T*he toilet.

What a fucking asshole, I thought, dipping the dishwashing sponge into it. Mr. Kolopanas didn't even buy the pair of gloves he promised. Not even a cleaning brush with the long handle. And the fucking bastard said he wanted it spotless? For two dollars and twenty-five cents an hour?

"Man," grumbling. "Fucking bitch."

The bathroom door opened.

"Sweetie, Mr. Kolopanas is leaving and he wants to see you before he goes."

I stood up from the floor of the stall and stretched. Mary. If it weren't for people like her, I thought, I'd go fucking crazy here.

"I'll be right there, Mary."

She was the oldest and most genuine of the group.

"Spoiled children," the old Lithuanian woman would say. "You're going to find men and women who act like spoiled children. They want everything. Give me. Me, me, me. Don't grow up to be like them, Louie, because you won't enjoy life. Poor things," she'd stare out into the cafeteria. "Look at them. They're so lost. Their greed will always make them empty. Don't know until too late. Yes, and they die too."

I walked into the filthy bare office.

"Yes, Mr. Kolopanas?"

"Next time you come in, knock. They don't teach you manners at home?"

I looked down at the floor of his office. The diner's commotion could be heard in the background.

"I am leaving soon. Everything finished in restrooms?"

"Yes . . . Ummm, Mr. Kolopanas?"

"Yes. What is it?" A carpet of money lay right on top of his desk. "I'm busy right now. I have no time to talk."

"I just wanted to know if I could get a raise?"

"A raise?" he laughed. "For what? The waitresses not paying you?"

"Kind of. But they don't give me too much and I wanted to know if I could get more."

"How much do I pay you again?"

"Two twenty-five."

"And with tips you must make what?" He flung his arms out. "About eight dollars every hour? A lot of money for a boy like you. What you do with money like that? Why you want more? You don't need more."

"But I don't even make that much," grabbing a pen and paper from his desk. "Look, I worked eight hours today and if you . . ."

"That's okay, that's okay," waving his hand to shoo me off. "We go talk to Mary, Sophie, and Joanne and have them give you more."

"But then they'll be mad at me! I can't work with people who are mad at me."

A smile curled along his lips.

"Do you want the money or not?"

"Yes, I ne . . ."

"Listen, I am too busy for this. If you want me to talk to them, we go and do it. If not . . ."

"But . . ."

"Do you want to work or not?" His smile disappeared. "I don't need this headache. You understand?" He buried his chin into his chest, lowering his head like a bull. He seemed to be preparing for another assault. His eyes reached the upper parts of their sockets. That malicious sight reminded me of Father Tom at his worst.

"Well, I quit then," taking off my apron and throwing it on his desk. "I hate fucking people like you! Fucking motherfucker! I hope your children die so people like you stop coming into this world!"

He stood up from his chair, eyes bulging.

"What are you gonna do?" I went for the door. "Huh? You can't make me do anything anymore. How does it feel? You fucking stupid asshole!"

I didn't even give him the chance to answer. Within minutes I was outside.

I ran to the park. Rain had begun to fall.

"Please, God," I cried. "Give me Kazlowski! Something. Something to hit. Anything! I'll take his face! Whatever! I don't care. Right now I just need somebody to hurt! Anybody that's mean!"

A lightning bolt cracked. The sky turned a muddy green.

"Right now I'm going to wait!" screaming across an empty baseball field. "But one day I'm not going to wait! One day I'll make everyone understand! Whether they want to or not!" I lifted my head. "And if you're not on my side, I'll find someone else who is! I'm really starting to get pissed off! I'm not fucking going to be like that one dude, Job. Not me! Fuck that! No one deserves that shit! Do you hear me? . . . We don't have what you have to take it! We're not like you! Man, are you even listening? Do you even fucking care? Fine then, I'm not gonna care either. Let's see how you like it."

20

*D*amn, Lou-Lou," Hugo broke in after Jose's name was mentioned on the intercom. "Your brother's in trouble again. I wonder whose ass he beat this time? I heard he got into a fight with that wrestling dude the other day. I heard your brother beat his ass good."

I turned around in my seat. "Shut the fuck up, bro', or else I'll beat your ass right now."

"What are you going to do?" wiggling his fingers in the air, "bring the UPCs after me?"

"Naw, bro'. All I need is my one pinky finger and your ass is down. So don't even start with me, you little scrub."

"Ooh, I'm scared, Lou."

"I won't even drop you because your stupid ass will start to cry."

"Luis," our history teacher, Mr. Monteleone, interrupted, handing me a set of papers, "may I say you did exemplary work these past two semesters. I was very impressed by your essays. You have a strong sense for detail. I can assure you that you will have a place in European Honors next year."

"Oh no. You're like the fourth teacher that's said I'm going to get into another honors class. I don't want to do any more work."

"Mr. Aguilera, I'm shocked. I would think that you would get bored sick doing work that is below your caliber. I take it then that you wish to limit yourself in the rest of your formative years here in the college prep?"

"But when am I going to have time for sports and work?"

"It's not like you play anyway, Lou," Hugo yelled. "Your ass was sitting down more on the bench whenever we had a game."

A burst of laughter filled the room.

"Hugo, that'll be enough from you. I don't see how your words are encouraging for Mr. Aguilera."

"Yeah, shut up, fly," DeLeon, another student, added.

"Oh, Mr. Monty, Lou knows I'm kidding. Don't you, Lou? You know I love you."

"Shut up, Hugo. You're such a nerd."

"Come on, Lou, tell him why you don't want to get any more honors classes. Say it, Lou. How you want to be with the UPCs for the rest of your life because it's cool."

"Shut the hell up, Hugo. You don't know anything about my life."

"In any case," Mr. Monteleone calmly continued, "I hope you consider the opportunities laid before you. It would be a waste to throw yourself away to idleness. You can't possibly spend the rest of your life being a—what do you call it—a UPC? Well, you could. But why would you?"

"I might."

"You don't strike me as the type of person who'll ever happily stay on only one plateau of existence . . . Sooner or later you're going to have to make a decision in life. I hope you're not too scared to make those changes that are vital to you."

"Yeah. I kind of was thinking about taking more honors classes anyway," turning to look at Hugo. "I guess I'm getting tired of seeing Hugo here anyway."

"Now, now, Luis. Each individual has his own unique talents. Hugo's may be very well disguised, but undoubtedly they exist." He smirked. "Somewhere. All nonsense aside, I hope everyone here realizes how important we are to one another. Without our interactions, the day-to-day basics needed in life would be gone. And what a sterile civilization we would have if we forgot the value of the one in front of our eyes. We must use our time in the utmost responsible manner if we wish to progress."

"I guess," half-minding his words. I began to drift away to the upcoming summer and to those things I wanted to do.

21

*P*ilsen.

"Brrrrrr . . . rrrrrrrrr . . . brrrrrrrrr . . . roooommm!"

It didn't matter to me that the sidewalks were covered with cracks in the foundation. That entire slabs of concrete lay dislodged in some areas, as if a war had occurred. The adults may have hated it, but the children adjusted, turning it into a wonderful terrain to play on, I thought.

"Brrrroooommmm. Brroom."

I joined him on the pavement. "Is your sister Norma here?"

"No," not caring to look up, "she went out."

"You know where she went or what time ago?"

"No. But my other brothers and sisters are here."

"So like how many brothers and sisters do you have?"

"Watch out! You're sitting on the mines! You're going to explode. You're on top of them!"

I looked down. "Just tell me where they're at and I'll be cool."

"Okay . . . There's Efrain, Edi, Norma, Lizandro, Angeles, Sonia, and Rosa."

"Man, you have a lot. I only have two brothers. One older, one younger."

"All of my brothers and sisters are older than me," continuing to play.

"I know Efrain. I met him at St. Vitus. I teach catechism there. I saw you there with him at Mass."

"Yeah, I like Efrain a lot."

"Yeah. He's pretty cool."

"Do you have comic books like him?"

"Uh-huh. I go buy them all the time. I think I'm going to get some next week with your brother."

"Which ones do you have?"

"I have the X-Men."

"Me too. Who's your favorite?"

"Nightcrawler."

"Yeah, he's cool. He's blue and has a tail and disappears whenever he wants to. And makes all this smoke when he disappears."

"Which one do you like?"

"All of them."

"It's good to like all of them," I said. "That makes it better. That way all of them can fight the bad stuff together."

"Yeah, I know."

"What's your name anyway?"

"My real name is Javier, but everyone calls me Javi."

"That's a cool name. So I guess I can call you Xavier. Like in the X-Men."

He lifted his head, smiling.

"I can tell you're just as cool as Xavier." I was transfixed by his face, primarily his shiny black eyes.

They seemed to mirror a vast, mysterious world with absolute delight. No matter where he existed, the totality of life was his own. As long as he remained a child.

"Yeah, he does things with his mind. Like move stuff and makes things happen. He's real smart and strong."

"Yep. He is."

"But not as strong as the little boy Akira. Do you have Akira?"

"Yes."

"Those are the only ones Efrain doesn't let me touch. He says I'm not ready. But I saw the movie already," gesturing to me that it was a secret.

"Me too."

"I saw it in Japanese. Did you see it in Japanese?"

"Yeah," thinking of our trip to the Music Box theater on the

North Side. "I did. In this cool place that has this moving sky with clouds projected on the ceiling while you're watching a movie."

"Cooooool. So you go to St. Vitus too?"

"Yeah. Sometimes. I go there with my mother on Saturdays and Sundays. Or when I'm suppose to teach catechism."

"You like going to church?"

"Sometimes."

"Don't you think it's boring?"

"Sometimes."

"Sometimes I play in church."

"I use to do that a lot. I still do."

"Do you get in trouble?"

"All the time. That makes it even more fun."

"Yeah, I know. But sometimes I want to fly out of there like how the superheroes do."

"But you do it at night. Don't you?"

He stopped playing. "How do you know?"

"I know. I use to fly like you a lot . . ."

"Do you want me to get Efrain?"

"Don't you want to talk to me anymore?"

"Yeah. I didn't know you wanted to talk to me."

"I do."

"Do you have brothers?"

"Two."

"Oh yeah," shaking his head. "You said that already."

"That's okay. People have to hear a lot to know what people are saying to them. I do too."

"Do you go out with them a lot?"

"I go out a lot with my older brother."

"Why don't you go out with your little brother? You should go out with your little brother. I bet you he wants to go out."

"I want to but I can't take him where I go."

"How come?"

"Because it's sometimes dangerous, Javi. Sometimes people fight where I go and people drink a lot."

"Like beer?"

"Yep."

"So why do you go if it's dangerous?"

"I don't know," trying desperately to find an answer, "'cause I like being with my friends. But you know that dangerous can mean a lot of different things? Right?"

"Yeah, like when I hear people shooting outside. Pow, pow, pow! It sounds like firecrackers. But it's dangerous . . . Do you ever have a hard time going to sleep?"

"All the time."

"What do you do about it?"

"I just don't sleep anymore."

"That's not good."

"It's okay. How old are you, Javi?"

"Five. How old are you?"

"Sixteen . . . So your sister Norma isn't going to be back right away?

"I don't know. Do you like her?"

"Yeah. You can tell, right?"

"Yeah. You get wushy when you say her name," sticking his tongue out and pretending to go into convulsions.

"I think Efrain can tell too. I only wish Norma could tell."

"Why don't you just tell her?"

"I kind of did. I kind of messed up too. I'm scared she doesn't like me anymore. Don't tell her I told you."

"I'm scared of a lot of things too. But when I feel like that, I bring out my cars and play outside."

"I don't think she'll play cars with me. But maybe next time when I come over I'll play with your stuff. If you let me."

"I don't care . . . That's why I got them."

"Yeah," starting to leave. "I know. I hate it when people don't let you play with their stuff too . . . Tell your sister I stopped by. Tell her I wanted to wait but I had to go to work."

"Okay. I'll tell Efrain you came too. How far are you going?"

"To the other side of the Damen Bridge."

"That's far."

"Not if you're a giant," getting on top of my bicycle. "Take care, Xavier."

"You too . . . Hey! Watch out for the mines! The mines!"

"I know," speeding away, "they're everywhere."

"You got it, big boy!"

ב ב

*Y*ou drew a picture for your mommy and daddy when you were in kindergarten. When you brought it home, they made you feel like it was part of the Sistine Chapel. They told you how beautiful it was. They told their friends how beautiful it was. They told you how much talent you had. And you swelled with pride . . . Well, I'm not your mommy. Or your daddy. I'm not going to hold your hand, stand back, and admire your immaculate creation. I'm not here for that. I'm here to teach and encourage you so by the time you leave here, you will hopefully know at least a fragment of what art is about."

No one said a word to this man wearing the khaki vest. He had asked us to arrange our wooden benches in a circle. We were all now looking at one another, waiting to see what else he had to say.

"I'm assuming a few of you here are convinced that you will pump an easy A out of this old windbag," he pointed a thumb at himself. "I might be wrong. But if I'm not, let me set things straight right now . . . If you want an A, you're going to have to work your ass at it just like you would in your math class, English class, or any other class. There are no shortcuts here. Art is to be taken seriously. I'm not saying you can't have fun with it. What's important is that you appreciate it and not take it for granted . . . Now because you're here, I'm under the impression that some of

217

you believe you can really draw. I suppose some of you even consider yourselves artists, in some vague sense of the word. Come on then, let me see a show of hands. Do we have any urban bohemians here? Who thinks they can draw? Paint? Anyone?

A few raised their arms. Soon more followed. The room buzzed of past accomplishments.

"Well then," raising his sights over the class, "will one of you kindly come here to the blackboard and demonstrate to me your particular talent? Better yet, let's make things easy. Can one of you," he grabbed a small carton from his desk, "draw what I'm about to draw?"

Mr. Range pulled a white chalk from the box. He left his seat and slowly walked over to the board where he quickly stretched his hand across the green surface and smeared a heavy white line.

"Ahhh, beautiful. This . . . is art."

The majority laughed. I waited, along with a few, for an explanation.

"Good, that's why I enjoy teaching sophomores," Mr. Range slowly looked at each of us, "you're a species like no other. Think you know it all and have been through it all . . . Well, it's certainly no Picasso," pausing before the white streak. "But it does reveal some charming quality to it. All right then. Mr. DeLeon? You're laughing. Is it because you think my exercise is funny? Do you feel I'm some kind of senile geezer? Or are you simply a happy-go-lucky kind of guy?" He rubbed the sides of his nose. "Which one is it?"

"None of them, Mr. Range," Jimmy cracked a smile and whispered something to the student sitting next to him. His companion laughed. "I just don't see what's so hard about what you just did. Anyone can do that."

"Is that so, Mr. DeLeon? So then why don't you get off your bench and come over here and prove it," pushing his glasses up.

Jimmy got up, gave a wink to the class, and waltzed over to the blackboard where he found a small thin chalk on the ledge. As he was about to begin, Mr. Range stopped him.

"Ah, Mr. DeLeon, you're already starting on a bad foot," Mr. Range held up the chalk in his hand. "If my memory is still intact, as it should be, then I believe this would be the chalk I used for my own work."

"Whatever you say, Mr. Range." DeLeon was unaware of the lesson I was watching unfold. "It doesn't matter to me."

"But, Mr. DeLeon, it does matter. You can't possibly confuse the chalk you have in your hand with the chalk I have in mine. How would you like it if I confused you with William over there?"

"Okay, Mr. Range. If you say the chalk you have is the one you want me to use, then I'll use it!"

"You don't seem to be catching my drift, Jimmy. How can you possibly confuse peaches with pears?"

"Mr. Range! I don't know what you're talking about! You tell me to draw this line you just drew and now you're talking about fruits. *Shazaam*, are you trying to trick me?"

"I'm not trying to trick you into anything. In the first place, I asked *can* you draw what I just drew. But what I've accomplished, you're nowhere near. Look here, son . . ."

"Son!" Jimmy cried in a high-pitched voice. "*Double shazaam!* I ain't your son!"

"Oh, Mr. DeLeon. I can already envision the year we're going to have. Let's not stray off the path. I'm quite aware of your personality . . ."

"How do you know how I am if this is the first time we've met?"

"Because, Jimmy," staring at him alone, "in all my experiences as a teacher and as a human being, I have come to the conclusion that you, Jimmy, are the kind that revels in trying to be the center of attraction."

"Everyone likes to be looked at, Mr. Range."

"I wouldn't say that, Mr. DeLeon. Not everything you believe in holds true with everyone else. If we were all on one page, you and I wouldn't even need to speak to let the other one know how we felt about things. The world would get along much better. But since that's not the case, I'm guessing what's vital is that we not forget the people around us and their differences. Everyone has the right to believe in whatever it is they wish to believe. How they act on these beliefs is a different story."

"So if what you're saying is true, then I can be the center of attention. Because that's who I am."

"To a certain extent, Mr. DeLeon. And because I'm such a gracious and loving host, I'm going to allow you part of your arena. But, remember, don't let things get out of control. This is still a classroom where there is always work to be completed. Just like in life."

"Okay. Now, are you going to let me draw this or what?"

"Do you have the right chalk?"

"Yes," he walked over and took the chalk from him. "Now I do."

"All right then, Jimmy. Go ahead. Give it your best."

Jimmy put himself right next to the line on the board. Carefully, he began to copy it right below the original. Every gradual curve and minute indentation were mimicked until the very end.

When he was done, no one in the classroom seemed to deny the resemblance of the two lines. I was undecided and kept silent. Something was wrong, I felt.

"It's a fine job, Mr. DeLeon. I expected that much from you." Jimmy smiled.

"Yes. It's a *fine* job, Jimmy. The only problem is that it is nowhere near being identical to my own. Not to say yours isn't a work of art," he walked over and examined Jimmy's results, "but it's certainly not mine."

"But it's the same, Mr. Range! Look at it! What's wrong with it?"

"Well," Mr. Range moved to the blackboard. "To the naked eye the two lines are one and the same. But if you look closer, you'll notice every little difference that makes them so distinct." He placed his face closer and closer to the blackboard. "I'm almost positive that if you had a microscope, you would find an infinite amount of discrepancies. Ah, here's one . . ."

"Of course, they're not going to be *exactly* the same. How can I do that?"

"You can't."

"So then why did you give me something to do when you knew I couldn't do it."

"Remember, I only asked if you could. Not if you would . . . You see, Jimmy, your pride answered the call, never once turning to the idea that once you create something, no matter what anyone else says, it can never be duplicated. Understand. Every stroke in a painting is blessed with an identity. Even if a stroke has been covered by layers of paint, that one single swish of the brush is distinct. By coming into existence it has changed the canvas, the work, and yourself. Do you catch my drift? Does everyone else here understand? Some of you will at this point and some of you won't. But that's okay. We all understand things at our own pace. Let's not become frustrated over the chaos. That's why we have questions—handy little things . . . Of course, individual growth comes when one allows oneself to be taught. That's where humility comes in. Which a lot of us here don't have, especially people who think they have it figured out. Who can really say they have it figured out? This dense pulp of life. You see, I believe we are skewed from the outset of our lives. But we each have the other to aid in unraveling the mess. And for those who don't know the meaning of the word *skewed*, I apologize. But don't be lazy and pass it up. Look it up, you lazy bastards," glaring from side to side. "Now what I want everyone to do is to pick up the instruments I've handed out. Hold them. Treat them as if they're an extension of your own body."

A few giggles.

"So predictable. But anyway, treat these instruments well and try to appreciate them. Somewhere out there, someone created what you are now holding. Someone gave it life. And it happens all the time. Every second in life there's life, no matter where you're at or how you are . . . Life may not give a shit about you. But you still have to give a shit about life. Or else you'll be living in an unfriendly world for a long time."

23

I have to head over to the hospital, Louie. My mother's turned for the worst. You think . . . you think you can come over and take care of the place for a while?"

"Yeah. Of course," my hand on the receiver began to shake. "How is she?"

"As expected. I think it's just a matter of time. But I need someone here to take care of the place. Make sure the dog is fed. There's enough food in the refrigerator if you get hungry. Other than that, I'll be back late at night. If you decide to leave at around ten or so, that's fine."

"No, Father. I'll wait for you."

"Make sure your mother knows where you are. I don't want her worried sick about you."

"Don't worry, I will."

"We'll talk when I get home."

"Okay."

He hung up the phone.

"Ma!" I yelled. "voy a ir a la iglesia!"

"Para qué?" she asked. "Qué pasó?"

"Creo que su mamá se está muriendo."

"Válgame Diós!"

"Yeah, Ma, I know. That's why I have to go," reaching for my rectory keys. "He needs me."

The black Labrador was asleep underneath the dining-room table, lying over a pair of worn slippers. They were "grandma's," I told myself. Father Tom's mother. She had left them behind the last time she had stayed.

"Poor baby," crouching before the dog. "You miss her. Don't you? I know you know how sick she is."

He stirred, opening his eyes slowly, and letting out a heavy sigh.

"Hasn't been the same around here these last few weeks. Everyone's really sad. Look, I'll be upstairs in Father's room if you need me, baby."

For the first time since I'd met him, Father's bedroom was in a state of disorder. I decided to do some cleaning to keep my mind off what was happening.

I took everything off his bed and began to look for some clean sheets. After I had made the bed, I made sure everything else in the room was in order as best as I could remember.

I then went to sit in Father's den, turned on the television, and waited for him to come home. The queasy feeling in my stomach prevented me from lying comfortably still. I rose, deciding to walk over to the church. I'd say a prayer, I told myself.

I entered St. Peter's. I felt the warmth and chill that I usually felt when I was there alone. Even though I never liked going into church by myself, especially at night, I kept coming.

"So tonight's the night?"

I needed to hear a voice. Since no one was ever around, I settled for my own.

"Why not next year or the year after that? Why tonight?"

I could hear every creak in this supposed house of God.

"I never forgave you for taking my grandfather away from me like that! Fuck . . . we were just getting to know each other! But I guess you know what's up. You're suppose to. It's your job."

I lay down on the altar's carpet. I let myself go, feeling the weight of myself upon the floor. My eyes gradually adjusted to the surrounding darkness.

"That's why people should take care of people when they're alive! Man, I should know. I know things get busy, but there's always a way . . ."

"Remember when I burned my hands carrying the incense?

Remember how Father Tom told me to keep holding it during Mass? How he said if Jesus could hang on a cross for three hours that I could hold on to the incense holder for three minutes? Man, I felt my fingers burning from the hot metal. But I didn't get my hands messed up. How come you always take care of me like that? Huh?"

Still no answer.

"You know what? I get tired of talking to myself. I think you're there sometimes, but I guess you can say I'm Thomas too."

A whistling draft howled through the empty hall.

"Look, I know he's not the nicest guy, but Father's been through a lot. We all go through a lot down here, you know. I think it's 'cause no one really feels safe down here. I mean . . . people are always trying to go for something, like it's going to make them feel better. Man, it doesn't help when everyone's fucking everyone else over. What can I say? Just promise me he'll figure it out before his time comes. That's all I'm asking! Sometimes I forget too, but I know you got my back."

I jumped up suddenly, facing the crucifix.

"And I know that other motherfucker is here too," looking straight at the crucifix. "Because if you're here, that bitch is here too." I swirled around. "I can feel you, bitch! One day it'll be just you and me. One on one. But not tonight, jerk. I got other things to take care of."

I walked out of the church and headed back to the rectory. At around nine, the dog awoke. He came to me, slowly making his way to my lap, where he stayed.

"We all get old. That's just the way it is. I think it's better she dies before she starts hurting too much."

I ran my fingers through his thin coat and listened to his breathing.

"Oh my God," in amazement, "you're crying. I'm so sorry," drawing him near me. "I really am."

He looked up at me. His eyes were red with tears. He knew before all of us, I thought.

"That's okay, baby. You just keep crying."

Time then passed at different speeds. Quick. Slow. All my perceptions were jumbled together. When the clock struck eleven-thirty, I heard someone downstairs.

224

"Louie? You still here?"

"Yes, Father. Do you need me to do anything?"

He came into the den. The dog immediately went along-side him.

"No," passing without even glancing, "it's over. I'll see you tomorrow. Thank you."

With that, he closed the door to his bedroom and I left.

The day of the funeral. Father Tom presided over the Mass. I wore the garments of a priest but performed the duties of an altar boy. After Mass, we left for the cemetery. And after she was buried and all the friends and distant relatives had sped away, only the closest family members and I remained.

Wife and husband, son and daughter. They stood at the top of a small mound with the burial spot in front of them. Arms wrapped around each other, heads bent down, they had each other to comfort. Just then I longed to have seen my grandfather buried. Would the pain have ended there?

I stared at them from the car, trying to imagine what they felt, trying to figure out what I should and shouldn't say at the brunch they were having afterwards. What would it be like? Would they want me there? I knew Father did. He had asked me to be there for him.

I felt sad. And yet happy. I wanted the whole world to see what I saw. To see the love he shared with me, the outsider.

I told myself never to forget that day on the mound nor his gesture of welcome.

24

There was that temptation to leave the group. Impatient as I felt, I waited in the breezeway, making sure the rest of the crew had paid. With each sounding beat from inside, my emotions tried to overpower the clamor of thought.

We were wearing all our traditional gear, anything adorned with the UPC symbol. Jackets. Hats. Football jerseys of our team, the Outsiders.

I noticed a group of four or five members of another party crew assembled nearby. They were younger than us. In a corner. Gazing. Gloating. Some admiring.

Tonight, we were fifty-plus.

"I think we should check our jackets in," Ruben announced. "What do you guys think?"

"No," Sergio replied, "I think we should keep them on. Let's wait to see what David says."

David walked in with his girlfriend.

"What are you guys waiting for?"

"What do you think, Dave?" Ruben spoke up. "Should we leave our jackets in the coatroom?"

"Naw, let's take 'em in. That way, if we have to leave we won't be waiting in line all day to pick 'em up."

"Yeah, and they won't lose them either," added Sergio, pushing his glasses up. "Besides, we want to show people we're here."

Everyone agreed and we entered the dark hall together. Rotating balls of light, coming from the center stage, made the faces in the crowd turn a muddy blue, green, and red. I was inside the glow now.

"Man, this shit is jammed packed!" leaning on Sergio.

"I know, Priest. Let's go find some place to stand, over by the front."

We walked in line along the edge of the mass, watching different pockets of intimacies occur. There were at least a thousand people, I thought. I focused in on the House Dogs on stage, performing their synchronized dance routine for the crowd. All four of them were keeping everyone in a state of frenzy with their rhythmic acrobatics. I thought of my own drills with Randy in Humboldt Park and his determination to make me a better dancer. The middle ground between being too technical and letting go was a thin line, he said. I agreed.

I swung my eyes from left to right. There were a good deal of other crews about, wearing their colors. Orange Crush was in one corner with their black and orange jackets. They were one of the oldest I knew, from the early eighties. The UPPs, Undercover Party People, were right next to them wearing white and purple. Each crew numbered about the same as us.

"Check it out, bro'," staring into the nucleus of the circle where the younger crews remained huddled. "There's the Exotic Ladies. They're wearing their new jackets, the ones my brother Jose helped design."

"Straight, Priest. But look who's right next to them. Those new motherfuckers. The LICs. They're looking at us all cold."

"Man. I can't stand those LICs."

"I know. They talk a lot of shit and start fights all the time. They're just as bad as the Funk Boyz. It's because of them they closed the party down last time. We better tell the rest of the boys they're here again giving us hard looks."

"Damn, bro'! Look! Even the Two-Six are here!"

"Where?"

"Over there," pointing my nose at them, "in the back. They're wearing their Playboy bunny shit all over. Fuck! This ain't no gang convention. I bet you they're the ones who are gonna start shit tonight!"

"What's wrong, Priest?" Smurf moved up.

"Man," turning to Smurf, "don't you see 'em?"

"Who? The Two-Shits? They're in full force, ain't it? Looks like they have a million munchkins with them. Don't worry, bro', they're all mostly peewees anyway. Except for maybe the ones in the back."

He was right. Their frontline was young. They were the ones randomly screaming and hollering obscenities at everyone. The ones behind them I was more worried about. They were quiet, measuring the situation. Looking around carefully. They seemed especially interested in us.

"Hey, Smurf, why do they have to keep checking us out?"

"The fuck do I know? Just watch your back, Priest, and watch your boys' back too. Okay?"

"Yeah."

"What's up?" Rudy came into the huddle.

Smurf turned to look at him. "Ah, the Priest is just worried about the Two-Six over there."

Rudy looked to me. "What's wrong, Demon?"

"Naw," feeling irritated, "they just keep looking over here, all crazy and shit. Man, if they want to start something, why don't they just go ahead and do it?"

"Look, Demon," Rudy patted my shoulder, "remember what we talked about in the meeting. We're not going to get involved in any gang fight. Besides, the Two-Six use guns and knives, bro'. We'll get slaughtered."

"Yeah, but what are we suppose to do if they start shit with one of us? Stand around and see one of our boys get fucked up?"

"That's different, Demon. If they want to fight, let them take the first shot. Hopefully, things won't get there anyway. Besides, I already checked them out. There's only ten real big guys with them. The rest are little punks. I don't think they'll want to fuck with fifty of us."

"Fifty-two," I said. "Minus one. Nalgas is still at work."

"Whatever. Fifty-two. Shit, Demon. Why do you always want to contradict."

"I just argue the truth."

"Well, don't go arguing the truth with the Two-Six because I don't think they'll be cool with it." Smurf and Rudy began to laugh. "Poor Demon . . ."

For the rest of the night I kept a vigilant eye on the Two-Six. I didn't want to be taken by surprise.

When the fighting began, we took whoever was involved from our group and shoved him behind us. We didn't want things to escalate beyond our control. It didn't occur to me that things already had.

As the Two-Six were hauled off by security, they kept yelling we were dead. In response, some of us laughed it off. Some repeated to them the same sentiment while others tried vainly to calm the disturbance.

It didn't matter. From that night on, we were all labeled TSK, Two-Six Killer. It meant we were their enemies so long as we existed.

25

*Y*ou made a mistake."

"Excuse me?"

"Yeah, you made a mistake, Father."

"Okay then," Father Tom said with curtness, "get to the point.
I don't have time for games."

"They're not games, Father. I'm serious. I don't know why you
asked me to find two people to work for you when all you were
going to do was fire them. Do you know how that makes me feel?
Especially since they're my friends?"

"I wouldn't have fired them if they had been doing their job the
way they were told."

"See, that's just it. You don't *tell* people to do anything. I think
that's wrong. Why can't you *ask* them?"

"I don't have to ask *anyone* anything if I'm paying them!"

"You're not listening to me, man."

"If they want to be *asked*, they can go back to that ghetto in
Pilsen and have their mother *ask* them to do their chores! And if
you want, you can go to."

"Pilsen's not a *ghetto*," I fired back. "People live there. It's their
home. It's some people's heads that are ghettos."

"Whatever, dude. Like I said, I don't have time for games."

"Okay, but they were doing their jobs."

"I'm not so sure. Is that why Rudy threw away a valuable antique vase from the church? What a fucking moron. He's lucky I fired him without charging him the cost of the vase."

"But, Father, you *told him* to throw away that vase in the dumpster. You said, 'throw-the-vase-that's-in-the-middle-of-the-altar.' Everyone heard you say that. Eddie. Me. Everyone. And that's what he did. Don't try to change the story and make me believe something else. I know what I remember—fucking trying to manipulate me. And then you fired his brother Mick along with him. Why? You didn't have to do that."

"Louie, I can fire whomever I want, especially a fat fuck like Rudy. I write the checks around here. Not you, Eddie, Rudy, or anyone else. If you don't like the way things are being done, then I suggest you pack your stuff and get the hell out of here along with the rest of your little brown friends!"

"Oh, so that's what I am," swallowing the lump in my throat. "Man, all I'm saying, Father, is you made a mistake."

"Excuse me! Who the hell are you to tell me I made a mistake?"

"But, Father, you mess up like this all the time. It's like you're really forgetful. No one here says anything 'cause they're too scared of you."

"Scared of what, Louie?"

"Scared to lose their jobs. Like Mick and Rudy . . . I mean, can't you see what you did was wrong? You've been acting like that for a while. Like you're better and shit. You can't treat people like that. Like they're your little fucking puppets. They're not toys, Father. They're real people. I mean, what's going to happen if I do something wrong because of your mistake?"

"Nothing's going to happen. After today, you're not going to be working here anymore. Now get your things and get the hell out of here!"

Always say the truth, they taught us in class. It didn't seem to be going too well at this point in time. But then when? When?, I wondered.

"Do I need to repeat myself, Mr. Aguilera? Get out of here before I throw you out on your little brown ass!"

I calmly looked at him. "No. I won't go. You're going to have to throw me out if you want me to leave. And if you raise your voice to me again, I'll raise my voice to you."

His nostrils flared. A series of parallel lines crunched against each other on his forehead.

"You're going to get out right now or I'm calling the police," his teeth gritted.

"Call the police!" I cried. "Go ahead. Do it! I'll tell everyone all about you! The way you've tried to touch me! The way you try to touch other people around here!"

"You're crazy! You know that?"

"You're the crazy one. Trying to make people believe stuff that isn't true. I'm not the only one who knows what's going on. You're only saying I'm crazy because you know Miss Barbara's here, listening to us. I'll tell her too! I'll tell everyone the truth! See, Father, I know you now. I know what you're about. It took me a while to figure it out, but I did it. Sometimes I couldn't tell, but now I know for sure all you care about is yourself."

"Get out!" moving closer. "Don't you dare tell me what the truth is, you snotty-nosed bastard! You think you're a big man all of a sudden? I taught you only a piece of the pie! Get this. You're nothing more than a little fish in a big ocean, Louie. I've eaten bigger fish than you in my lifetime. You want to bring me down? Idiot! You're new to this game!"

"See, Father, you're wrong. I'm not playing your fucking stupid game! You know why? I know I'll lose. And anyway, I don't want to know anything about your fucked-up game. It's mean. All it is is a bunch of fucking lies. People lying to each other left and right, non-stop. Fucking hypocrites. It's stupid to try and make it work that way. That's how come stuff only lasts for a little while. You think I feel good that I know they're closing down Quigley a year before anyone else knows. Even the principal? I have friends there, Father, that I'm never going to see again. Don't people mean anything? What, we can't even trust the Church either? No, Father, I'm going to play my own game now, with my own rules and shit. That way, you won't even know what's going to hit you. And I can't wait to see when other people start doing it. 'Cause you know you can't stop it."

"I'm warning you, Louie. One of these days you're going to get a bullet in the back of your head for talking such nonsense."

"Who's going to do it, Father? You? Go for it. I'm not afraid to die. Not anymore. I know there's a God up there waiting for me.

That motherfucker takes care of me every day. That bastard's been with me since before I met you and anyone else."

"You really are insane. I ought to . . ."

"Like I said, Father, go for it. I got people backing me up also. If it comes down to war, then I'm ready for it," shrugging my shoulders. "What's wrong, Father? Why aren't you saying anything anymore? Surprised to see that I think for myself? See, Father, all I do is watch. People maybe think I'm some kind of a pussy because they don't see me say anything to people like you, but I do things without even them knowing. That's the way I am. It's the best fucking way. Like I said, Father, I'm not going to play these mind games with you or anyone else. I'm going to be who I am and treat the nice people around me with respect. If people don't respect me, then I'm going to do what I'm doing to you right now, hold up a mirror and show you what kind of person you are. I'm good at that."

The floor in the room next door creaked. A shuffle of footsteps. Miss Barbara.

"Louie, if you're going to keep talking like this, I think we should take it upstairs."

"I don't care where we talk. It's you and her who's afraid of the truth anyway. No matter what you do with it, shit always comes out."

Father Tom closed the door behind us and indicated that I should sit down. I remained standing.

He rubbed his eyes and waited for a few minutes to pass.

"I haven't been that bad of an old queen to you?" he finally said. "Have I?"

"Sometimes you're cool, Father, but sometimes you're really mean. I don't have anything against you liking guys and the other stuff you're into. That's your own business. But I think there's something wrong with you being a priest and doing things like that. People look up to you, Father. You made vows and stuff. It's fucked-up when you say you're something and you're doing something else. It's not right. It's not like you didn't know it was a big job when you took it."

"Had you going there for a while?"

"Kind of. I figured it out but didn't want to say anything. It's no big deal to me. But I'm not sure I should be around here anymore. I don't know if I can trust you."

"And the truth of the matter is, I think you've outgrown this place as well. Can you believe that there were times when I thought you and I could just leave one day and go to Italy?"

"I don't grow out of things, Father. There's always something new to find in shit. But I guess I just don't trust my own feelings here. Especially not with people who aren't straight with me."

"We've come a long way, you and I. I always knew you were a lot smarter than what you led people to believe. Maybe too smart for your own good."

"I just wish people would pay attention to things around them."

"People are too busy, Louie."

"You're the one that always says not to make excuses. If people have time to play stupid mind games, why don't they have time to think and do the right things?"

"It's not that easy."

"Yes it is. People just dig their own holes. I know because I sometimes dig my own holes. Sometimes I'm selfish and keep wanting but don't give anything back. That's when I fuck up."

"Well, you're extremely fortunate that you've come to this epiphany so early in life. Others aren't quite at that stage yet."

"Great, so people like me have to suffer because of all the shit that's going on."

"Remember, Louie, you were probably once flinging that shit as well. None of us are perfect. And look what I have to deal with. You don't think I miss my freedom?"

"I guess . . . I'm just frustrated. I don't know."

"You should take some time off. Go to Mexico. You always seem to come back in good spirits when you go there."

"Maybe. But I can't just be going to Mexico every time there's trouble. That's kind of what my dad did when he came here. That didn't work out. Nah, I have to figure out what I'm going to do here."

"Good luck. I can always give you my shrink's number."

"You go to one of those doctors?"

"Sometimes. Want the number?"

"No. I'll figure it out on my own. I'm pretty sure I can do it by myself."

"It's going to take time that way. There's medication for depression, you know? It helps."

"Fuck that. Anyway, only I know what's going on inside my head."

"All right then. Let me write you a check of what we owe you so you can head on out of here." He went over to his desk and pulled his personal checkbook from the drawer. "You know I'm going to miss you being around here," writing out a check and handing it to me.

"I'll come back sometime," taking the check from him and folding it.

"I'm sure you will. There's still the business of some meetings here," he smiled.

"I know," reflecting on the UPCs. "You know I'm not a little kid anymore, Father. I know who I am."

"Of course."

I shook his hand and gave him a heartfelt hug. Downstairs from the corner of my eye I saw Miss Barbara behind her desk. She was in her office, what used to be Father Tom's room. She was working diligently at preserving whatever she could of her world. She didn't even say good-bye when I left the rectory, although I did hear a short sigh of relief.

Fuck her, I thought.

26

*A*fter fifteen minutes of greeting latecomers, the room quieted down. We positioned ourselves along the tables assembled in rectangular form. The look on Sergio's face worried me.

"I think we all know what this meeting is about," he said. "It started with that one party at Highlander's awhile back. From what I know, that's the first time the Two-Six and UPCs mixed it up. The only good thing that happened that night was that security was able to throw them out. I don't know what would have happened if a big fight had started."

"We would have killed them!" someone jeered. "That's what would have happened."

The room filled with assured laughter.

"Ha, ha," Sergio said sarcastically. "Some of you guys might think this is funny, but this shit is serious. I hear people saying at Juarez we're at war with the Two-Six. Whether it's a rumor or not doesn't matter anymore. If people are coming up to one of us and saying this sort of shit, it might as well be the truth. I know some of us have cousins or brothers who are Kings or D's. I just want to say that if they ask you if we're at war, tell them no. The last thing we need is for the Two-Six to think we get backup from the Kings or D's. Now about the last party we went to. Who's fucking idea was it to go there?"

No one answered.

"Well whoever it was, great fucking idea! I hope you know that it put a whole bunch of the boys in a fucked-up situation."

"Fucking put us in the middle of Darkside," Mauricio interjected, "where all those fucking bunnies live . . . Nothing but Two-Six there. Straight up. Motherfuckers started capping at us. Fuck, they almost hit Rudy, the Priest, Jose, and everyone else who was there."

"Shit, at least we had a priest on duty to give the last rites!"

Again the laughter.

"Seriously," Sergio shook his head. "This is getting all fucked-up. I saw someone even tagged UPC and TSK next to each other on some wall by Damen and Cermak. Now I'm not saying it's someone inside our crew—it could be—but what I'm saying is someone out there wants to see us get it on with the Two-Six. There's no way we're going to go there. We didn't start out gangbanging and we're not going to end up gangbanging. If there's anyone here who's tagging that kind of shit, you better walk out right now. 'Cause if we find you doing that shit, your ass is gonna be grass."

"So what are we suppose to do? The Two-Six already think we're at war with them!"

"We're going to have to be more careful where we go from now on and what we do."

Moans let out all over the room.

"Look," Sergio responded, "things aren't the same anymore since we first started hanging out. You see all these new little crews have gangbangers backing them up. I know for a fact the Kings were talking to some of us—and I'm not mentioning any names—about backing us up if we backed them up. I don't think anyone here joined UPC to do that. Also, I think we let in too many new guys who don't give a shit about the crew. There's suppose to be over fifty of us, but only like twenty or thirty come to the meetings. I think that's why we have so many little cliques going on right in our crew. What the fuck is that all about? We're suppose to be together."

"Yeah, well, if you and Juan and Big Izzy didn't try to control everything, then maybe things wouldn't be this way," someone chided from across the tables. "People aren't coming 'cause it's like their thoughts don't even count."

"We vote on everything," was the reply.

"Yeah, but only on the things you guys over there want to talk about. And then you're doing all these deals behind people's backs. Who made you guys the leaders?"

"That's fucking bullshit! We're the ones who worked our ass off to get the name out there from the beginning! How are you going to push someone like Demon away, or Rudy, or Luis, when they've been in it from the start? . . . I don't see him complaining, just doing stuff for the boys. What I see is some of us are just talking all this shit but not doing anything about it! I've *never* told anyone not to do anything! But it's up to every person in the crew to do something with themselves for the crew. How am I gonna trust some of the people who don't even show up to the meetings with important shit? Yeah, some of us have night jobs now. I understand that. But some of us just don't make the effort. I know it's weird for some of you to say stuff in front of a group, but you can come to any of us later on. Like Demon. He mentioned using the church hall for a party and he took care of it. No one talked shit then about him handling it. He wasn't even pissed off that we all used up the money when he was in Mexico. But did you say anything about him then? No, you were too busy getting drunk."

"Poor Demon," Rudy cried.

"Look," Sergio continued, "all I'm saying is things are getting nastier and nastier. I guess we can't just keep having fun like we use to. Some of you are even saying this is getting old. Maybe it is."

Silence.

"Check it out, even house parties have been getting raided more and more by the five-o. Rookies fucking think we're gangbangers? It's everyone's fault. The only thing I can say is we still have those two narcs who are willing to work with us."

"Who, bro'?" Juan interrupted. "Batman and Robin?"

"I know they gave themselves funny names," Sergio smirked, "but their last names are really Rodriguez and Ventura. Hey, they've been around to know what's up. For some reason they really like us."

"Oooh," everyone murmured.

"Not in that way, assholes," Sergio smiled. "I don't think they want to see all these party crews turn into gangs. I think it'd be more of a pain in their ass if they did. I even heard a couple of you guys mention they had escorted you out of a party a couple of times."

"Yeah, so what the fuck are two narcs going to do for all of us?"

"For right now, that's all we got. We'll just have to see what happens now . . . Another thing we have to talk about is the hall party we're going to throw in a couple of months. I don't know if anyone has heard, but the Priest said he could maybe get us the church hall again."

"Who?" someone interrupted.

"You know who, motherfucker. The Priest. Demon. Stop interrupting. I know no one wants to be here for the next two hours like last time."

"What about beer?"

"No beer until after the party!" Sergio responded. "I don't know about you guys, but I don't think the priest would be too happy if we got beer."

"Fuck what Demon thinks!"

"I'm talking about the real priest, Mauricio. Not our Priest."

"Oh, that's different," Mauricio said, "he might have to marry me sometime."

More laughter.

"Anyway, it's going to be in two months so we got to see who and who is going to do what. I'm thinking Orlando is going to take care of the dj's again. And we're going to get our fliers made where we usually have them made. The money we'll grab from the last party we threw. I think Dave still has the money."

"I don't know," Juan said, "he didn't even show up to this meeting. Maybe he skipped town with the change."

"Now, guys," Sergio said, "we all now why Dave's not here, so let's not pick on him when he's not around."

"Why not, Sergio?" Luis said. "We pick on you when you're not around."

"Okay, that's enough. See, that's how bullshit gets started. Why do people start messing around like that when there's so much other shit to do? Getting back to business. We should be able to get the same number like last time. About five hundred or six hundred . . . Let me see. What did I forget?"

"How much are we going to charge at the party?" Moneybags asked.

"Oh yeah, it's going to be like five bucks. Don't worry, Money-bags, you're going to get in for free. If everything goes good we'll make about two thousand that night and probably throw another one in two months . . . Oh, and one thing left that I forgot to say. We're going to need someone to chaperone the party again. I'm serious, guys. That's how the priest wants it."

"Fuck what the Pr . . ."

"Not that priest, Juan. The other one. Anyway, we're going to have Demon and Cubby's mother take care of us."

"Will they drink with us after the party?"

"That's up to them," Sergio answered. "So I guess we covered everything we were suppose to cover. What I'm going to do now is talk to the guys who are going to be in charge of the party, and the rest of you can do whatever it is that you guys do. Remember the stuff about the Two-Six. I don't want to be receiving calls from anybody's mom that one of yous got shot . . ."

"*Yous?*" Mauricio joked. "How many *yous?*"

"You know what I mean . . . If you're going to go out in your jackets or anything representing UPC, make sure you're not alone."

"Yes, mommy," Tony said.

"Shut up, white boy," Luis joked, "now you're going to know what it's like to be Mexican."

"That's okay," Tony replied, "people already give me shit about hanging out with you spics."

"All right then," Sergio finished. "I'll see all of you guys in about a month."

"If the Two-Six don't kill us!" Mauricio yelled.

27

Our trek brought us to a small metal bridge overlooking waters that seemed cleaner than the Chicago River. Instead of rust-coated barriers and cracking concrete, I was pleased to find a thick wall of trees along the banks. The only horror was that the wooded area was confined to about fifty feet inland. Industrial edifices made sure of this.

"So no one else wanted to come except us?" I asked as we crossed the bridge.

Alfred, gripping the steering wheel with both hands, frowned. "Everyone else I called said they were busy doing something."

"Oh, and they can't take a day out of their lives to visit someone who was there for them when they were growing up?"

"Calmado," Gregorio patted my shoulder from the backseat. "She's going to be happy to see us at least."

"Oh, I know that. But it kind of sucks nobody else cares."

"How do you know they don't care?" asked Gregorio. "Maybe they do have important things to do."

"Like what?"

"Maybe they already went," Alfred insisted.

"Maybe, maybe, maybe . . . I'm getting tired of all this maybe shit! I think if one of us were really sick, Sister Therese would be right there for us. Every time she taught she was."

"Not everyone's like that, Luisillo," Gregorio persisted in calming me down.

No shit, I said to myself.

Again I looked out of the passenger window and then over to Alfred. Soon, we would both be in a new school, I thought. The marching. The sit-outs. The media attention. What a waste of time.

Not mine. I hadn't participated. What for? I was an insider and had known the outcome all along.

The Archdiocese wasn't about to sell the downtown campus. Father made it clear that the price for that location soared with each passing year. The alternative—preserve it as a historical landmark and resettle all of the students onto the South campus—was also out of the question. Why? Because there were more blacks moving into that neighborhood. And the Church couldn't afford the supposed instability that would be caused by that movement. The whites wouldn't hear of it, Father said. Besides, he tried to argue, the South Side campus wasn't producing any priests. Neither was the North Side campus, I remarked. He only grunted disapproval.

Of course, there were more things going on, he said. But you had to be part of the "game" to know those things.

All I knew was that he asked me to remind him to take me out to the Ritz for breakfast on my first day at the "real seminary." Real seminary! What fucking bullshit. And everyone at school thought I was insane. Fuck them for not listening.

I felt a cozy August wind blow warm air into the car.

"So did Sister sound sick when she was on the phone?"

"No," Alfred replied. "But it's not like she's going to tell me anyway. That's not how she's like."

"Man, I remember how that woman took so much because of us. Especially with the shit I use to do," muttering to myself.

We rounded the corner and drove onto the street where we were instructed to go. A couple of blocks down the lonely road and we found the place. It was a humble one-floor institution. Trees were sparsely spread around the school evenly. There was a good deal of open space all around.

"Man, this place looks dead."

"I don't think I could ever live around here," Gregorio added.

"I kind of like it," I said, "'cause no one's around."

"I wonder where the convent is?" Alfred interrupted.

"It's probably this other building," Gregorio pointed to a small brick house across the gravel parking lot.

"It has to be," Alfred parked.

"Well, let's go and find out," opening the car door.

The three of us walked over and Gregorio rang the doorbell. After a few minutes, Sister Therese answered.

"I was beginning to think you boys had gotten lost. After you called to tell me you were coming, I wasn't too sure I had given you the proper directions. Did you boys enjoy the ride here?"

We nodded our heads and smiled.

"Sister," Gregorio pulled at his neck tenderly, "is it okay if I get a drink of water—no ice?"

"Actually, I made some fresh lemonade," welcoming us in. "Still making sure the throat's taken care of?" she smiled.

"Of course. I already said to you that I was going to be a famous singer."

"Comedian maybe," I joked. "Singer? No way. You don't sound too good."

"Louie, still out to conquer the world and the people in it with your charming words?"

"Always."

"But you're going to have to learn a little bit of diplomacy to do so."

"He's never going to get that," Alfred said.

"Don't be too sure," her eyes sparkled, finding their way to mine. "We didn't even think he would graduate from grammar school alive."

"That's true."

"And what about you, Alfred? How are your brothers doing?"

"Good, everyone's good."

"I'm happy to hear that. Well, let me show you boys the place."

She took us on a brief tour, showing us her modestly small, perfectly organized room, the rest of the convent, the school grounds, and the school itself.

"What do you boys think?"

"It's small," I said bluntly.

"Well, there's no need for anything like St. Peter's here. There's only three of us now. Connie recently went on to the main house a few weeks ago. She's going to stay there from now on."

"Is Sister Consuela all right?" Alfred asked.

"She'll be fine there. She just needs to be away from the little monsters you once were."

"Yeah," rubbing her shoulder. "I guess we were bad."

"Nothing that I couldn't handle."

"But you're Sister Therese. You can take on anything."

"Don't say that too loud, Gregorio. They might just send me back to teach in Chicago."

"Like there's any more schools to teach in over there," I said. "They're closing so many of them."

"Things aren't so hot right now in Chicago, are they?"

"They don't know what they're doing," Alfred said. "They forget that the real Church is about people."

"And who taught you boys this?"

"You did," we said together.

"Yeah, Sister," I said. "I don't think we're ever going to forget all the stuff you taught us."

"I'm happy you boys are here. It means a lot to me."

"But you're not really happy here, Sister," I said. "Are you?"

"Why do you ask that?"

"You know I can tell."

"Still good at that?"

"I don't have anything else. I have to be good at one thing at least."

"You are good at more than one thing, Louie. In fact, the three of you boys are bright young men. I'm not simply saying that to inflate your egos. It's still up to each one of you to figure out what your gifts are and what you're going to do with them."

"I wish we were all back at St. Peter's."

"It doesn't work that way. We have to keep building and looking ahead. Of course, that doesn't mean we don't look back every once in a while and reflect on our doings. That's important too. We have to replace some of those old boards on the wooden floor. But, hopefully, the foundation we have so far under our feet is strong enough to support the weight of ourselves and the things to come."

"Hopefully," I repeated.

"Besides, there's no way I would go back to St. Peter's even if it was still open. Not with my heart condition," she went to sit on a recliner. "I've had my share of the cross. Your class completely took my first wind right out," she winked.

"Sorry, Sister," we said.

"For what? It was a fun ride."

The rest of the day we spent discussing her present situation and old stories. With little left to say, we bid farewell, leaving her on an unpaved road.

The last time I will see her, I thought dismally. I was sure of this.

28

All I'm saying, Jean, is that it's those damn wetbacks who are pushing this country to hell . . . Goddamn Mexicans, they're . . ."

"Shhhhh," Mrs. Connor's effort to hide her neighbor's views were in vain. "There's one of them sitting with William Senior in the family room right now, Carl," she continued in a cautious whisper. "I don't want him thinking we're that type of people. It's nothing against you, mind you, but he is one of William Junior's friends. We'll talk about it . . ."

"Don't listen to them," the elderly policeman, sensing my agitation, confided to me from his lazy-chair. "You just drink your beer. Let them gossip all they want. Mr. Kinley never watches what he says anyway. He's also off the mark if you haven't noticed by now . . ."

Then why invite him to your home?, I thought. Why even tolerate what he has to say?

". . . Now you were saying something about the movie?"

"Oh yeah," stumbling back to my thoughts. "I saw *The Great Escape* with my dad a long time ago. It's one of my favorite movies. I like it 'cause they start digging underneath the Nazis to get out."

"Right, reducing the chance of confrontation," Mr. Connor remarked. "Fighting doesn't get you anywhere."

"It takes care of the bad guys," drawing a long drink.

"No, they keep coming anyway," he shuffled uncomfortably in his seat, "from everywhere," concentrating on the screen. "I'm going for another beer. Want one more?"

"No," lifting myself from my spot on the sofa. "Is it okay if I go upstairs to rest?"

"Of course. You're our guest. Will and the boys should be coming home soon . . . I'm happy you could make it out here this weekend, Louie. Sorry you couldn't make it here earlier in the year . . . I don't understand why Will didn't invite you when the rest of the kids were here for vacation. That's when things really get good."

"I was probably busy," going up the stairs. "But thanks for having me here anyway. I really like your summer home."

"So you don't want another? It'll ease the nap."

"It's cool."

I walked casually to the guest room, placing myself in front of the window overlooking the lake. The sun's setting was producing a radiant glow over the water's surface. Numerous flashes of black ripples impeded it from turning into a simple reality of light. Both extremes produced an illusion of ants hurrying in and out of nowhere. A simple existence of life and death for them. But soon both would be gone, I reasoned. And tomorrow they would have another chance at it.

I lowered myself on the hard bed, stretching my arms in preparation for supposed flight. I remembered a weekend retreat sponsored by my former seminary. We had spent most of our three days emptying ourselves to each other, divulging painful years through the prepared meditation of those in charge. Our teachers had asked us to examine the life we had lived thus far and our relationship with a silent God. There in the isolation of their experiments we found peace. They seemed to smile at themselves and our graceful arrival at their understanding.

Our nights were far more adventurous, in seemed. Some had come better prepared, with flashlights and the history of their brothers' experiences. I felt fortunate not to have either one. As with many other things, I anticipated nothing. I was rewarded with the feeling of surprise.

The after-hours frolic ended with minor warnings from the patrolling priest. I was sure all along that he knew of our whereabouts and was simply letting us experience the workings of friendship. Hmmm. I held the memory intact. How different would things have been if I had asked Jose what to do?

"Lou!"

Will's arrival grounded my rare opportunity to reflect. I left the room and headed to the kitchen where I had heard voices. His mother and father were no longer around.

"My mom says you met Mr. Kinley," producing marshmallows, chocolate milk, and a variety of other sweet items from the grocery bags.

"Don't worry, Lou," our friend John added, "we'll make a white boy out of you yet this weekend. We got everything good. No tacos for you."

"Hey, guys, leave Lou alone," Brian nudged John. "Someday we might need him to teach us how to make burritos. Right, Lou?"

I grinned, seeing that from all the things laid out on the kitchen counter, none were what I had paid for, what I had asked for. I said nothing, too exhausted to argue with them. It wouldn't make a difference anyway, I thought. The things had already been bought.

the last night

1990—1991

29

*D*on't even sweat it, Eddie," I said, gawking at the gothic structure before us. "There's got to be some place around here that'll hire us. We're in the middle of downtown, bro'."

I kept looking at our school, imagining how surreal it must look from above, sitting among high-rises and skyscrapers. What was even more bizarre was having the Magnificent Mile, the city's most expensive shopping district, only half a block away.

"I hope we get a job, Louie," the sophomore stepped up his pace. "I really want one. I want those turntables bad."

I smiled, remembering Tear. He had gone to another school.

"Let's try that place," after a few minutes of walking down Rush Street. "It looks straight."

"Guadalaharry's? I don't know, Louie. It looks like a bar. You think they'll hire us?"

"You never know. There's a restaurant on top. It doesn't look bad."

We walked into the cream-colored building. I laughed, knowing better than to accept the decorations as authentic Mexican.

We found wooden stools turned upside down on top of the bar. A blonde woman with a tuxedo-like uniform came forth from a backroom.

"Can I help you boys?" her voice hoarse.

I stepped forward. "We want to know if you're hiring."

"For busboys?"

"Anything, I guess."

"Wait here," she smiled. "I'll call the manager."

"What do you think?" Eddie whispered.

"She looks friendly. That's kind of good. If they didn't need anybody, we wouldn't be here anymore. We'll see what the manager says."

A stocky, rose-cheeked fellow with a thick mustache and short hair emerged from the same place as the woman. He straightened the jacket of his olive suit.

"Dave Bruna," extending his right hand to each of us. "So what can I help you with, guys?"

"We were wondering if you needed anyone to work here or the restaurant upstairs?" I said.

"You guys seem pretty young."

"I'm seventeen."

"And I just turned sixteen this summer," Eddie added.

"You're of legal age then. Good, that's one thing out of the way. The fact that you both know English also tells me you two are legal? Am I correct?"

"Uh-huh. We go to school down the street."

He flinched. "I heard on the news they closed that seminary?"

"No," I said, "they kept that one open and closed the one we use to go to on the South Side."

"Hmmm. Must be disappointing to have your school closed so late in the game."

"Yep."

"You boys doing good in school? I'm not going to have Padre come over here with a paddle, am I?"

"Yes. My grades are always good. What I need is a job."

"I have good grades too," Eddie added.

"Well, I can see that you came prepared to look for a job," Dave indicated to Eddie. "You're looking sharp today."

"Thanks," Eddie caressed his tie. "I'm use to dressing this way."

"You should take some pointers from your friend," turning to me. "Jogging pants and sneakers aren't going to land you a job around here. People will think you just got off the boat."

"I've worked since I was around thirteen," I said confidently.

"When I become a lawyer and get paid thousands of dollars, then I'll wear a suit."

"Not bad," smiling. "Are you that quick when you work?"

"Quicker."

"Well, let me tell you guys the truth. We're currently hiring two or three busboys for the evening shifts upstairs. Or else I wouldn't have you standing here like a couple of imbeciles. The last three were fired because of immigration problems. Things are beginning to get tight around the ship. I can't guarantee you'll be hired today but why don't you fill out these two applications and get them back to me by tomorrow."

"We can fill them out right now. Right, Eddie?"

"Sure, right away."

"Good," Dave said. "I like that. That tells me something about you guys. Fill them out and leave them with the waitress when you're finished then."

"Excuse me, Mr. Bruna?"

"Call me Dave. What do I look like to you? Some aging bastard?"

"Okay, Dave. How much do you pay the busboys here?"

"On a good night you're looking at anywhere between thirty and forty bucks plus your hourly. Around here, that's decent for a busboy. Does that suit you?"

"Yeah," I said. "It's okay."

"Now I take it you two are inseparable?"

Eddie agreed.

"Well then, let me make this clear. If I do hire you, I don't want any horseplaying going on upstairs. No flirting with the waitresses. People are starting to get more sensitive about things like that. Which is a bunch of bullshit if you ask me because they're just throwing it all under the rug anyway. Another thing. The only thing I'm anal about is punctuality. The third time you're late, you're fired."

"No problem."

"Okay then, get your applications done and get the hell out of here."

After we finished the applications, Eddie and I waited outside.

"Do you want to go to other places and fill out some more applications?"

"Naw. He's going to hire us."

"Why do you say that?"

"'Cause. I can tell. Why else would he tell us all the rules? Besides, I don't want to work anywhere else."

"But what if we could find another place that pays more?"

"So what? I'd rather be here, making less and being happy than working with a bunch of snotty assholes that are gonna fuck up my whole day. It's bad enough that a lot of the people who come to eat are jerks. Anyway, Dave seems straight. You see the way he was talking shit to me about not being dressed well. He wasn't like a hypocrite about it—just keeping it inside his head. There aren't a lot of people like that, Eddie. That's respect."

"But what if he doesn't hire us?"

"He will. He knows we're down with our shit, bro'."

"We're going to have a blast working together." Eddie pulled me close to him. "I bet you we're going to meet a lot of fine honeys too."

"Man, you know it," massaging the back of his neck. "You and me baby! The dynamic duo!"

"Forever."

"Yeah," smiling at Eddie, "forever."

30

*S*o what are you going to do, Louie? He's been talking shit about you all week."

"I know, Jes," opening my locker. "Motherfucker even threw a gang sign up at me the other day like he was all hard. Pussy ass North Side bitches. Bring them down to the South Side and they'll see what hard is."

"They don't know jack," Jesse continued. "Necesitan un pinche palo up their asses."

"What are you talking about, bro'? They already have poles up their asses. Especially since we got here and took over their school big-time. Fuck Q North! Fuck all these lame ass motherfuckers who think they're gangbangers! Did you see how that one motherfucker kept combing his hair in Mass? Man, he's more worried about his new gym shoes and the fucking pretty-boy clothes he wears. And they're all like that. Man, that ain't hard."

"Fucking Louie," Jesse laughed. "You always have to come up with something."

"Got to, bro'," grabbing my things. "It's who I am."

"Look, here comes some of them now."

A pack of five or six were cruising down the school hall. The one we were talking about passed by me, brushing against me forcefully.

"Hey, bitch!" I yelled. "Watch where you walk!"

They went down the stairs, laughing to themselves.

"Motherfucker," closing my locker and sprinting forward. "I'm going to beat his ass now. He just better not drag those other bitches into it."

"Don't worry, Louie. You know I'll back you up."

"Aw, Jes, you don't even have to say that. You and me have been doing this shit since we were freshman, bro'. I just don't want this shit to blow up for no reason. You know?"

We stopped at the edge of the stairs.

"Hey, bitch! You got a problem?"

He turned around and looked up. "Yeah, I don't like your punk ass."

"So what are you going to do about it?"

"Why don't you come down here and find out?" spreading his arms out.

Seconds later I was in front of him on a landing between two flights of stairs. One going up. One going down.

"I'm here," confronting him.

He shot a gang sign inches from my face.

"Put that shit down. We're not on some stupid street corner that you don't even own, motherfucker."

"Make me put it . . ."

I swung my left arm and hit him right on his face. His friends held back. Jesse, I thought.

The one I hit looked down at the ground and covered his nose. He then glanced up at me in shock.

"You hit me . . . You hit me . . ."

"Man, shut up. I didn't even hit you hard."

"I can't believe you hit me."

"Believe it, bitch," someone yelled from the top of the stairs.

"Shut the fuck up," I yelled back. "This ain't your shit."

"Come on, Louie," Jesse whispered. "This bitch ain't do-ing shit."

"I know. I'm telling you. They're all little momma's boys."

"I have a handful of students who say you were the one who made initial contact."

"I did," answering the disciplinarian. "But he's the one who

258

started it! First he pushes me. And then he threw up a gang sign to me. And that's not the first time! I wasn't just going to stand there and take it from him."

"What about walking away and coming over to report it? Did you ever consider that?"

"That's not the way the real world works."

"Let me tell you something about the real world," he said calmly. "It's composed of different sorts of people. We don't live in a world where everyone believes violence is a solution. There are people who have opposed it. Read your history. There's a fellow by the name of Gandhi you should know about."

"I know who he is. I wrote a ten-page report on him last year and also did a video project on him. I was the one who shot him."

"There you go. So then you know a bit of his teachings?"

"Yeah, but that stuff won't work today. People don't want to hear stuff like that anymore."

"Remember, the world is only what we make of it, Mr. Aguilera. I assure you there are people out there who don't want this cycle of violence to continue."

"Yeah, where? To me, it looks like everyone's out just for themselves."

"I understand this past year has been confusing for you," his voice cracked, "and for everyone else here. Not only did the people from South lose their school, but you—and I'm sure a lot of other people here at North—lost precious faith in the transition. Frankly, these are difficult times you're in. The other day I heard a report on the news that someone was killed for the shoes he was wearing. Shoes!" He paused. "I don't envy you. Our values and our systems of values are deteriorating as a society. The boundaries of violence are quickly evaporating. I can't say there's never been fighting in school. Jesus, I remember being in one or two brawls myself when I was your age. But things have scaled dramatically upward or downward—whichever way you want to see it. These days, you don't fight simply to combat. You fight to maim. To cripple. To kill. When a place like this, which is supposed to be a sanctuary, starts seeing this sort of trouble, then we've really outdone ourselves as beasts. What's to become of us when it reaches our society's extremities?"

"I know what you're saying. But nobody wants to do anything about it."

"I'm surprised, Mr. Aguilera. I look down at your student record and see hardly a blemish. Soccer, freshman year. Cross-country, sophomore and junior years. Honor roll in all three years at South. So what's all this about?"

I smirked. Everything, I thought, everything that you don't think about or want to talk about.

"I see there was a couple of disciplinary actions taken against you before. Not too shabby. I'm sure there's a few more things you've thought your way out of."

I grinned long and wide.

"Are you having problems at home, Luis?"

"For a while I did," I said dryly. "I got use to them already."

"You shouldn't. That seems to be the problem today. People are too comfortable with the way things are. If it's not that, it's that people seem to not care what is happening, so long as they're not in the middle of it. I imagine you're the kind that likes to get in the middle of things?"

"Yeah, even when my big brother and little brother would fight each other I would do something mean to both of them. That way they would come after me and they wouldn't fight each other anymore."

He laughed. "An interesting twist on the divide and conquer strategy, except you still end up only fighting. So then you're the middle child?"

I nodded my head.

"I hear it's hard to be there."

"I always feel like I'm in the middle. You get use to it."

"Sounds lonely."

"Yeah," muttering under my breath, "that's the word."

"I'll tell you what I'm going to do. I'll give you three days of detention. Nothing more. But you have to promise me that there'll be no more fighting. What you did was wrong and would normally call for suspension. But seeing the circumstances as they are, things merely got out of hand. Wouldn't you agree?"

I nodded.

"None of you are bad," he went on. "I hope you can realize that in him as I realize that in you. Now go back to class, Mr. Aguilera. And learn."

He rose from behind his desk.

"Try to make the best out of the year and the rest of your life," leading me out the door.

We smiled at each other, watching a parade of students pass us by.

31

*Y*ou're telling me all this time you were hanging out with the UPCs you never put it all together?"

"Naw," embarrassed. "I mean, I can sit here and tell you the difference between the Kings, the Two-Six, the Disciples, and other gangs by the way they dress and act, bro', but I can't say exactly what's the difference. That shit about Folks and People. I don't get that either."

"It's a whole different world, Nigga," Jesse finished filling the litter box.

"That's why I wanna go get some beers and talk about it. You know what's up, Jes."

We walked out of his apartment and found ourselves in front of his brother's car.

"Aren't we going to take yours, Jes?"

"Didn't you hear what happened to it?"

"Naw. What happened?"

"La Raza firebombed my sweetheart a few days ago."

"Oh man, I'm sorry. How do you know it was them?"

"Ain't nothing but Raza around here. Besides, they've been trying to steal the car for the longest. My brother had that ride all hooked up too. Even if you got behind the wheel and had the car keys, the car wouldn't turn on."

"For real? So how would you turn it on?"

"We wired the car so that you had to press a button before trying to turn it on. If not, there'd be a cutoff switch to the engine."

"That's fucking bad. But where'd you keep the button?"

"Nigga, I'm not going to tell you everything," he smiled. "But if you really want to know, you can have it anywhere. You can have it running underneath the seat. Up your ass if you want."

"Cool."

"It's a trip, ain't it?"

"Yeah. So La Raza blew your shit up because they couldn't steal it?"

"Wouldn't you get pissed off if you worked on getting a ride for months and the day you were about to get it something so stupid like that happened to you?"

"I guess so. But that's fucked-up. It was so dope."

"No joke, bitch. We already went to the junkyard to see what parts we could get for it so we can fix it up. Hopefully, we'll finish it up before winter comes."

"Why don't you just buy another one?"

"Nigga, please, just 'cause your lady gets sick doesn't mean you trade her in for another one."

"Yeah, I guess you're right."

"Let's get into the car, bro'," Jesse furnished a set of keys from his black baggy trousers. "I'm not in the mood for any of these putos to start shit with me today. Don't look up now but there's been a car driving around the block since we've been out here talking. I'm pretty sure it's Raza."

We got in the car.

"But I thought La Raza were cool with you?"

"Where'd you get that?"

"Well at South, J.C. was La Raza. You talked to him, didn't you?"

"Yeah, but you have to think, Louie. Nigger comes from the old school. Those motherfuckers know what it is to respect. Besides, J.C.'s a Raza from 18th. These pussys are from 57th. Raza's not Raza."

"Yeah, that's right. J.C. told me who he was with. Man, I can't believe I forgot! I hate it when that shit happens . . . I cruised with him a couple of times when I was a junior. I don't know why, but he never wanted to go right on 18th Street. And that's his 'hood."

"I wouldn't either, bro'. There's a different gang on every corner over there. You see all the bullet holes he's got in his car? That boy's been capped at so many times."

"Yep."

"He told my brother he got them all in one day when he was going down that street."

"It's crazy," watching him insert a stereo pullout into the metal cabinet. "And he lives right off of 18th? With his boys staying close by?"

"What can you do? That's the way it is over there. It's 'cause over there it's mostly guys who just got off the boats. It ain't like in Little Village where you have all Kings on one side for about a mile and then all Two-Six on the other side. That's been their 'hood for a while."

"Man, I remember being a freshman on the way to school one morning and we stopped by a doughnut place. We were waiting in the drive-thru when some little kids—probably freshmen—starting flashing the crown at J.C. He told me to pull out the gun from the glove compartment. That was the first time I ever grabbed a gun in my life."

"It was a .22? Right?"

"Yep. Shit felt weird. I gave it to him. You should have seen those dumbfucks. They were kissing his ass after that. Telling him sorry. This and that."

"They were probably little wannabes," Jesse began to drive. "See, Louie, that's the thing about Kings. They're not punks like other little bitches. We're almighty."

He stressed the word *almighty* in such a way that I finally understood the meaning of the word. I had heard it used a lot in church during prayers and sermons. But I had never heard it said in such an overall complete way.

"But what's the difference between the Kings and everyone else, bro'?"

"For one, the Kings have been around a lot longer than anyone else. We've been riding high in Chicago since the days when they use to wear zoot suits. I think the Latin Kings use to be called the

Humboldt Park Knights back in the day. That's up where the P.R.s live, by where you and the gym teacher go tutor after school. Yep, back in the day. That's when they use to fight with knives and fists, nigga."

"Shit, not anymore."

"No shit. And it's gotten crazier and crazier a lot faster too. I bet you if J.C. pulled that piece out today, some punk ass bitch would pull out something bigger. It don't matter. Kings are everywhere anyway."

"Just like everybody else."

"No, bro'. We're everywhere. You think a guy can just forget about being a King? If you're straight, that shit's in your heart always. I even know cops who are still Kings and help out the boys once in a while. Kings are the biggest Hispanic gang in the city. There's about fifteen thousand in Chicago. That's what the cops say. I bet you there's about four thousand real hardcore motherfuckers out there. Even five-o knows what's up. There's even black and gold in Mexico."

We turned into the parking lot of the supermarket. Inside we headed to the liquor department and bought a twenty-four pack of Corona.

"Hmmm. That's funny. Don't tell me you drink Corona just because it means 'crown' in Spanish?"

"Naw, bro', I drink it because it tastes good. But it doesn't hurt that it's got gold," he smiled. "See, Louie, other people that are kind of like you don't understand what we're about."

"What do you mean people that are kind of like me?"

"Well, you're pretty smart up there," pointing to his head, "but you kinda know what's up and kinda don't. What's good is you're not a coconut."

"Man, I can't stand those motherfuckers. They think just because they're educated that they can turn their backs on where they came from and forget all the shit their parents had to go through. It's like they look down on the gangbangers. Shit, they just didn't get all the breaks. That's all. Some of them are pussys and some of them are cool."

"That's right," Jesse said. "Everyone wants to fit in and when you can't find anything to fit into then you have to make your own thing. Shit, gangs aren't just a bunch of guys on a street corner. They're everywhere. Everyone wears colors. The biggest gang in the city wears color."

"Who's that?"

"Think about it . . . Five-o."

"Yep," I said. "I guess I never really found my one thing for real. Maybe I just don't want one."

"Maybe you're suppose to be everywhere for the rest of your life. Did you ever think about that?"

"Naw. It sounds kind of cool."

"You crazy motherfucker."

Back at Jesse's home, I rummaged through the kitchen cabinets, searching for a bottle opener.

"Mira, bro'," Jesse said. "Since we're at my crib, I'll take care of you."

I sat at the table and watched him cut a lime into eight equal pieces. He squeezed a piece of lime through the bottle's opening and then dropped it into the bottle. He then carefully poured some salt on the rim and inside the neck of the bottle. Afterwards, he began swirling the bottle in his hand at a slow rate.

"Do you got that rhythm because of practice?"

"Bro', would you rather drink piss?"

"Chill, cabrón. You know I'm just fooling with you."

He kept swirling the bottle.

"Only from you, Louie. I take this abuse only from you."

"I know."

"By the way, Louie, I was going to ask you. Are you still mixing?"

"I still got my tables. But I do it only for myself. Why? What's up?"

He handed me the bottle. "I want you to make me a tape with all the classics. I don't like this new shit they're playing."

"Yeah, I can make you a tape. Do you want me to put some old new wave on one side and house on the other?"

"Anyway you think is straight."

"Cool."

He started preparing his own bottle.

"You know what's fucked-up, Jes?"

"What?"

"The way the news call the Kings a *street gang*. They don't call Cosa Nostra a *street gang*."

"You know how it is, bro'. Even in the bad shit, we're looked down on. They either don't understand how deep this shit is or don't want to give us the respect. It's also because a lot of wanna-bes are giving the real Kings a bad name. Posers, bro'. They ain't even peewees! If it wasn't for us, they wouldn't even have a name. And they still think they're down! Fucking pendejos, they'll be cruising in their mommy and daddy's new car with music pumping out of a company radio, wearing gold chains strapped like they're big pimps. All of a sudden they'll see someone on a corner throw up the crown at them or flash all five fingers in the air and they'll throw it right back. Nigga, by the end of the night all their windows are smashed. Bitches couldn't even tell they were being false-flagged by some peewee because they don't know who's really who."

I started to laugh, taking a quick chug.

"That's why I think you're straight, bro'," resting my Corona on top of my lap. "You say how it is."

"Have to throw down for People."

"That's right. Kings are People. Hey, Jesse, how did that shit start out anyway? Sounds just like Crips and Bloods to me."

"Crips and Bloods is something else, bro'. That's an L.A. thing. The originals say Folks and People started in jail in the early eighties. I think in Joliet or County. Some motherfuckers wanted to separate gangs in two different categories so that there would be more control. What I heard happened was that gangbangers turned either Folks or People. Gangs like the Two-Six, Disciples, Gangster Disciples, and a whole bunch of other motherfuckers became Folks. The Latin Kings, Vice-Lords, and a whole shitload of other motherfuckers got to be People."

"Fucking weird, dog."

"Bro', all this shit is organized like you can't believe. What I hear is that it was the Kings and G.D.s who started the whole fucking breakup between Folks and People. No one else in the city has that much pull like the Kings and G.D.s, except for probably the El Rukn's and the mobs. But those motherfuckers are all into some other serious shit. I'm telling you, Louie, you have to pay close attention to everything around you, bro', or else people will fuck you up because of what you don't know. You can't be walking down the street today anywhere with the wrong color combination or your hat tilted the wrong way."

"By the way, when are you going to get rid of that nasty goatee you have on your face? One of these days, people are going to confuse you for a King."

His mustache, along with the goatee, formed an upside-down pitchfork. Until then, I hadn't noticed the idea behind it.

"Now you're thinking, Louie. It's all about representing."

"Yeah, I use to want to wear Converse sneakers until I found out the five-pointed star stood for People."

"You're lucky you never wore black and gold. Then they would've thought you were a straight-up King."

"Hey, bro', I'm not that stupid."

"It's not about being stupid, bro'. It's about being ignorant. There's just so much shit going on all the time that you don't see the shit in front of you. It's these little details that tell you a lot about someone. See, since the Kings are People, then they put up the number five because that number stands for People. And anything to the left is People also. So niggers who are People tilt their shit to the left."

"Oh, so when some gangbanger's crossing his arms together like when I see him doing it on the corners, that's saying he's either People or Folks—depending on how they cross them?"

"Bingo, bitch. And Folks is a whole different story. Folks use the number six. Nigger, why do you think you see all of these stars of David next to G.D.? Because the Gangster Disciples are Folks and that's their main symbol, a six-pointed star. That along with the pitchfork."

"That's fucking bad. It's like another language."

"I thought you knew?"

"I do, but not like that . . . Damn, bro', there's a lot of shit to this."

"Nigger, it gets even more complicated. There's shit that I can't even tell you."

"Why?" I asked.

"'Cause my ass wouldn't be here if I could . . . I don't know about you, Louie. It's from hanging out with all the geeks at South.

You'd be with the black nerds and the white nerds at their table at lunch. All the time, bitch. Nigger, for a while I was scared you were going to turn coconut on me."

"Naw, the way I see it, bro', you have to get a little bit of every-thing to make life interesting."

"Bitch, you sound like a ho."

"I ain't no whore, motherfucker. At least I don't live a boring existence like some other people who stick to one thing."

"I know you're not saying that to me."

"Hell no. You know what's up. You hang around with the weirdest motherfucker there is."

"Yeah, bro'. No one can say you and me ever had it boring."

We picked up our bottles and clanked the necks against each other.

"Like that one time you were going to throw down with that one pussy who said he was an Ambrose or an SD," I said. "I had your back right there."

"Nigger, we had fun at South."

"Yep. Even if it did get all fucked-up. It was worth it."

In an hour we finished nearly half of the beers. That's when it started. I asked him about the literature. I asked him how one would know if one was a real King, fascinated by the longevity and immensity of such an organization.

"I'll explain it to you the way my brother explained it to me," he said. "Every King has his set of dots and if that nigger can't tell you his dots then you know he's phony. And the way he says his dots, you know he knows what's up."

"Are you talking about the dots that are on top of the five-pointed crown? Like when they spray paint on the back of garages and buildings?"

"Mira, bro'—I'll explain it to you so that you can understand. Each King is an owner to two sets of dots. The first set is like a generic one. Those dots represent things like obedience, loyalty, love, respect, and honor. The other dots are like a passcode. Let's say you're a King from the North Side and some nigger comes up to you and asks you what you're all about and he's a King from the South Side. Then you tell him your dots. Only Kings know what that means."

"What about this Inca shit I'm hearing? I hear that the main leaders are now being called 'Incas.'"

"Fuck that. That's just little-kid shit. We really don't know who started that, but it ain't real."

"Yeah, but if they're saying it . . ."

"Look, bro', that's some peewee's invention. All hype bullshit." He shook his head and frowned. "Before, they didn't even wear tear-drop tattoos to show off that they've been in jail . . . Come on, bro', think about it, how can you be proud of being caught and caged? Everyone just thinks it's cool. And even though it don't make sense, everyone wants to be down with that. And some haven't even been locked up ever."

"They're posers then?"

"You got to figure some of them are. But that's with anything. Motherfuckers come out of college with their diplomas, all big and bad, and some of them cheated their way in and cheated their way out."

"But I thought no matter what, all Kings were almighty crowners?"

Jesse did a doubletake.

"Not everyone's really down for the crown, bro'," he said. "Just because they say they are doesn't mean they are. Like I said, that's with everything. You know how it is. Everybody has to make a name for themselves, make themselves special from the things that went on before. Shit, no one's ever going to be as bad as the niggers who started the whole shit going. They were the shit."

I knew what he was saying. I once wore colors. Blue and white. And everyone wanted to be a part, I thought dismally, especially after the work had been done.

"What's wrong, bro'? You look sad."

"I was just thinking about when I was UPC. When they use to call me Demon. Hardly anyone calls me Demon or Priest anymore, Jes. I remember I would walk on the street and people would come up to me and ask me if I was the Priest. It's like everyone knew me."

"You're still Louie though, cabrón. That's who you'll always be."

"I guess."

"How did that shit ever end anyway? I never asked you."

270

I sighed. "It's a long story."

"You got some place to go?"

"No."

"Then?"

"Well . . . a lot of shit happened. The UPCs came right after the original crews. The original crews were like Orange Crush, Latin Taste, and a whole mess of other motherfuckers I don't even know. Then we came along. It was us, crews like the Exotic Ladies, Undercover Party People, Party Society, Nasty Boyz, Majestics, you name it, bro'. No one really fought anybody, except for a couple of small fights here and there because of stupid shit. All the crews did was party . . . Then we started shouting at each other and representing. Then people started getting crazy. I remember slam-dancing to industrial music one time and knocking out people left and right. I guess some people didn't like that. And then crews started to war against each other little by little. They started to get backup from gangbangers. And everything got fucked up."

"Yeah. You told me about how the Two-Six were always after you guys."

"They hated us, bro'."

"Yeah, you told me it was your brother Jose who got hit at that one party at Highlander's. They went for the big guy right away. When that nigger left South, no one else was around to take his place. Why'd he leave again?"

"I don't know. I think he was just getting tired of my old man complaining about having to pay for school. At least he didn't drop out. He went to public school. I think he's going to get married to this one girl soon. I hardly talk to him or my little brother."

"Are you for real?"

"Yeah, he hardly stays at the crib anymore. Anyway," I continued, "we even went to this one party on Darkside."

"What! Were you and your boys high or something?"

"Naw, bro'. Fuck drugs. That shit fucks you up. I once saw this one girl at this party who almost OD'd. Man, I don't even remember seeing any of my boys ever doing weed. Maybe some of them did, but I never saw them."

"But, nigger, you didn't know Darkside is the heart of the Two-Six?"

"Now I do," smiling. "Like eight of us went into this house party and there was nothing but Two-Six there. The older ones. They didn't say anything at first. We even had our UPC jackets on. Soon, more of our boys showed up and things started getting really weird. You could tell the Two-Six were all high too. They started getting bold, dog. Some more of their boys—big motherfuckers—showed up and that's when we decided to leave. We were almost on the corner by our cars when they started capping at us. Motherfuckers, that's the second time someone tried to shoot me. Like that one time we went to a house party the Funk Boys were throwing. All of us paid our five bucks . . . Bro', that's the most expensive plastic cup I ever bought. Niggers had run out of beer by the time we got there and the motherfuckers didn't say shit. You know they knew. So anyway, me and my boy Moneybags went upstairs to collect. He was like the cheapest motherfucker around. He was the one who passed all the cans of soda underneath the tables at Atotonilco's for us. You should have seen it. One of the Funk Boys pulled out a .22 on us. Man, I was shitting bricks, dog. But fucking Moneybags kept arguing. He wanted his beer or his five bucks back. What a bitch. I don't know how that nigger's still alive."

Jesse laughed.

"It's funny. Around the time we called it quits, some of our boys went to the drive-in. They went with their ladies and met up with some of the other boys. They were wearing UPC baseball caps and their jackets. The Two-Six were there too. One of them clipped one of my boys. Well, my boys pulled out before it got real crazy. Except that the motherfucker they hit—I think it was Louie—he went home to get his father's gun. He came back to the drive-in, pulled out the pistol, and pulled that motherfucking trigger. Man, that shit was so rusty, Jes. The whole fucking thing fell apart right there. I think his grandfather had it from the Korean War or some other war. Of course, the Two-Six then beat the shit out of him. Bro', they should have known better than to do that with Darkside only a few blocks away. Shortly after that, we decided to call it quits. People wanted to start it up again this year. Like my little brother Izzy. Him, big Izzy, and Juan talked about it. But I guess it never happened. I guess that's why Izzy joined Party Society. He just wanted to be in that shit so bad."

"Jose went on to become KGB?"

"Yeah."

"How about you, bro'? Why didn't you join another crew?"

"Bro', I can't do that anymore," pounding my fist across my heart. "It's over. That died with the UPCs."

32

*D*id you hear that? He's dead!"

"What?" I said. "Who's dead?"

"Mr. Range," Hugo answered. "They just said it right now in the announcements!"

"Stop fucking around, Hugo!"

"I'm not! Didn't you hear it?"

"I must've missed it."

"That's it, Lou," Jimmy added, "say good-bye to Mr. Range."

"Naw, man, I can't believe it," covering my face. I began to rub my temples. "What the fuck!"

"Lou, are you okay?"

"Oh man," feeling jittery, "this is fucked-up. He wasn't suppose to die . . . He was so fucking cool. Fuck! Why the fuck did he have to goooo? . . . He was like the only teacher that really knew us, Hugo. He was like the only one."

"I know."

"We didn't even get to spend our senior year with him! He taught us, Hugo! He taught us about art. He never wanted anything else but us to know what he knew!"

"Don't worry, Aggie, I bet you he's in a better place."

"Oh man! All those awesome times we had with him in class. I wonder if he was hurting when he died. I hope not."

"I hope so too. His wake's tonight and tomorrow. You want to go?"

"I don't know. I'm sick and tired of seeing people cry. I'm sick and tired of all of this shit."

"Come on, Lou. You'll feel better if we go."

"Man, I'm never going to find anybody like him ever again."

"Come on, Lou, that's not true . . . Don't say that, Aggie. There's people like that all the time."

"No, for real."

"Damn, Aggie, don't get so depressed."

"What am I suppose to feel? I should have told him how I felt."

I'm such an asshole, I thought. I talk all this shit and think all this shit and don't even know what I'm saying! I should have looked for his number. I should have called him up and asked him everything I wanted to ask. I wanted to tell him about my last trip to Mexico. I needed to know what he thought about that painting I saw out there in the museum when I went alone. The painting with all those melting clocks. The painting by Salvador Dalí. I should have just called him to thank him for everything else. I should have . . .

"Come on, Aggie, I'm right he . . ."

33

*Y*ou got a problem, bro'?"

The flirtatious wink to the girl in front of him had set him off.

I looked to my far left. He was the one they called Nigger. His hair was cut close to his skin. The D's were beginning to wear their hair this way, I told myself. I recognized him from when I was a UPC.

"You look familiar, bro'," coming at me again. "Why don't you stop looking at my sister, bitch?"

"First of all," leaning on my porch rail. "I ain't your bro'. You might be my bitch, but I ain't your bro'. And second of all," pointing back, "this is my crib. This is my neighborhood. I don't know why they rented the back apartment to your lowlife self next door but you better watch your shit around here."

"So you think you're hard?" staying at the bottom of the steps. "Fuck you! You ain't nothing but a faggot with that fag haircut you have on. Why don't you cut that stupid ass mop? You fuckin' fag!"

"Fuck you, bitch! At least I don't use some girl for protection. Why do you put your sister in front of you like that? Huh, bitch? I can't even believe she'd walk with a lowlife like you."

Rivas, his real name, began to fume.

"Don't even bring my sister into this, bitch!"

"Why? What are you going to do?" getting off the rail. "You

276

gonna get your pussy ass bitches to come after me again and try to beat my ass?"

"Yeah, I knew I knew you," he said.

"Yeah, you can't even handle me by yourself, asshole!"

"I don't need anyone to fuck you up, bitch!"

"Sure, bro'," stepping to the edge of the apartment porch, "come on then! Let's go!"

I climbed down one step of the stairs. Slowly. So as to not lose my advantage, I thought.

"Come on, Mike! You don't want to fight with this piece of shit!"

"Hey!" yelling to his sister. "We'll go when I say!"

"What's wrong, Mike," taunting him, "ain't your sister gonna back you up? I bet you she'll fight better than you. I wonder how many times she's saved your ass . . . Let me guess, your ass was kicked out of your home 'cause your ma probably got fed up with you? I think what I'm saying is right, 'cause you don't seem to be talking shit anymore. So now what's up, bro'? Now who's hard?"

Rivas started up, but his sister held him back.

"What, bitch? Why so quiet? Didn't you like what I said? Can't face the truth like most people?" His face had turned red. "Yeah, bitch," continuing the onslaught, "now who's fuckin' hard? You sure ain't. You call yourself a human being? Fuck that. You ain't nothing but an unwanted bastard! Your own mother threw you away!"

"Man," having trouble finding the words he wanted, "you ain't nothing but a pussy ass bitch! If my sister wasn't here right now, I'd fucking beat your ass."

"If you think you're all that, do it!" raising my arms and waiting for him to come.

His sister started caressing his arm, trying to comfort him.

"You know what? Why don't you just go home? You ain't doing shit here. You're just wasting my time. Go home. Oh, that's right, you don't have a real home. That should make you feel better. Go beat on them . . . Hey, I hear you like beating on girls too. Why don't you go beat on your sister or something? Punk mother-fucker!"

"You're dead, bitch," walking away.

"Excuse me? Did you say something?"

"You're dead, bitch."

The second time softer than the first.

"Yeah, bro'," I scoffed and pulled my hair back. "Whatever. Get in line. I know a lot of other motherfuckers who wanna beat my ass."

This time Mike didn't say a word. He looked me right in the eye, slowly lifted his finger and slid it over his throat. He smiled a wicked smile, pointing his finger right at me. His mouth moved, but no sounds came forth. I read his lips.

"You're—dead—bitch."

I remained still.

34

*H*ey, Carlos!" shouting to an open window. "Carlos! Let's go get a slice of pizza at Leona's!"

"Sure," my cousin stuck his head out.

I sat on the front steps and began lacing my shoes.

"Aren't you gong to take a shirt, then?"

"Yeah, let me just finish this."

Seconds later, Carlos appeared at the front door of the apartment.

"Hey, Lou, do you know what all that racket is going on next door?"

"I don't know what's going on over there," shaking my head. "Maybe it's that idiot Mike . . . Hey, are you really hungry?"

"I'm starving. Our mothers haven't gotten back from Mass yet."

"I don't understand why they want to spend a beautiful Sunday like today at church."

"Its beyond me, Lou."

"I don't think I'm ever going to church again because of what they did with Q South, Carlos. That shit was fucked-up. You know it all had to do with money. The Church is just going to lose a lot of people that way because they sold their souls like that."

"We better go, Lou. My stomach's starting to talk trash."

"Okay," finishing the last "rabbit ears" on the shoestrings.

"Lou, didn't my aunt ever teach you the other way to tie a shoe?"

"Yep, but I don't like to do it that way. I don't know why, this way is more fun for me."

"That's fucking great," he chuckled, "I haven't seen anyone do that since we were at St. Peter's."

I stood up, feeling invigorated.

"So what do you think about this bozo that lives next door?"

"Are you talking about Nigger?"

"Is that what they call that Mexican guy, Lou? With the spiky hair?"

"Yeah. He use to be LIC. Now I think they're called LIDs."

"Why?"

"LIC use to stand for Latin Image Crew. But since they get backup from the Disciples, they turned Latin Image Disciples."

"Weird."

"Yep."

"So, Lou—before I forget—are you excited about going to college?"

"Well, you tell me," jumping off the last step onto the sidewalk, "you're the one who went to that school, not me."

"Let me just say this, Lou, when you get there you're going to meet some pretty strange people, at least strange in what you and I are use to. They don't fuck around with work. They're pretty intense in their," he held up both hands, "'academic' shit. The whole place is pretty white too. Like real white."

"So, what do you think we grew up in? This place is still mostly Polish, except for the Mexicans and a couple of Chinese families I've seen move in."

"I knew you were going to say that, but I'm telling you, Lou, the way it is over there is totally different from what you're use to. No matter what you say."

"Yeah, well I'll deal with college once I get there. Come on, let's go get some pizza."

Carlos began to walk steadily toward the corner.

"You know what? Let's go down 37th Street. Maybe Roxanne will be out."

"I thought you broke up with her, Lou?"

"That doesn't mean I can't be her friend."

"You still think about her?"

"Yeah, man. It's like the song. She's always on my mind."

When we reached the corner of our block, we turned and went down 37th Street.

"So why'd you break up with her?"

"I don't know. I got tired, I guess. We went out for almost two years. Besides, I'm probably going away to college in September. I want to check it out over there and not worry about her."

"You just wanted to start dating other girls, Lou."

"No, she means a lot to me but I do kinda want to get away from her and start something new. There's nothing wrong with that, is there?"

"No," Carlos abruptly lifted his head.

"What's wrong?"

"Can't you hear it?"

I stopped my walk in midstep.

"Yeah, I hear it. It's that fake house music they play on the big radio station now. Man, I think I smell something too."

He raised his nose to the air. "Are you thinking what I'm thinking, Lou?"

"I think it's weed, bro'! I think. I've only smelled it two times at a party. Someone's smoking up big-time, that's for sure."

"I bet you it's those assholes next door." Carlos stopped at the mouth of our alley.

"Yep," advancing, "you're right, Carlos. I see that asshole Rivas with his boys."

"There he is!" someone shouted from the backyard of our neighbor's apartment.

"Fucking, Lou, they're coming this way. Let's get the fuck out of here!"

"Why? We live here too. What are we suppose to do? Run in our own neighborhood? Fuck that! If they're going to come after me, let them come. It doesn't matter what I do anyway. If they really want me, they'll get me. But maybe next time I won't be with anyone else."

"I don't know, let's just go! I don't think you and I can handle all of them."

"Chill, bro'. We'll see what happens. I know I can take at least four of them down."

The first wave came straight toward us. A second had jumped across the alley into a neighbor's yard.

"See, bro', they're going to get me one way or another. Ain't nothing I can do."

Eight of them stood in front of me now.

"Hey, bro', we heard your silly ass has been talking a lot of smack!"

"Listen, I don't know your ass. The only one I know from all of you is Mike. And I'm going to tell it to you the way I told it to him. I ain't your fucking bro'. Now, what goes on between him and me is none of your business. If he's got something to say, let him say it to me right now."

"I don't think so, pretty boy, that isn't the way it works. You fuck with one of our boys, you fuck with all of us!"

"Look, I ain't got shit with you boys. It's between Nigger and me."

I wondered how much longer this talk was going to go on before one of them finally decided to do something.

"No, bro', we said that's not the way it works," someone repeated.

"Yeah . . . there's what? About eight of you motherfuckers against me and my cousin? Fuck it, I'll take all of you on. One by one, but Mike has to go first!"

Mike's voice erupted from the back of the gang.

"Fuck that!"

The next thing that came was a crashing glass. It came from behind. I turned around. The second wave had come down on me. One of them was holding the remnants of a beer bottle neck in his hand.

I felt streams of warm liquid run down the back of my neck, down my shoulders, and onto my back. I put my hand behind my head and felt pieces of cold pebble-sized objects stuck in my long and curly hair. I drew the hand to the front of my face, unable to make sense of the amounts of red liquid covering my fingers.

"Beat his ass!" I heard Mike command.

Someone with a baseball bat came over to my right side and swung at my head. I ducked, but someone else from the other side smacked me in the leg with what I felt was a pipe. I buckled.

A second bottle broke. Again on the head. This time I fell to the ground. Hit after hit dropped on my head. I felt a numbness. I felt feet kicking my midsection where my ribs were located. Blows landed on the front of my legs, but the majority of the hits pelted my head.

I started to kick like a wild dog. One of mine landed.

"Get his fucking legs!" someone yelled. "Grab them, bitch!"

Something hard quieted them down. Fucking pipe, I thought. They went back to my skull.

"Mike, you're a fuckin' pussy!" I yelled. "You're all fuckin' pussys! Fuckin' bitches! Just wait until I get up . . . Just wait until I fucking get . . ."

"You're not going to get up, motherfucker!" someone laughed.

Something inside told me to put my head in between my arms before it all caved in. Why was this happening to me?, I thought. Why?

Everything was a mess. God, please God, make it stop, I heard myself say. Make them stop.

"Stop!!! Pleeeeaase!!!"

But the beating continued. My head and heart sank low. I began to do what was still my own. I began to cry. I heard them laughing and then quiet down as if the second phase of the thrashing necessitated complete concentration. I made my plea again. To them and God. But it wouldn't stop.

"Leave him alone!" Carlos cried. "Why don't you guys just stop already? You're going to kill him!"

"That's what this bitch wants," a voice said.

I decided to die.

"Let him go! I said leave my brother alone!"

Israel's roar stopped us all.

I sat up on the pavement, gasping for air.

"You want to mess with my brother?" he continued. "Huh? Let's see how you jagoffs do against the two of us!"

Israel wielded a baseball bat, painted blue and white, Party Society colors.

I looked to my side, stood up, and reached for the one closest to me. He looked scared and tried to run away. Tried, because it seemed that his feet had suddenly become anchored by the weight of the present change in situation. Each step he made seemed to ask for tremendous effort.

I grabbed the front of his shirt and shoved him against the wall of a building.

"I'm so sorry you didn't kill me," I whispered in his ear, seeing his bloodshot eyes, "'cause now I'm going to kill you and when I'm finished with you I'm going to rip every piece of your body and eat it piece by piece." I shoved him good and hard against brick. "Do you hear me? I'm going to kill you, and then I'm going to come after your family and kill them! I don't care how many of them there are! I don't care how big they are! I don't care if they're little babies! I just want to make sure they don't make animals like you anymore! That I never have to deal with shit like you anymore!"

He stopped struggling. He didn't cuss. He just said one thing.

"Please, let me go."

"I'm not going to let you go. Never! You're going to die right here, and I'm not even going to use any bat on you! I'm not going to use a gun. I'm not going to use a bottle. I'm just going to use my hands. I'm going to make you suffer the way I was suffering. Maybe even worse. Are you scared? Huh? Answer me!"

I extended my arm, sweeping it across his face.

"I'm not even going to punch you!" I yelled. "You want to know why? Because you're not a person, you're a thing. Something like you doesn't deserve to get hit like that. Something like you deserves less."

I slapped him again. No one was around to help him. The few who had remained were now at the mercy of my brother. This one kept asking that I let him go.

"I already told you I'm not going to let you go. Do you hear me? I'm going to fucking haunt you for the rest of your life, motherfucker! I'll go all the way to hell if I have to! Look at me!"

I turned him around. His eyes filled with horror.

"That's right, bitch! Look at what you did! You're never going to forget this face. I'll always be there. Every time you go to sleep. You didn't think I was going to get up? Huh? There's no way you'll ever get away from me. Not until I let you go. And that won't be for a long time."

"I think they're bringing backup!"

"What did you say, Izzy!?"

"Look, here comes some of them again. I think they have a gun!"

I let go and stood next to my brother.

"Don't worry, I got my own backup," he said.

He pulled me by my shirt and began running down 36th Street. I followed closely.

Two blocks down, we reached a school playground. He let out a whistle. His boys came out of nowhere.

"What's up, Izzy?" one of them yelled.

"They're capping at us! They just jumped my brother and now they're capping at us! Look at what they did to him," putting his hand on me.

"That's fucked-up, bro'."

"Who the fuck did it?" another asked.

"The LIDs, bro'."

"Man, fuck the LIDs! This ain't even their 'hood. Why they busting shit around here? Let's go fuck 'em up, Izzy."

"That's what I'm saying."

By then a group of about twenty had congregated. Some were armed with bats. Cars began pulling up on us as well.

"Who are all these motherfuckers, Izzy? They're not PS?"

"Don't you worry about that," racing back to the alley. "I told you I had backup, Lou."

"Man, they really fucked you up," a wide-eyed boy, about fifteen, ran up to me. "Your shirt's all red with blood! Man, they really fucked you up! Don't it hurt?"

"Not anymore. I just want to go kill those motherfuckers now."

"Don't worry, we'll take care of those bitches!"

"Thanks."

"Oh shit, here comes the five-o," he said.

But no one really seemed to care.

A patrol car pulled up. "Where do all of you boys think you're going?"

"Man," I said bitterly, "where have you been? Can't you see what they did to me?"

"Relax," the officer said, "what's going on?"

"*You relax,* I'm going to go fuck someone up!"

"It's a goddamn lynch mob," said his partner. "That's what's going on."

They left and weren't seen again for another thirty minutes.

35

*M*a told me you got your ass kicked yesterday?"

"Come on, Jose," whining from my bunk bed, "don't yell."

"No one's yelling, dork. It's all in your head. So how long have you been in bed?"

"Why do you want to know?"

"Because, bro', you're beginning to smell."

"Fuck you. What time is it anyway? It looks like it's dark outside."

"It's ten o'clock."

"That late. Shit, I got to get to the U of C tomorrow."

"Why?"

"I'm in some stupid summer program there. I feel like such a guinea pig. I have to go Mondays, Wednesdays, and Fridays."

"Why do you have to go on a Tuesday then?"

"What do you mean? Isn't it Sunday still?"

"No," he teased. "Today's Monday. Tomorrow's Tuesday. And the next day is Wednesday. . . . Are you sure you didn't lose a couple of pieces from your brain? I saw Ma had some really weird-looking cabbage in the pozole today."

I began to laugh. "Damn, Jose," stopping halfway, "it hurts."

"No, duh. They stitched you up, didn't they?"

"Yeah. In three places."

"Don't worry, you'll get use to it. And, remember, you'll never feel like anything hurts ever again."

"How do you know?"

"Let me see . . . The last time I got beat up this bad was when I was ten or eleven. Every fight since then has felt like you sneezing on me."

"Stoppp, Jose, don't say anything that'll make me laugh. I can't laugh. Everything hurts."

"Why'd you let them hurt you, goofy ass?"

"I wasn't going to run."

"So instead you let them play baseball with your head. What a dork."

I didn't respond.

"Don't cry," Jose said. "Take it all in. Tell me who were the guys that did it to you."

"No."

"Why not?"

"'Cause, I don't want you to get mixed up in this. And tell Izzy I don't want him doing anything else either. This is my shit and I'm going to take care of it."

"Look, I'm not going to let anyone get away with this."

"They're not, Jose. If I don't get them, I know God will."

"What are you talking about?"

"I don't want you getting in trouble, Jose. Soon you and Grisel are going to get married and have a kid. I don't want anyone fucking around with that."

"No one's going to do anything to me."

"Yeah, but you never know. Everything we do sooner or later catches up to us."

"That's if you let it, Louie."

"No, Jose, that's the truth. People can't run that fast . . . You know what's fucked-up? I remember running in this meet when I was in cross-country at Quigley. We went to this really beautiful place where there was these huge hills to run it. But when people started coming down the hill, someone fell. Man, so many people ran over that one guy with their spikes and everything. That kid was bleeding when he came back. And I heard some other runners laughing and saying how they weren't going to slow down no matter what because they wanted to have good times . . . Why are people like that? Don't people know that the race is not about one person winning? That it's about the run and having everyone do their best? Man, shit like that makes me not want to do anything anymore."

He went over to the window and opened it, letting fresh air in.

"So you're positive you don't want me to do anything about what happened? You know that all you need to do is give me a name."

"Naw, it's cool. Besides, this is my business. No one else's. But you can do me one big favor."

"What's that?"

"Talk to Izzy, bro'. Make sure you tell him what I told you. Tell him I don't want him to do anything stupid."

"Izzy? He's not going to do anything dumb. He's smarter than that. He has better grades than you."

"No, Jose, you should have seen him when they were beating me. I've never seen my little brother like that. It was like he was on fire or something. Like he gave me this energy to get up and fight. I couldn't even tell who he was at first. I swear to God. He knew exactly what to do and how to take care of them. They ran, Jose! All of those motherfuckers ran when they saw him! It kind of scared me to think that he knew what to do. It's weird. He's different."

"He grew up, dork. What's the big deal?'

"Maybe we should've hung out with him more when we were little."

"Too late now," he retorted. "I wouldn't worry about it. Izzy's not stupid. He knows what he's doing."

"Maybe we should've let him become a UPC when he wanted to," I rambled on. "That way he wouldn't have had to join PS."

"You don't know that."

"Yeah, but things are so different now, Jose. It's not the same."

"Relax. You think too much about everything. It's not that bad."

"Yes it is! You're KGB and Izzy's PS. Both of them are at war with one another. That makes you and him at war too. Don't tell me that's not fucked-up? Please talk to him, Jose. He's always looked up to you. No one ever listens to me. I don't even listen to myself."

He chuckled. "Easy, Charlie Brown. You're just a little out there. Everything's going to be okay. I promise I'll talk to him. Just for you. But he has to do what he has to do. Personally, I don't ever want to see any of my brothers getting beat up like this again."

"You know what, Jose? Ma told me that she's thinking about sending me to Mexico for a month. She's scared I'm going to get a gun somewhere and kill one of those motherfuckers. Or that they're going to come after me again."

"Have you thought about killing someone?"

"No, but if I'm going to kill someone, I'm not going to do it with a gun. I'm going to do it with my bare hands. I'm not going to be a coward."

"Just remember one thing, Louie, once you do it, it'll never leave you alone."

"I know," thinking of the abortion. Of this and other things I had never spoken to anyone about. "I know."

"Dad hasn't come to see you?"

"No. And I don't want to see him."

"Why?"

"Why should I? He wasn't here when it happened. Besides, what's he going to do? . . . Hey, Jose, I'm thinking about living over in Mexico with my uncle Cosme and aunt Chepina. They once told me that they'd pay for my school out there. Hey, it wouldn't be too bad. At least there I wouldn't have to deal with the gangbangers or with people giving me dirty looks because I'm Mexican."

"What about U of C? I thought they gave you a scholarship or something to go there?"

"Yeah. I got some money, but I don't know if I want to go there. I'm tired of getting shitted on because of the color of my skin. If that happens there, I don't know what I'm going to do. Remember when we first got here? Remember how some of the old ladies around here would grab their bags like we were going to rip them off?"

"Shit, they use to do it a lot. But that's a long time ago. It's in the past."

"Yeah, but stuff like that still happens. I'm tired of that shit, Jose."

"Hate to say it, but Mexico's got bad people too. They're not all cool."

"I'm tired of people then."

"No you're not. You're just saying that because you're pissed off right now. You always do this. Say stupid shit you don't mean."

"Like I said, I can't even trust myself."

"Go back to sleep, Louie," Jose left the room. "You have to rest."

"Okay," trying to leave the madness.

Minutes later I recalled my uncle Cosme's Spanish words. Rest is for the dead, I repeated in English. I rose out of bed then, feeling all energy depleted and stepped over to my equipment, clicking the power strip on.

As I turned on a turntable and searched through my plastic milk crate for a record, a question came to mind. Whatever happened to the woman in the park? How had it gone for her after we had made the connection?

Just then I found the twelve-inch vinyl I needed. The one I was dependent on to make me feel good. The name of it was "Love and Music." It played like new.

There wouldn't be any more questions that night.